THE ECONOMY OF TURKEY SINCE LIBERALIZATION

Also by S. Togan

FOREIGN TRADE REGIME AND TRADE LIBERALIZATION IN
  TURKEY DURING THE 1980s

Also by V. N. Balasubramanyam

ECONOMY OF INDIA
INTERNATIONAL INVESTMENT (*edited with David Sapsford*)

The Economy of Turkey since Liberalization

Edited by

S. Togan
Professor of Economics
Bilkent University, Ankara

and

V. N. Balasubramanyam
Professor of Development Economics
Lancaster University

First published in Great Britain 1996 by
MACMILLAN PRESS LTD
Houndmills, Basingstoke, Hampshire RG21 6XS
and London
Companies and representatives
throughout the world

A catalogue record for this book is available
from the British Library.

ISBN 0–333–60900–X

First published in the United States of America 1996 by
ST. MARTIN'S PRESS, INC.,
Scholarly and Reference Division,
175 Fifth Avenue,
New York, N.Y. 10010

ISBN 0–312–12694–8

Library of Congress Cataloging-in-Publication Data
The economy of Turkey since liberalization / edited by S. Togan and
V. N. Balasubramanyam.
p. cm.
Includes bibliographical references and index.
ISBN 0–312–12694–8
1. Turkey—Commercial policy—Congresses. 2. Turkey—Foreign
economic relations—Congresses. 3. Turkey—Economic policy-
-Congresses. 4. Turkey—Economic conditions—1960-   —Congresses.
I. Togan, Sübidey. II. Balasubramanyam, V. N.
HF1583.4.E28   1996
330.9561—dc20   95–5640
                                                                              CIP

© S. Togan and V. N. Balasubramanyam 1996

10   9   8   7   6   5   4   3   2   1
05   04   03   02   01   00   99   98   97   96

Printed in Great Britain by
Ipswich Book Co Ltd, Ipswich, Suffolk

Contents

List of Figures

List of Tables

Preface

The essays in this volume were discussed at a conference held at the Bilkent University at Ankara in Turkey. The participants in the conference included economists from both Turkey and Britain with an interest in trade and development issues. The collaboration between Turkish and British economists proved effective and fruitful; while the Turkish economists spoke with the authority of first-hand knowledge on most of the issues discussed at the conference, economists from Britain were able to provide a detached, if not always an objective, assessment of the issues. The composition of the participants drawn from the Universities of Lancaster and Nottingham in England and various Turkish universities and official agencies in Turkey, including the Central Bank of Turkey, provided for a wide-ranging discussion of the issues. As convenors of the conference we would like to express our gratitude to all the participants including the authors of the papers and their discussants for their valuable contributions. We hope this volume of essays will provide readers with an overview of the motivation, process and consequences of Turkey's experiment in economic liberalization, and inspire further work on economic liberalization in general and Turkey's economic policies and performance.

Lancaster   S. TOGAN and V. N. BALASUBRAMANYAM

Acknowledgements

We would like to express our gratitude to Mr Colin Perchard, formerly Councillor for the British Council and Cultural Affairs in Ankara, and Associate Professor Ahmet Ertugrul, General Manager of Turk Eximbank (Export Credit Bank of Turkey) for financial assistance for the conference. We would also like to thank Professor Mithat Coruh, President of Bilkent University, for his support and encouragement. Our thanks are due to Mrs Carol Barlow for cheerfully putting up with our many demands for secretarial and editorial help.

Participants in the Conference and Contributors to the Volume

Sydney Afriat, Professor of Economics, Bilkent University, Ankara.

Oktan H. Aktan, Professor of Economics, Hacettepe University, Ankara.

Abdurrahman Ariman, Association for Foreign Capital Coordination, Istanbul.

V. N. Balasubramanyam, Professor of Economics, Lancaster University, Lancaster.

Merih Celâsun, Professor of Economics, Middle East Technical University, Ankara.

Mithat Coruh, President, Bilkent University, Ankara.

Aylin Ege, General Directorate for EC Affairs, State Planning Organisation, Prime Ministry, Republic of Turkey, Ankara.

Yavuz Ege, State Planning Organization, Ankara.

Hasan Ersel, Vice Governor, The Central Bank of the Republic of Turkey, Ankara.

David Greenaway, Professor of Economics, University of Nottingham, Nottingham.

Orhan Guvenen, Director, State Institute of Statistics, Prime Ministry, Republic of Turkey.

Robert C. Hine, Senior Lecturer in Economics, University of Nottingham, and Professor, College of Europe, Bruges

Candan Karlitekin, Research Department, Turk Eximbank (Export Credit Bank of Turkey), Ankara.

Gulten Kazgan, Professor of Economics, Istanbul University, Istanbul.

Oliver Morrissey, Lecturer in Economics, University of Nottingham, Nottingham.

Ziya Onis, Associate Professor, Department of Political Science and International Relations, Bosphorus University, Istanbul.

David Sapsford, Professor of Economics, Economics Department, Lancaster University, Lancaster.

P. N. Snowden, Senior Lecturer in Economics, Economics Department, Lancaster University, Lancaster.

Fatma Taskin, Assistant Professor of Economics, Bilkent University, Ankara.

Sübidey Togan, Professor of Economics, Bilkent University, Ankara.

Ercan Uygur, Professor of Economics, Ankara University, Ankara.

A. Erinc Yeldan, Associate Professor of Economics, Bilkent University, Ankara.

Bahri Yilmaz, Associate Professor of Economics, Bilkent University, Istanbul.

1 Introduction

S. Togan and V. N. Balasubramanyam

The dominant theme in development economics in recent years is the liberalization programmes undertaken by a number of developing countries, either unilaterally or as a part of the World Bank structural adjustment lending programmes. One such programme, which poses a number of analytical issues, is that undertaken by Turkey in 1980. Although Turkey experimented with liberalization of the economy during the 1970s, the measures she implemented then were half-hearted and spasmodic. The 1980 reform package, in contrast, was comprehensive and bold, including not only liberalization of the foreign trade regime but also widespread financial reform and macroeconomic stabilization policies. The economic consequences of the experiment continue to be a matter of debate. The new regime, which came into office in 1993, headed by Mrs Tanau Ciller, a former Professor of Economics, continues to battle with an inflation rate of 109 per cent (the latest figures for percentage change in CPI over the last twelve months), a declining lira and a sizeable public sector borrowing requirement amounting to 16 per cent of the country's GNP. It is all too easy to lay the blame for the current economic problems at the door of the 1980 reforms, dubbed '*the infamous package*' by certain sections of the financial press. Whether or not the current economic problems are a consequence of the reforms is arguable. It is, however, to be noted that despite the relatively high inflation rate Turkey has registered annual growth rates well above those of other OECD countries and the economy is known for its resilience in the face of adversity. It is for these reasons and because Turkey is about to implement another package of reforms designed to contain inflation and improve the competitiveness of her exports and her credit rating, that an evaluation of Turkey's liberalization experiment would be of value.

Turkey's liberalization experiment has been the subject of a number of studies. Most of these studies, however, are not easily accessible and it may also be fair to say that neither the Turkish experiment nor the extensive analysis of it by Turkish economists have received the attention they merit. This volume of papers, written by a group of economists based in Turkey and in Britain, is intended to introduce students and practitioners of development economics to the dramatic

1

experiment in liberalization undertaken by Turkey and the rich variety of issues it poses. These papers also provide a background for analysing the economic problems Turkey is currently experiencing.

The papers are arranged in three broad groups. The first group consists of two papers which analyse trade and industrialization issues in the context of the liberalization programme. The first of these papers, by Sübidey Togan from Bilkent University in Turkey, provides an exhaustive empirical analysis of the structure and performance of Turkey's foreign trade following the liberalization of the trade regime undertaken in 1980. Utilizing well-known statistical measures and concepts, Togan estimates the height of protection afforded to various industries, the degree of bias against exports prevalent during the 1980s, and evaluates the extent to which liberalization was successful in correcting the bias against exports. He concludes that although the programme of liberalization was successful in reducing the bias against exports, it did not entirely eliminate it. Togan's paper is worth reading not only for its analysis of the impact of the trade regime in place on the competitiveness of Turkey's exports, but also for the manner in which it copes with a vast amount of data to draw meaningful conclusions. The second paper in this group, by David Greenaway of Nottingham University and David Sapsford of Lancaster University, analyses a currently fashionable theme – the relationship between trade reform and the terms of trade. The attractive features of the paper are its lucid survey of the existing literature on the relationship between trade liberalization and the terms of trade and the sophisticated econometric techniques it deploys to test the hypothesis that liberalization leads to changes in terms of trade. Greenaway and Sapsford, on the basis of the econometric evidence they assemble, conclude that it is changes in terms of trade that may have influenced liberalization of trade in Turkey, rather than the other way round.

The second group of papers deal with issues relating to foreign direct investment (FDI), foreign aid and financial liberalization in Turkey. Balasubramanyam of Lancaster University analyses the reasons for the relatively low level of foreign direct investment in Turkey in the recent past and evaluates the likely impact of the programme of economic liberalization on inflows of FDI into Turkey in the future. He also argues that if Turkey could achieve macroeconomic stability and establish credible liberalization measures, she could attract increased volumes of FDI without offering generous tax concessions and other incentives to foreign firms. Oliver Morrissey of Nottingham University discusses Turkey's experience as a recipient of foreign aid. His analysis of Turkey's experience with structural adjustment loans, a particular form of conditional aid, provides a number of lessons for other developing countries. Amongst other issues, Morrissey discusses the case for gradualism in the adjustment process and the case for utilizing aid funds for investment in infrastructure facilities. Drawing upon Turkey's experience, he also suggests lessons for the World Bank in administering its structural adjustment policies. The final paper in this group, by Nicholas Snowden of Lancaster University, discusses aspects of liberalization in the financial sector. Changes in the regulatory environment in this context can produce awkward problems of transition. These are reviewed systematically in the Turkish context and some new issues in financial liberalization raised.

The third group of papers considers specific policy-oriented issues, such as Turkey's case for the membership of the European Union and the export promotion policies of Turkey. Membership of the EU is high on the agenda of policy makers in Turkey. In a wide ranging essay, Robert Hines of Nottingham University considers the various obstacles Turkey faces in her bid for membership and concludes that a pragmatic solution for Turkey would be to join the European Free Trade Association in the first instance. Such a move would not only provide some of the advantages of membership of the EU, such as better access to EU markets, but also pave the way for eventual membership of the EU. Fatma Taskin and Ernic Yeldan discuss the link between exports on the one hand and employment, growth and functional income distribution in Turkey on the other. They argue that export-based expansion of the economy could not be sustained in the face of the deteriorating real income shares of wage labour and little capital accumulation. Export expansion itself was achieved by suppressing domestic absorption through wage reductions and currency depreciation. They show how this process, however, could not be sustained and that the strategy hit its political limits in the late 1980s. Okan Aktan of Hacetetepe University in Ankara provides a critical evaluation of the impact of export subsidies and exchange-rate policies on the export performance of the Turkish economy. The paper argues that the multitude of export promotion measures introduced during the 1980s were not sufficient to eliminate the bias against exports created by the import-substitution policies pursued during the years prior to liberalization. Furthermore, the scaling down of export promotion measures during the second half of the 1980s and the subsequent overvaluation of the lira were responsible in large measure for the slowing down of the growth of Turkish exports.

Turkey is unique amongst the developing countries for many reasons. It is perhaps the only Islamic country which has embraced Western mores and institutions, it is also a country which can boast of a highly educated elite and a literacy rate well above the norm for other developing countries. Turkey's experiment with liberalization is perhaps unique both because of the broad sweep of reforms it envisaged and the determination the country has shown in sticking to the reforms in the face of adversity. For these reasons the analysis of Turkey's liberalization experiment provided by the nine essays in the volume should be of value to both practitioners and students of development.

2 Trade Liberalization and Competitive Structure in Turkey during the 1980s

Sübidey Togan

1 INTRODUCTION

All present-day industrial and developing countries have, at one time or another, protected their manufacturing industries. Turkey is no exception. It has protected import-substituting industries over exports and industry over agriculture during the three decades 1950–79. During this period, Turkey followed an inward-oriented development strategy. Until the mid-1960s it was engaged in replacing the imports of non-durable consumer goods by domestic production. By the mid-1960s Turkey was able to satisfy the domestic demand for those commodities. It then had a choices of two strategies: it could either embark on exportation of manufactured goods, or it could move on to the second stage of import substitution. Turkey chose the latter strategy and replaced the imports of intermediate goods and consumer durables by domestic production. But these commodities had different character-istics from those replaced at the first stage. They were highly capital intensive, they required the availability of skilled and technical labour and were subject to economies of scale, with efficient plant size being large compared to domestic needs. Correspondingly high protection of these industries was required. High protection was achieved through tariffs, quotas and over-valued exchange rates. As a result, the incremental capital output ratio increased considerably and eventually the maintenance of the pace of growth became more and more costly.

The quadrupling of oil prices between 1973 and 1974 and the 1974–5 world recession adversely affected the Turkish economy. The oil bill rose sharply. The economic difficulties of the European economies led to a slowdown of emigration and a decline in workers remittances. Despite the external shocks amounting, according to Balassa (1981), to 5.4 per cent of GNP, Turkey attempted to preserve its growth momen-tum through rapid reserve decumulation and massive external borrowing.

5

Successive governments refused to adapt their economic strategies to the new environment and pursued expansionary policies. Under the impetus of the public sector, investment programmes grew sharply. The investment/GNP ratio increased from about 19.1 per cent in 1973 to 24.1 per cent in 1977. Since consumption was not simultaneously constrained, GNP grew at the unsustainable rate of 7.8 per cent per annum during 1974–6. The gap between national savings and investment widened. During this period, when financial markets were repressed by way of mandatory ceilings on deposit and borrowing rates, the public finances deteriorated sharply. As public investment programmes increased considerably, the government also imposed policies such as under-indexation of the prices of public enterprises and over-employment by these institutions. These policies, in turn, caused dramatical deterioration of the accounts of state economic enterprises. As a result, the public sector borrowing requirements increased to about 11.7 per cent of GNP in 1977. Money supply and, hence, inflation exploded. The government, in order to keep the inflation rate from increasing further, kept essentially to a fixed exchange-rate system. Although Turkey introduced a series of minor exchange-rate adjustments, the spread between Turkish and world-wide inflation rate increased. The real exchange rate appreciated. The government tried to avoid the adverse effects of the exchange-rate appreciation by increases in export rebate rates and increased control on foreign capital movements. But as a result of the policies followed, imports grew and exports stagnated. By 1977 the net capital inflow was nearly double that of export value. The heavy borrowing soon led to high external debt. The share of short-term debt increased rapidly. Consequently, the widening current account deficit developed into a payments crisis in 1977 and Turkey lost its international creditworthiness. Shortage of foreign exchange restricted the inflow of imports that were required for production as well as capacity expansions needed for future growth. The crisis was accompanied by recession and also political instability. By late 1970s it was apparent that the strategy followed was no longer sustainable.

In January 1980, the government introduced a comprehensive policy package designed to restore price stability, achieve viable growth, increase the efficiency of resource allocation through greater reliance on market forces and introduce 'outward orientation' in economic policy.

The stabilization programme introduced in January 1980 made use of a wide range of policy instruments. The financial position of state economic enterprises was improved through a combination of price increases, reduction in wage expenditure and scaling down of investment programmes. The budget deficit was reduced by widening the income tax base, raising some indirect tax rates and improving tax collection procedures. Monetary policy was tightened. Action was taken to increase the efficiency of the financial system and foreign trade and foreign exchange movements were liberalized to a very large extent. The liberalization episode that began in January 1980 marks a turning point in Turkish economic history. For the first time in its recent history, the country aimed explicitly at making the economy more 'market oriented'.

The purpose of this paper is to analyze quantitatively the trade liberalization episode to Turkey's liberalization experience that began during the 1980s. In Section 2 we consider the characteristics of the Turkish foreign trade regime, and in Section 3 the competitive structure of the Turkish economy. The paper concludes with policy recommendations towards the rationalization of the Turkish foreign trade system.

2   TRADE LIBERALIZATION

A trade system is called neutral if it operates under perfect competition as it would in the absence of government interference. Any movement in a trade regime towards neutrality is defined as trade liberalization, and a change which increases the deviation from neutrality is seen as reversal of liberalization. Trade liberalization, thus defined, manifests itself in three ways. First, trade liberalization is a move from rationing through government regulation to the use of price mechanisms in the form of tariffs. Second, a move towards neutrality lowers the average levels of nominal and effective protection and subsidy rates and reduces the dispensions within the system of these rates. The third manifestation of trade liberalization is a move towards a system where the real exchange rate and the sectoral real effective exchange rates remain relatively stable over time with no violent fluctuations.

2.1   Import regime

In the immediate post-war years, Marshall aid was granted to Turkey, and Turkey became a member of the Organization for European Economic Cooperation, thus promoting Turkey's ties with the West. In 1950s, the anti-etatist Democratic Party took power from the, until then, monopolistic Republican Party. At the beginning of the 1950s, the government followed liberal policies. But after the massive crop failure of

1954, the country turned to import substituting policies, and hence to protectionist foreign trade policies. Licensing was to be required for all imports, with many import commodities transferred to the quota list. All importers were required to possess an 'importer's certificate', and a system of multiple exchange rates was inaugurated. In 1954, Turkey replaced specific tariff rates with *ad valorem* rates, and tariff rates were increased considerably as reported by Baysan and Blitzer (1988).

In 1958, the government agreed on a stabilization programme prepared with the assistance of the IMF. The Turkish lira was devalued and Turkey moved towards a more unified exchange-rate system. The various separate lists of imports were replaced by import programmes, which stated import regulations and procedures that importers had to follow to obtain import licenses. The first import programme appeared in the *Official Gazette* on 23 September 1958. Thereafter, import programmes became the major instrument of import control.

During the 1960s, a new, socially progressive constitution was adopted. The constitution required the establishment of the State Planning Organization and formal economy-wide planning through five-year plans and annual programmes. With the introduction of economy-wide planning, economic policy exhibited greater concern for industrialization. During this period, Turkey explicitly followed an inward-oriented development strategy through high protection of industry. High protection was achieved through restrictions, regulation, tariffs, quotas and overvalued exchange rates.

During the 1960s and 1970s, all imports into Turkey were regulated by annual import programmes. Each programme was published in the *Official Gazette*. The import programme itemized commodities under the liberalization list, the quota list, and a list enumerating the commodities to be imported under bilateral trade arrangements. Importation of goods not enumerated in any of the lists was prohibited. Of these lists, the quota list and the liberalization list were of major importance. The liberalized lists contained commodities considered essential for the achievement of development plan objectives when domestic productive capacity was unavailable. They consisted mostly of capital goods and raw materials. The liberalization list was further divided into a free import list (liberalization list I) and a restricted list (liberalization list II). Commodities on the free import list consisted mainly of raw materials and spare parts, while commodities on the restricted list were mainly processed and semi-processed goods and raw materials.

The quota list covered commodities of which there was some domestic production or which were considered not essential by plan objectives such as consumer goods. As soon as domestic production of an import competing product began, the import was transferred from the liberalized list to the quota list. When domestic production of a commodity was sufficient to meet the domestic demand, the item was removed from the quota list. Since commodities not specified on the import lists could not be imported, complete protection was then granted to local producers.

Importers wishing to import any commodity on liberalization lists I and II during the 1960s and 1970s had to go through a complex set of procedures. Procedures for items of liberalization list I were simpler than those for items on liberalization list II, which in turn were simpler than those on the quota list items.

Anyone wishing to import a liberalized list I item had to first obtain an 'importer's certificate' from the local Chamber of Industries or the Chamber of Commerce. The Chamber issued the certificate as long as the person was a bona fide producer or wholesaler. The certificate entitled the holder to select items relevant to the holder's business. Once the import programme was announced, the holder of an 'importer's certificate' valid for commodities on liberalization list I could make an application for an import licence from the Central Bank. The applicant gave the description of the goods he wished to import, the quantity and the unit price. He made a 'guarantee deposit' at the local bank, which would be transferred to the Central Bank. The guarantee deposit rates varied over time. They amounted in 1966 to 70 per cent for items on liberalization list I, 100 per cent for items on liberalization list II, and 10–30 per cent for items on the quota list. Thereafter, the Central Bank issued import permits for the amount applied for on a 'first-come, first-served' basis as long as foreign exchange was available. A licence, once issued, constituted a valid claim against foreign exchange. To import the commodity the holder of the import permit had to have a letter of credit in hand. The importer having the import permit and letter of credit could place his/her order. When the goods arrived at the customs office, the custom officials checked whether the imported items conformed to the description on the import permit. The importer then paid all duties and surcharges associated with importation and cleared the goods from customs.

An importer wishing to import items on liberalization list II had to obtain, in addition to the procedures described above, the approval of a government agency prior to the issuance of an import licence. The purpose of the 'permission certificate' was to increase the difficulties associated with importing, and thus to restrict imports. The import programme specified the government agency the 'permission certificate' had to be obtained.

In the case of imports of goods on the quota list, the procedures were more complex than either of the liberalization list procedures. To study the procedures, first one must consider the way the value of each quota item in the import programme was determined. In that process, the State Planning Organization, the Ministry of Commerce, the Central Bank, the Ministry of Finance and the Union of Chambers of Commerce and Industry took part. The Union represented the interests of the private sector, whereas the Ministry of Finance represented the interests of public sector enterprises. There were two type of quotas: commodity specific and user specific. The commodity specific quotas were further allocated between industrialists and importers. Importers were those who imported for the purpose of resale without processing, whereas industrialists were those who were using the quota goods in their own production process. Legally, imports to industrialists could not be resold. Each commodity specific quota value was subdivided into the amount to be allocated to industrialists and the amount for importers. On the other hand, the user specific quotas were divided into investment goods quotas and those covering the needs of certain assemblers and manufacturers. Goods imported under these quotas required the approval of the State Planning Organization to insure that the activities were in conformity with the plan objectives.

Allocation of quotas after the publication of quotas followed different procedures for industrialists and importers. in the case of industrialists, the public and private sector shares of individual quotas were first worked out by the relevant ministries and Union of Chambers. Once the private sector share was determined, the problem was to allocate the amount among the industrialists. At that stage, we may note that some of the items in the import programmes were designated as being subject to the control of individual ministries. When no ministry was specified the application was made to the local chamber of industry which forwarded it to the Union of Chambers. Industrialists wishing to import those items applied to the relevant ministry for a 'requirements certificate'. These certificates were issued in proportion to the plant capacities of the applicants. The amount allocated to each importer was shown on the 'requirements certificate'. This certificate was forwarded to the Central Bank, with which the Central Bank issued the import license. On the other hand, the allocation procedures in the case of importers were simpler. Once the import list were published, importers made their requests with an authorized bank, which forwarded the application to the Central Bank. The Central Bank summed the value of requests by quota categories, and when the sum exceeded the quota, the bank allocated the quotas by scaling down proportionately so that the quota was filled.

Imports were subject to tariffs and tariff-like charges. The latter consisted, as reported in Krueger (1974), Baysan and Blitzer (1991) and Krueger and Aktan (1992), mainly of the municipality tax, stamp duty, wharf tax and production tax.

The import regime explained above remained in force until the 1980s. In 1981, the quota list was partly phased out. In that year a large number of commodities were transferred from 'liberalization list II' to 'liberalization list I'. A major reform was introduced in January 1984, when all imports were classified into three lists: the 'prohibited list', 'imports subject to permission' and 'liberalized list'. Commodities that could not be imported under any circumstances, such as arms and ammunition, were specified in the 'prohibited list'. 'Imports subject to permission' specified the items that could be imported with prior official permission, and the 'liberalized list' enumerated the commodities that could be freely imported.

At the time of the import system reform, the government replaced the production tax, which applied to domestic production and import of certain commodities, with the value added tax (VAT), which applied to almost all commodities. Moreover, it imposed a new surcharge, the 'housing fund tax', on some imports to finance housing construction for poor and middle-income families. In addition, two surcharges on imports were imposed under the titles of the 'support and price stabilization fund tax' and 'resource utilization support fund tax'. Thereafter, the import duty and housing fund tax rates were revised at least once every year during the 1985–92 period.

During the 1980s, imports were subject to tariffs and several tariff-like charges: the municipality tax, transportation infrastructure tax, mining fund tax, stamp duty, value added tax, housing fund tax, resource utilizatin and support fund tax, and support and price stabilization fund tax.

2.1.1 Quantitative restrictions

As emphasized above, the quota list specified the dollar value of imports and implied a binding quantitative restriction on imports. It was partly phased out in 1981. Table 2.1 shows the share of commodities in the 'restricted list' (liberalization list II) in total imports. As can be seen from the table, the share of commodities in the 'restricted list'

TABLE *2.1*   *Share of 'restricted list' imports in total imports*

	Restricted imports (million US $)	Total imports (million US $)	Share of restricted imports in total imports (%)
1970	192	948	20.3
1971	260	1171	22.2
1972	413	1563	26.4
1973	478	2086	22.9
1974	697	3778	18.4
1975	1163	4739	24.5
1976	1143	5129	22.3
1977	1160	5796	20.0
1978	784	4599	17.0
1979	973	5069	19.2
1980	947	7909	12.0
1981	831	8933	9.3
1982	272	8843	3.1
1983	163	9235	1.8
1984	17	10757	0.2

SOURCE: Various issues of the Annual Report, Central Bank of Turkey.

declined from 24.5 per cent in 1974 to 9.3 per cent in 1981 and 1.8 per cent in 1983.

In 1984, a major trade reform was introduced, when all imports were classified into three lists: the 'prohibited list', the 'imports subject to permission list' and the 'liberalized list'. Prior to 1984, a large number of commodities had already been transferred, starting with the 1981 import regime from the restricted list (liberalization list II) to the free import list (liberalization list I).

The 'prohibited list', introduced in 1984, originally contained about 500 commodities. The number of these commodities decreased substantially in the following year; the number was reduced to three in 1985 and was kept thereafter at that level.

Table 2.2 shows the share of commodities in the list 'imports subject to permission'. As can be seen from the table, this list constituted about 46.5 per cent of all imports in 1984. The share declined to 21.9 in 1986 and 6.1 per cent in 1988. In 1984, the list covered a wide range of commodities, but by 1988 it was used in only 11 of the 49 sectors, the most important of which included the pharmaceutical products, printing and publishing, and other non-metallic mineral products sectors. In the case of pharmaceutical products, the share of imports

TABLE 2.2   *Share of imports 'subject to permission' in sectoral imports (%)*

I–O code	Sector name	1984	1986	1988	Total
1	Agriculture	0.10	1.90	0.00	100
2	Animal husbandry	10.55	1.40	0.00	100
3	Forestry	0.00	0.00	0.00	100
4	Fishery	0.00	90.62	0.00	100
5	Coal mining	0.44	0.00	0.00	100
6	Crude petroleum	100.00	0.00	0.00	100
7	Iron ore mining	0.00	0.00	0.00	100
8	Other met. ore mining	0.00	0.00	0.00	100
9	Non-metallic mining	50.40	48.25	0.00	100
10	Stone quarrying	0.00	0.00	0.00	100
11	Slaughtering & meat	0.00	25.99	0.00	100
12	Fruits & vegetables	0.00	0.41	0.00	100
13	Vegetable & animal oil	0.00	0.00	0.00	100
14	Grain mill products	0.00	4.33	0.00	100
15	Sugar refining	3.41	53.10	0.00	100
16	Other food processing	0.25	1.10	0.00	100
17	Alcoholic beverages	94.52	0.04	0.00	100
18	Non-alcoholic beverages	0.00	100.00	0.00	100
19	Processed tobacco	0.00	100.00	0.00	100
20	Ginning	0.00	0.00	0.00	100
21	Textiles	7.95	3.71	0.00	100
22	Clothing	0.00	41.95	0.00	100
23	Leather & fur products	0.00	0.08	0.00	100
24	Footwear	0.00	0.00	0.00	100
25	Wood products	1.33	0.26	0.00	100
26	Wood furniture	0.00	100.00	0.00	100
27	Paper & paper products	0.08	7.47	6.18	100
28	Printing & publishing	0.03	39.64	39.41	100
29	Fertilizers	0.00	9.28	0.00	100
30	Pharmaceutical products	0.00	48.18	49.34	100
31	Other chemical products	0.00	9.74	5.58	100
32	Petroleum refining	99.09	0.00	0.00	100
33	Petroleum & coal products	0.00	0.00	0.00	100
34	Rubber products	27.22	5.43	0.00	100
35	Plastic products	93.13	94.23	0.00	100
36	Glass & glass products	12.38	20.56	0.00	100
37	Cement	0.00	0.00	0.00	100
38	Non-metallic mineral	53.28	32.40	30.29	100
39	Iron & steel	91.29	62.95	20.57	100
40	Non-ferrous metals	83.10	83.70	12.35	100
41	Fabricated metal products	65.51	49.53	0.05	100

cont. on page 14

TABLE 2.2 *continued*

I–O code	Sector name	1984	1986	1988	Total
42	Non-electrical machinery	52.90	18.47	5.11	100
43	Agricultural machinery	46.63	7.38	0.00	100
44	Electrical machinery	31.95	31.67	13.09	100
45	Shipbuilding & repairing	100.00	95.42	0.00	100
46	Railroad equipment	0.00	0.00	0.00	100
47	Motor vehicles	58.48	57.08	13.39	100
48	Other transport equipment	1.24	1.24	0.00	100
49	Other man. industries	20.44	22.61	0.01	100
Mean		46.46	21.86	6.08	100

SOURCE: Author's calculations.

subject to permission was about 48.2 per cent of all sectoral imports in 1986, and 49.3 per cent in 1988.

By 1990 all of the different types of quantitative restrictions were completely phased out.

2.1.2 *Nominal and effective protection rates*

It is well known that in the absence of quantitative restrictions and foreign exchange controls, quota premiums will disappear. Hence any divergence between domestic ex-factory price and the tariff-inclusive landed cost of an imported commodity can be attributed to the trade margins of the wholesalers. This means that tariffs, levies and other expenses, e.g. the tariff equivalent of guarantee deposits required for imports, will represent the nominal protection rate (NPR) on the commodity.

Economists have long recognized that the profitability of a business activity can be changed by measures which affect the selling price of the final product, the costs of the intermediate material inputs, or a combination of both. The literature on effective protection maintains that when there are intermediate inputs, effective protection to value added is what matters and not the nominal protection. Put another way, if both the final product and the material inputs used to process that product can be bought or sold on world markets at given prices, under free trade conditions and with a given exchange rate, this would provide a certain value added (cost of labour, land and capital inclusive of an acceptable profit margin). Tariffs and tariff-like charges alter the product price and the cost to the enterprise of the intermediate inputs, thus widening or narrowing the value added. Effective protection is simply the difference between the observed value added at tariff inclusive domestic prices and what the value added would be under free trade at world prices; and the effective protection rate is this difference expressed as a proportion or percentage of the free trade value added.

Table 2.3 provides estimates of nominal and effective protection rates. The nominal protection rates have been obtained under the assumption that there are no quantitative restrictions and that quota premiums are zero. From Table 2.3 it can be seen that the economy-wide nominal protection rate (NPR) has declined from 70.2 per cent in 1984 to 28.3 per cent in 1991. Noting the fact that quantitative restrictions had been eliminated completely by the end of 1980s, the reductions in nominal protection rates have been larger than indicated above. Similarly, the economy-wide effective protection rate (EPR) declined from 74.71 per cent in 1984 to 38.38 per cent in 1991. More significantly, recent policies have narrowed the inter-industry distribution of the NPR and EPRs, as evidenced by the values of standard deviation figures for NPR and EPR. When determining the average rates, we have weighted the sectoral nominal rates by sectoral outputs valued at world prices, and the sectoral effective rates by sectoral value added evaluated at world prices.

The most striking conclusion to be derived from Table 2.3 relates to the height of protection in Turkey. From the table we note that, among the 49 tradeable goods industries considered, there were 30 industries in 1983, 32 in 1984, 24 in 1988, 11 in 1990 and eight in 1991 which had NPRs higher than 50 per cent. On the other hand, there were five industries in 1983, three in 1984, seven in 1988, 15 in 1990 and 17 industries in 1991 which had NPRs less than 20 per cent. A similar consideration applies to the EPRs. There were 27 industries in 1983, 30 in 1984, 28 in 1988, 24 in 1990 and 23 industries in 1991 which had EPRs greater than 50 per cent. Similarly, there were seven industries in 1983, six in 1984, eight in 1988, nine in 1990 and eleven industries in 1991 which had non-negative EPRs less than 20 per cent. There were two industries in 1983, 1984 and 1988, which had negative EPRs between 0 and − 100 per cent; and the number of sectors with EPRs less than − 100 per cent amounted to four in 1983, three in 1984, two in 1988, zero in 1990 and one in 1991.

After having shown the level of protection we now turn to a more detailed examination of the characteristics of tariff revisions. For this purpose we compare the 1983 figures with the average of 1990–1 figures.

TABLE 2.3 Sectoral protection rates (%)

I-O code	Sector name	Nominal protection rates					Effective protection rates				
		NPR83	NPR84	NPR88	NPR90	NPR91	EPR83	EPR84	EPR88	EPR90	EPR91
1	Agriculture	25.05	36.12	53.00	9.86	22.45	22.35	34.49	59.98	13.81	28.92
2	Animal husbandry	21.66	25.89	21.65	11.57	12.72	13.91	15.24	7.32	21.13	16.13
3	Forestry	36.37	41.11	17.61	4.68	5.90	45.62	50.38	19.11	13.50	16.21
4	Fishery	40.67	45.03	82.82	55.93	55.25	38.43	42.74	88.10	64.42	63.88
5	Coal mining	81.02	85.38	29.21	17.70	16.96	100.43	105.83	34.90	31.34	30.51
6	Crude petroleum	24.36	29.49	24.34	34.11	30.91	39.11	44.48	44.05	46.66	43.29
7	Iron ore mining	15.91	20.27	12.43	4.35	3.55	10.80	15.31	9.55	10.95	10.55
8	Other met. ore mining	15.74	20.10	36.82	4.36	3.56	14.05	18.78	44.08	13.43	12.80
9	Non-metallic mining	102.06	107.07	70.91	20.65	31.66	124.81	130.73	81.53	32.79	46.57
10	Stone quarrying	25.80	27.59	17.55	8.20	7.28	21.95	23.37	18.15	15.58	15.03
11	Slaughtering & meat	78.28	78.68	40.00	10.03	20.54	364.66	301.94	79.59	16.43	40.85
12	Fruits & vegetables	140.71	145.54	94.85	69.97	69.30	-1949.80	383500.00	227.29	413.51	244.96
13	Vegetable & animal oil	56.71	61.29	16.23	17.90	12.65	83.18	83.57	9.76	25.19	12.00
14	Grain mill products	46.80	51.16	104.75	38.61	45.19	182.87	117.38	-793.92	512.60	261.01
15	Sugar refining	139.66	144.43	103.17	44.71	44.09	-21.47	-24.86	-19.75	141.83	105.01
16	Other food processing	108.36	131.73	104.24	39.79	48.36	-1159.90	-1580.20	346.76	93.21	107.93
17	Alcoholic beverages	90.42	95.02	224.82	232.34	182.25	623.82	709.79	870.41	642.31	382.30
18	Non-alcoholic beverages	63.99	68.35	172.62	152.37	151.70	129.73	142.73	-16921.00	902.08	1001.50
19	Processed tobacco	372.79	378.68	78.16	87.63	86.96	-1841.20	-2815.80	97.58	180.96	157.38
20	Ginning	7.42	9.67	22.52	4.35	3.55	-12.03	-15.62	-0.71	12.67	-2.55
21	Textiles	109.07	104.44	64.20	34.37	34.49	330.77	285.01	114.50	70.32	68.43
22	Clothing	154.89	160.46	169.45	122.03	123.07	234.38	258.88	25418.00	5969.60	6106.00
23	Leather & fur products	152.48	157.05	40.77	15.85	17.36	779.91	819.27	55.46	30.97	27.76
24	Footwear	157.00	161.75	57.56	54.48	51.89	187.95	191.10	74.82	93.66	86.95
25	Wood products	83.25	88.67	24.64	42.30	39.33	154.14	162.91	36.47	128.31	109.15
26	Wood furniture	129.49	133.85	163.32	84.72	46.04	198.92	205.79	657.91	151.94	68.79
27	Paper & paper products	63.23	63.97	19.77	26.66	25.69	113.71	113.97	40.05	56.04	54.08

#	Industry										
28	Printing & publishing	26.07	26.83	21.70	35.13	12.17	11.04	12.03	27.00	53.89	17.04
29	Fertilizers	31.12	35.48	20.69	12.49	12.21	17.30	23.89	13.52	17.02	16.79
30	Pharmaceutical products	26.89	30.47	27.48	37.97	32.44	22.16	26.04	29.14	48.38	44.49
31	Other chemical products	51.46	45.17	47.48	28.93	25.43	61.23	48.54	66.61	49.04	43.04
32	Petroleum refining	57.60	62.88	41.27	26.24	24.49	105.41	110.84	82.07	27.14	27.14
33	Petroleum & coal products	65.26	69.85	11.56	23.84	13.78	76.30	82.09	0.02	32.12	13.31
34	Rubber products	53.78	61.70	52.78	37.93	37.00	49.43	63.34	68.07	61.09	60.59
35	Plastic products	250.98	256.34	105.04	54.91	50.80	-890.50	-753.93	310.20	124.99	116.66
36	Glass & glass products	67.13	74.29	146.51	79.75	40.62	91.00	102.29	238.68	123.39	59.88
37	Cement	48.16	5.87	8.41	32.52	25.22	103.35	4.05	8.35	82.70	62.34
38	Non-metallic mineral	54.05	58.75	42.31	42.57	34.74	74.66	88.71	64.51	76.71	62.77
39	Iron & steel	39.53	42.48	31.56	9.74	9.37	55.19	59.39	57.44	22.48	22.45
40	Non-ferrous metals	61.93	53.43	35.20	12.59	11.66	146.78	113.08	59.69	31.54	30.58
41	Fabricated metal products	82.17	86.87	95.91	35.77	33.94	159.43	179.10	388.68	96.44	91.48
42	Non-electrical machinery	53.58	57.06	73.43	23.62	21.17	55.78	59.84	107.66	39.54	35.85
43	Agricultural machinery	47.37	60.43	84.16	27.25	23.68	43.33	68.44	167.68	43.48	39.66
44	Electrical machinery	49.45	58.96	76.43	33.36	33.26	47.46	63.69	109.94	54.39	56.28
45	Shipbuilding & repairing	63.27	66.79	90.35	38.56	37.88	67.16	71.76	120.82	57.31	56.99
46	Railroad equipment	19.28	23.64	43.71	26.14	3.55	2.12	6.71	47.80	37.90	3.94
47	Motor vehicles	65.00	70.70	106.62	59.42	45.14	87.36	94.93	185.01	103.30	76.33
48	Other transport equipment	14.62	19.01	34.08	6.50	3.56	17.47	22.06	42.38	16.88	13.81
49	Other man. industries	70.09	125.76	69.12	21.30	19.52	75.62	197.39	92.44	38.56	36.50
	Mean	65.22	70.19	55.42	28.68	28.25	70.99	74.71	68.56	39.12	38.38
	Standard deviation	63.75	65.39	48.28	40.49	35.80	213.01	205.39	212.72	116.26	65.83

SOURCE: Author's calculations.

First, we note that in 1983 the highest NPR, were granted to the following sectors; processed tobacco and products (372.79), plastic products (250.98), and footwear (157). The highest EPRs in 1983 were provided to the leather and fur products (779.91), alcoholic beverages (623.82), and slaughtering and meat preservation (364.66) sectors. In the same year, the sectors receiving the lowest NPRs were ginning (7.42), other transport equipment (14.62), and other metallic ore mining (15.74). Similarly, the sectors receiving the lowest EPRs were fruit and vegetable canning (− 1949.8), processed tobacco and products (− 1841.2), and other food processing (− 1159.9). Comparing the 1983 figures with the average figures for the period 1990–1, we note that NPRs have decreased in 44 sectors and increased in five. Among the five sectors for which the NPRs increased, the greatest increase occurred in the alcoholic and non-alcoholic beverages sectors. On the other hand, the greatest decrease in NPR occurred in processed tobacco and products, plastic products, and leather and fur products sectors. In the case of EPR, we note that during the period 1983–91, the protection rates have increased in 19, and decreased in 30 industries. The largest increase in EPR occurred in the sectors of clothing, fruit and vegetable canning, and processed tobacco and products, the largest decrease in EPR occurred in the sectors of leather and fur products, slaughtering and meat preservation, and textiles. By 1991, the sectors receiving the highest EPRs were alcoholic beverages (182.25), non-alcoholic beverages (151.70), and clothing (123.07); and the sectors receiving the highest NPRs were clothing (6106), non-alcoholic beverages (1001.5), and alcoholic beverages (382.3). During the same year, the sector of ginning (3.55), iron ore mining (3.55), and railroad equipment (3.55) were granted the lowest NPRs. Similarly, the lowest EPRs were provided to the sectors of ginning (-2.55), railroad equipment (3.94), and iron ore mining (10.55).

Ordering the sectors according to their EPR figures for the years 1990 and 1991, we note that among the first ten industries of the two orderings, the non-alcoholic beverages, alcoholic beverages, grain mill products, fruit and vegetable canning, processed tobacco and products, wood and cork products, sugar refining and plastic products sectors appear in both listings. Hence, these are the most protected sectors in the Turkish economy. The data further reveal that for sectors for which the EPR is less than zero but larger than − 100 (−100 < EPR < 0) the value added at the official exchange rate is less than the value added of its foreign counterparts. As such, these industries represent the least protected sectors in the economy. The numbers of such sectors were two in 1983, 1984 and 1988, zero in 1990 and one in 1991. From Table 2.10 it follows that the ginning sector has consistently been the least protected industry in the economy. Table 2.4 presents NPRs and EPRs for broad industry groups. In the upper part of this table, industries are classified into nine industry groups and in the lower part into four trade categories: export, export- and import-competing, import-competing, non-import-competing. The classification of the sectors into four trade categories follows the rule adopted in Balassa *et al.* (1982).

Calculations presented in the first part of Table 2.4 reveal significant characteristics of the tariff system. There is a marked tendency for tariff rates to escalate from lower to higher stages of fabrication. In general, the tariff rates are lowest for primary activities, followed by mining and energy, and highest for manufacturing. For instance, in 1990 the NPR (EPR) was 10.86 (16.5) per cent for primary activities, 18.27 (29.27) per cent for mining and energy, and 36.23 (53.09) per cent for manufacturing. The escalation of subsidy rates is also evident among the subsectors of manufacturing, within which the lowest protection rates apply to intermediate goods and higher rates to consumer and investment goods. For instance, in 1990 the NPR was 25.87 per cent on intermediate goods, 37.87 per cent on investment goods and 52.34 per cent on consumer goods. During the same year the EPR was 23.29 per cent on intermediate goods, 56.97 per cent on consumer goods, and 68.17 on investment goods.

The second part of Table 2.4 reveals that, throughout the 1980s, the protection rates on export industries were higher than those on export- and import-competing, and non-import-competing industries. This indicates that Turkey's recent success in expanding its exports has been achieved under protection. The government protected the export industries, as evidenced by the high values of EPR in export industries compared to those in other industries.

2.2   Export regime

Since the adoption of the first five-year development plan in 1963, Turkey has encouraged economic activity through a complex system of incentives. Domestic investments were encouraged through investment allowances, tax deductions, low-cost credits and tariff reductions, and exemptions on imported machinery and material inputs. Until 1980, domestic production was further assisted through import licensing, quantitative restrictions on imports and over-valued exchange rates. These measure discouraged exports by raising the profitability of

TABLE 2.4 Protection rates by major commodity groups and trade categories (%)

Commodity groups	Nominal protection rates					Effective protection rates				
	1983	1984	1988	1990	1991	1983	1984	1988	1990	1991
Commodity groups										
I. Primary activities[a]	24.57	33.14	42.15	10.86	19.21	22.03	31.17	46.50	16.52	26.09
II. Mining & energy[b]	56.05	60.10	28.92	18.27	17.83	73.92	78.64	37.45	29.85	30.01
III. Manufacturing	81.83	85.40	61.83	36.23	34.02	104.08	104.19	99.62	62.77	47.71
1. Consumer goods	129.09	133.98	88.07	52.34	53.33	178.34	162.91	24.96	79.06	51.14
Processed food[c]	92.92	102.99	77.13	32.40	38.31	192.70	159.23	-55.65	94.87	66.78
Beverages & tobacco[d]	316.22	321.84	103.86	111.40	103.85	623.82	709.79	870.41	642.31	382.30
Non-durable & durable consumer goods[e]	123.98	122.90	96.46	60.26	57.84	135.29	126.96	28.79	26.50	15.21
2. Intermediate goods[f]	57.97	59.21	38.04	25.87	22.37	73.41	74.23	102.38	52.38	41.06
3. Investment goods	61.53	68.00	87.87	37.87	33.05	89.52	102.65	208.94	72.93	64.90
Machinery[g]	61.69	68.51	83.31	31.57	30.05	93.59	108.69	223.13	66.69	64.14
Transport equipment[h]	61.06	66.57	100.60	55.47	41.43	76.96	84.01	165.16	92.18	67.24
4. Other manufacturing industries[i]	70.09	125.76	69.12	23.79	20.73	75.62	197.39	92.44	38.56	36.50

Trade categories

I. Export industries[j]	131.29	136.78	93.01	55.04	54.35	298.33	282.09	171.39	89.35	71.01
II. Export- and import-competing industries[k]	46.70	49.01	42.79	17.22	15.86	59.30	63.57	65.14	32.52	30.66
II. Import-competing industries[l]	52.95	58.20	51.13	30.95	26.66	63.39	69.92	64.08	44.27	39.88
IV. Non-import-competing industries[m]	47.16	52.61	45.14	21.02	24.11	52.30	59.48	67.64	32.21	37.14

NOTES:
[a] Includes sectors nos 1–4.
[b] Includes sectors nos 5–10.
[c] Includes sectors nos 11–16.
[d] Includes sectors nos 17–19
[e] Includes sectors nos 21, 22, 24 and 26.
[f] Includes sectors nos 20, 23, 25 and 27–40.
[g] Includes sectors nos 41–44.
[h] Includes sectors nos 45–48.
[i] Includes sectors no. 49.
[j] Includes sectors nos 12, 16–23, 36 and 41.
[k] Includes sectors nos 8, 9, 29, 31, 39, 40, 42, 43 and 49.
[l] Includes sectors nos 3, 5, 6, 7, 10, 13, 27, 30 and 44–48.
[m] Includes sectors nos 1, 2, 4, 11, 14, 15, 24–26, 28, 32–35, 37 and 38.

SOURCE: Author's calculations.

production for domestic markets over foreign markets. To counteract these adverse effects, incentives were provided to exports. Exports were encouraged through tax rebates, preferential credits, and tariff exemptions on imported inputs and packaging materials. However, these incentives were not sufficient enough to eliminate the then prevailing bias against exports.

In 1979, Turkey ran up against the limits of foreign borrowing and was forced to reschedule its debts to Western governments and foreign commercial banks. A precondition for rescheduling was the acceptance of the IMFs structural adjustment programme implemented on 24 January 1980. By 1985, Turkey's current account deficit was a manageable $1 billion. The balance of payments turnaround during the 1980s was achieved largely by dramatic improvements in exports. Exports increased from $2.9 billion in 1980 to $13.6 billion in 1991. The increase in exports experienced during the 1980s was achieved through a consistent export-promotion policy, which relied on three main instruments: exchange rate policy, which affects every tradeable good, and credit policy and fiscal incentives, both of which tend to produce biased sectoral effects.

In January of 1980, the Turkish lira (TL) was devalued by almost 50 per cent, from TL 47.10 to TL 70 per dollar. The then existent multiple exchange-rate system was eliminated except for import of fertilizers, and fertilizer inputs. After May 1981, the exchange rate was adjusted daily against major currencies in order to maintain the competitiveness of Turkish exports. In August 1988, a major reform was introduced and a system of market-setting of foreign exchange rates was adopted. The real depreciation of the Turkish lira, achieved through the exchange-rate policy followed during that period, provided a great incentive to Turkish exporters. Besides the exchange-rate policy, the government also relied on credit policy and fiscal incentives.

The government extended credit at preferential rates of interest to producers/exporters of selected products. During the first half of the 1980s, a substantial difference existed between the general lending rate and the rate of interest applied to export credits. However, that system was abrogated in 1985. After 1987, preferential credits to exporters were extended via the newly established Eximbank.

The fiscal incentives provided to exporters during the 1980s included: export rate rebates; cash grants financed by the 'Support and Price Stabilization Fund'; duty-free imports of intermediates and raw materials; exemption from the production tax, which was replaced later by exemption from value added tax; foreign exchange allocations;

exemption from corporate income tax; rebates from the 'Resource Utilization Support Fund'; exemption from various taxes related to alternative export transactions, and exemptions from freight rates. In addition to these subsidies, the exports of certain agricultural commodities were and still are subject to tax.

Table 2.5 shows the subsidy rates for each of the 49 tradeable sectors. From the table it follows that the economy-wide nominal subsidy rate declined over the period from 31.98 per cent in 1983 to 13.04 per cent in 1990. More significantly, recent policies have narrowed the inter-industry distribution of nominal subsidy rates. The standard deviation of nominal subsidy rates declined from 19.76 in 1983 to 8.13 in 1990.

The most striking conclusion to be derived from Table 2.5 relates to the level dispersion of subsidies in Turkey. From the table we note that amongst the 49 tradeable goods industries considered, there were eight industries in 1983, one in 1984 and 1986, and no industries in 1988 and 1990, which had nominal subsidy rates higher than 50 per cent. Additionally, there were ten industries in 1983, 15 in 1984, 23 in 1986, 17 in 1988, and 39 industries in 1990 which had a non-negative nominal subsidy rate less than 20 per cent. In 1986 there was one industry, in 1988 two industries and in 1990 three industries with negative subsidy rates.

After having discussed the level of subsidy, we now turn to a more detailed examination of the characteristics of export incentive policies. First, we note that in 1983 the highest subsidy rates were granted to the sectors of fabricated metal products (101.055), printing and publishing (73.364), and paper and paper products (73.226). In the same year, the sectors receiving the lowest subsidies were ginning (3.618), processed tobacco (7.439), and agriculture (7.713).

In 1984, the subsidy rates were reduced over all sectors. The highest reductions in subsidy rates were achieved in fabricated metal products, wood and cork products, wood furniture and fixtures. Comparison of the nominal subsidy rates for 1986 with those for 1984 reveals that subsidy rates were raised in four sectors and were reduced in the remaining 45 sectors. The sectors for which the nominal subsidy rates were increased included leather and fur products, processed tobacco, and ginning. In contrast, the largest reductions in subsidy rates during 1986 were achieved in the sectors of fabricated metal products, clothing, and other food processing. During the period 1986–8, subsidy rates increased in 27 sectors, and decreased in 22 sectors. The sectors for which the subsidy rates increased during the period included the grain

TABLE 2.5 Sectoral subsidy rates (%)

I-O code	Sector name	Nominal subsidy rates					Effective subsidy rates		
		1983	1984	1986	1988	1990	1983	1984	1990
1	Agriculture	7.713	7.707	4.539	22.900	5.588	4.786	4.337	2.730
2	Animal husbandry	9.880	9.032	6.120	6.169	4.175	12.553	10.606	4.006
3	Forestry	8.420	7.965	6.803	3.293	-0.492	7.455	6.867	-1.703
4	Fishery	17.367	16.317	12.499	12.125	4.577	16.092	14.603	2.024
5	Coal mining	12.243	10.323	9.796	10.895	9.816	12.584	9.616	9.303
6	Crude petroleum	11.734	9.794	9.267	10.512	9.606	10.068	7.684	8.200
7	Iron ore mining	21.177	18.985	17.598	17.485	10.596	20.860	17.904	9.049
8	Other metallic ore mining	22.804	19.904	17.747	18.009	9.716	23.575	19.966	8.770
9	Non-metallic mining	20.040	17.652	15.525	15.416	9.784	23.200	19.805	9.288
10	Stone quarrying	33.252	28.467	23.721	12.585	9.448	34.979	28.578	6.536
11	Slaughtering & meat	36.536	27.464	20.143	12.746	12.581	207.420	132.126	25.386
12	Fruits & vegetables	26.203	19.265	13.858	16.247	8.679	-504.476	1324.200	35.423
13	Vegetable & animal oil	27.056	22.181	18.877	20.591	13.264	49.854	35.388	20.720
14	Grain mill products	16.332	11.257	10.877	39.745	14.338	74.865	32.559	109.344
15	Sugar refining	29.334	22.735	18.184	16.625	16.616	42.526	29.228	44.062
16	Other food processing	21.589	15.937	-1.992	-1.666	0.365	-220.038	-199.662	14.100
17	Alcoholic beverages	31.286	23.903	18.461	21.295	7.586	84.157	63.494	14.601
18	Non-alcoholic beverages	29.818	22.971	18.420	21.132	8.176	60.639	44.683	24.828
19	Processed tobacco	7.439	1.127	11.768	11.570	13.485	-20.614	3.344	26.349
20	Ginning	3.618	2.601	4.415	-11.469	7.366	1.863	-0.851	13.494
21	Textiles	33.429	25.268	12.205	10.872	8.683	91.064	55.723	6.440
22	Clothing	44.860	35.461	15.448	10.893	8.076	91.070	65.686	43.879
23	Leather & fur products	44.847	36.803	117.327	24.339	20.648	254.957	188.171	36.670
24	Footwear	41.116	31.663	25.737	32.261	26.658	59.160	43.222	42.042
25	Wood products	72.747	31.360	23.999	25.825	8.835	227.758	90.742	22.402

26 Wood furniture	70.572	29.617	25.386	26.186	9.145	153.458	58.940	14.429
27 Paper & paper products	73.226	33.068	27.157	31.290	31.610	164.989	60.449	59.418
28 Printing & publishing	73.364	32.457	25.886	24.006	10.965	103.976	39.764	12.098
29 Fertilizers	40.691	33.061	27.761	20.906	13.099	58.444	45.061	10.226
30 Pharmaceutical products	35.327	27.897	22.598	28.094	10.056	49.910	37.738	8.614
31 Other chemical products	35.895	30.088	26.998	26.730	16.082	52.783	37.852	16.216
32 Petroleum refining	41.837	39.223	36.783	36.322	28.329	78.282	58.044	13.050
33 Petroleum & coal products	45.664	42.401	39.962	34.109	22.379	55.949	41.995	12.568
34 Rubber products	39.237	36.219	26.177	33.723	19.414	46.602	42.537	22.105
35 Plastic products	40.296	36.292	26.300	25.606	12.578	-127.377	-90.872	8.681
36 Glass & glass products	33.313	24.271	19.916	20.658	9.714	44.012	29.346	6.884
37 Cement	34.855	26.318	21.874	20.725	9.736	70.423	31.915	9.303
38 Non-metallic minerals	37.577	28.193	22.949	28.834	17.309	55.225	38.604	21.641
39 Iron & steel	54.366	39.705	30.149	45.550	37.657	128.936	83.205	87.471
40 Non-ferrous metals	57.351	41.347	31.101	31.385	15.199	176.896	102.320	23.317
41 Fabricated metal products	101.055	54.914	27.912	31.201	11.299	305.249	151.465	14.744
42 Non-electrical machinery	43.694	40.731	25.370	26.045	14.941	72.973	65.848	20.647
43 Agricultural machinery	47.752	45.895	31.074	43.489	21.504	89.607	87.112	33.977
44 Electrical machinery	59.189	32.787	26.692	28.007	19.491	105.146	51.497	33.513
45 Shipbuilding & repairing	33.625	26.766	15.295	12.324	-2.208	38.790	29.407	-7.933
46 Railroad equipment	14.959	12.642	8.330	7.315	1.462	8.915	3.626	-11.224
47 Motor vehicles	40.766	34.745	23.354	37.474	4.077	66.455	50.406	-14.501
48 Other transport equipment	30.395	23.659	12.188	24.145	-4.008	40.068	30.254	-8.005
49 Other manufact. industries	41.001	32.850	34.367	30.603	12.148	63.479	62.065	15.183
Mean	31.978	24.125	18.488	22.590	13.035	37.519	30.838	12.250
Standard deviation	19.760	11.617	16.427	11.365	8.133	115.861	189.638	22.513

SOURCE: Author's calculations.

mill products, agriculture, and iron and steel industries. The sectors for which subsidy rates decreased included leather and fur products, ginning, and stone quarrying industries. During the period 1988–90, subsidy rates increased in four and decreased in 45 industries. The sectors for which subsidy rates increased included ginning, other food processing, and processed tobacco. The sectors for which subsidy rates decreased included motor vehicles, other transport equipment, and grain mill products. By 1990, the highest subsidy rates were paid to iron and steel (37.657), paper and paper products (31.61), and petroleum refinery (28.329). On the other hand, the sectors of other transport equipment (−4.008), shipbuilding and repairing (−2.208), and forestry (−0.492) received the lowest subsidy rates.

Table 2.6 present nominal subsidy rates for broad industry groups. In the upper part of the table industries were classified into nine industry groups, and in the lower part into four trade categories. Calculations presented in the first part of Table 2.6 reveal significant characteristics within the subsidy system. There is a marked tendency for subsidy rates to escalate from lower to higher stages of fabrication. In general, the subsidy rates are lowest for primary activities, followed by mining and energy, and highest for manufacturing. For instance, in 1984 the nominal subsidy rate was 8.31 per cent for primary activities, 15.43 per cent for mining and energy, and 31.64 per cent for manufacturing. The escalation of subsidy rates is also evident among the subsectors of manufacturing, within which the lowest subsidy rates apply to consumer goods. Higher rates were applied during the 1980s to investment goods and in 1990 to intermediate goods.

The second part of Table 2.6 reveals that, throughout the 1980s, the subsidy rates on export industries were lower than those on export- and import-competing industries, which, in turn, received the highest subsidy rates among the four trade categories.

Nominal subsidy is concerned with the impact of incentives on product prices. Effective subsidy (ESR) is concerned with the impact of incentives on production activities, taking into account incentives to outputs and tariffs and tariff-like charges to the intermediate inputs of these activities. Calculations of the ESR for 1983 and 1990 in Table 2.6 reveal that the average ESR for the economy as a whole decreased from 37.52 in 1983 to 12.25 in 1990. Furthermore, the inter-industry distribution of effective subsidy rates narrowed during the period. The standard deviation of effective subsidy rates declined from 115.861 in 1983 to 22.513 in 1990.

Consideration of the frequency distribution of ESRs reveals that among the 49 tradeable sectors considered there were 10 (1) industries in 1983 (1990) which had an effective subsidy rate higher than 100 per cent. There were 16 (2) industries in 1983 (1990) with effective subsidy rates within the range of 20–50, and 8 (24) industries in the range of 0–20. in 1983 (1990) there was 1 (6) industry with negative effective subsidy rates with values greater than −100, and there were 3 (0) industries with effective subsidy rates less than −100.

In 1983, the sectors with the highest effective subsidy rates were fabricated metal products (305.249), leather and fur products (254.957) and wood products (227.758) industries. The sectors with the lowest effective subsidy rates were fruits and vegetables (−504.476), other food processing (−200.038), and plastic products (−127.377). In 1990, the sectors with the highest effective subsidy rates included the grain mill products (109.344), iron and steel (87.471), and agricultural machinery (59.418) industries. The sectors with the lowest effective subsidy rates were motor vehicles (−14.501), other food processing (−14.1), and railroad equipment (−11.224).

During the period 1983–4, effective subsidy rates increased in four and decreased in 45 industries. The largest increase in effective subsidy rates occurred in the sectors of fruits and vegetables, plastic products, and processed tobacco. The largest decreases in effective subsidy rates were achieved in the fabricated metal products, wood products, and paper and paper products industries. During the 1984–90 period, effective subsidy rates increased in eight, and decreased in 41 industries. The largest increases in effective subsidy rates were achieved in the sectors of other food processing, plastic products, and grain mill products. Effective subsidy rates decreased in the fruits and vegetables, leather and fur products, and fabricated metal products industries.

Table 2.6 present the effective subsidy rates for the broad industry groups introduced in Table 2.4. From the table we note that effective subsidy rates escalate from lower to higher stages of fabrication. The effective subsidy rates are lowest for primary activities, followed by mining and energy, and highest on manufacturing. In 1983 (1990) the effective subsidy rate was 6.38 (2.55) per cent for primary activities, 17.63 (8.64) per cent for mining and energy, and 77.80 (23.26) per cent for manufacturing. The second part of Table 2.6 reveals that in 1983 (1990) the highest effective subsidy rates applied to export- and import-competing industries, as in the case of nominal subsidy rates.

TABLE 2.6 Subsidy rates by major commodity groups and trade categories (%)

Commodity groups	Nominal subsidy rates					Effective subsidy rates		
	1983	1984	1986	1988	1990	1983	1984	1990
Commodity groups								
I. Primary activities[a]	8.62	8.31	5.29	16.54	4.86	6.38	5.62	2.55
II. Mining & energy[b]	18.06	15.43	13.78	12.16	9.71	17.63	14.10	8.64
III. Manufacturing	43.11	31.64	24.65	57.76	16.87	77.80	63.75	23.26
1. Consumer goods	30.08	22.05	12.57	13.60	9.42	19.58	71.91	23.79
Processed food[c]	26.24	19.84	11.14	13.85	9.13	-8.16	91.48	23.91
Beverages & tobacco[d]	15.01	8.40	13.92	14.69	11.63	-4.35	12.59	24.65
Non-durable & durable consumer goods[e]	38.99	28.16	14.52	12.99	9.44	130.46	89.86	22.36
2. Intermediate goods[f]	45.66	34.74	31.44	31.46	22.62	87.85	53.28	26.01
3. Investment goods	61.22	40.63	25.79	31.00	12.68	147.01	84.04	13.98
Machinery[g]	69.03	43.40	27.21	30.08	15.83	175.41	96.75	22.92
Transport equipment[h]	38.27	32.47	21.61	33.71	3.41	59.38	44.79	-13.60
4. Other manufacturing industries[i]	41.00	32.85	34.37	30.60	12.15	63.48	62.07	15.18

Trade categories

I. Export industries[j]	38.97	26.15	16.21	11.38	7.95	23.91	55.02	14.30
II. Export- and import-competing industries[k]	46.16	36.62	28.53	33.77	23.20	87.39	62.04	37.20
II. Import-competing industries[l]	37.37	25.11	19.88	22.91	12.27	46.21	27.54	11.25
IV. Non-import-competing industries[m]	24.46	19.78	16.13	23.11	12.09	30.74	20.72	7.89

NOTES:
[a] Includes sectors nos 1–4.
[b] Includes sectors nos 5–10.
[c] Includes sectors nos 11–16.
[d] Includes sectors nos 17–19
[e] Includes sectors nos 21, 22, 24 and 26.
[f] Includes sectors nos 20, 23, 25 and 27–40.
[g] Includes sectors nos 41–44.
[h] Includes sectors nos 45–48.
[i] Includes sectors no. 49.
[j] Includes sectors nos 12, 16–23, 36 and 41.
[k] Includes sectors nos 8, 9, 29, 31, 39, 40, 42, 43 and 49.
[l] Includes sectors nos 3, 5, 6, 7, 10, 13, 27, 30 and 44–48.
[m] Includes sectors nos 1, 2, 4, 11, 14, 15, 24–26, 28, 32–35, 37 and 38.

SOURCE: Author's calculations.

2.3 Real exchange rate

Towards the end of the 1970s, Turkey followed a fixed and multiple exchange-rate policy. With the stabilization measures of 1980, Turkey devalued the Turkish lira (TL) by almost 50 per cent. The multiple exchange-rate system was eliminated except for imports of fertilizers, and fertilizer inputs. After May 1981, the exchange rate was adjusted daily against major currencies in order to maintain the competitiveness of Turkish exports. In August 1988, major reform was introduced, and a system of market setting of foreign exchange rates was adopted.

The success of liberalization policies depends in the long term on developments of the real exchange rate. The appreciation of the real exchange rate contributes in the long run to expansion and the depreciation to reduction of the trade deficit.

From Table 2.7 we note that the real exchange rate is defined as

$$\emptyset = (Ep^\$/p)$$

where E denotes the exchange rate, the price of foreign currency in terms of Turkish lira, $p^\$$ is the foreign price index measured by the GDP price deflator, and p is the domestic price index measured by GDP price deflator. The real exchange rate appreciated considerably during the 1970s, leading to the balance-of-payments problems of the late 1970s. During the 1980s, the real exchange rate depreciated until 1988, contributing to a large increase in exports. Thereafter, the trend in the real exchange rate was reversed.

2.4 Anti-export bias and sectoral real effective exchange rates

A natural question that arises is whether the expanded export incentives and the tariff reductions analyzed above have reduced the bias against exports entailed by import-protection and export-promotion measures. This question may be answered by calculating the profitability of producing for export relative to domestic market, approximated using the measure

$$\pi = (1 + s) / (1 + t),$$

where s denotes the subsidy rate and t the protection rate. In the following, we consider for the subsidy rates the nominal and effective subsidy, and for the protection rates the nominal and effective protection rates.

Table 2.8 presents the anti-export bias figures for the 49 tradeable sectors evaluated using the figures given in Tables 2.3 and 2.5. From the table it follows that, on average, anti-export bias prevailed during the 1980s. The average value of anti-export bias evaluated using nominal figures was 0.864 in 1983, 0.792 in 1984, 0.83 in 1988, and 0.914 in 1990. The average value of anti-export bias evaluated using effective figures was 0.896 in 1983, 0.79 in 1984, and 0.84 in 1990. The figures indicate anti-export bias, since the average figures for the economy as a whole are less than unity throughout this period. The average value of anti-export bias continues to increase over time. This development clearly represents changes in a healthy direction. Since, under a liberal trade regime, the measure of anti-export bias would equal unity and variance zero, we note that there still remains an area for considerable improvement.

Consideration of sectoral anti-export measures using nominal subsidy and protection figures reveals that in 1983, 12 industries had π values greater than unity (indicating export bias), and 37 sectors had π values less than unity (indicating anti-export bias). During 1983, the highest π figures applied to the printing and publishing (1.375), other transport equipment (1.138), and iron and steel (1.106) sectors; and the lowest figures to the processed tobacco and products (0.524), plastic products (0.4), and fruit and vegetables canning (0.524) sectors. By 1990, the ordering had changed and 11 industries had π values greater than unity, while 38 industries had π values less than unity. During 1990, the highest π figures applied to the iron and steel (1.254), iron ore mining (1.06), and other metallic ore mining (1.05) sectors. The alcoholic beverages (0.324), non-alcoholic beverages (0.429), and clothing (0.487) sectors were receiving the lowest π figures. The trade policies that were followed during the period 1983–90 resulted in considerable increases in the π values of the leather and fur products, processed tobacco and products, and plastic products sectors, and in decreases in π values of the printing and publishing, and alcoholic and non-alcoholic beverages sectors.

Consideration of sectoral anti-export measures using effective subsidy and protection figures reveals that in 1983, 18 industries had π values greater that unity (indicating export bias), and 31 sectors had π values less than unity (indicating anti-export bias). During 1983, the highest π figures applied to the printing and publishing (1.837), sugar refining (1.815), and fabricated metal products (1.562) sectors; and the lowest figures to the processed tobacco and products (-0.046), plastic products (0.035), and other food processing (0.113) sectors. By

TABLE 2.7 Real exchange rate

	IL/$ [a]	DM/$ [b]	TL/DM [c]	Effective exchange rate (TL/$) [d]	Turkish GDP deflator (1968=1) [e]	OECD GDP deflator (1968=1) [f]	Islamic countries GDP deflator (1968=1) [g]	Share of Islamic countries in Turkish exports (%) [h]	Foreign price (1968=1) [i]	Real exchange rate (AVG=100) [j]
1960	4.870	4.200	1.160	4.8120	0.6580	0.7557	0.8751	1.00	0.7569	39.782
1961	9.000	4.033	2.231	8.9814	0.6861	0.8029	0.9013	1.80	0.8047	75.704
1962	9.000	4.000	2.250	9.0000	0.7513	0.8254	0.9085	0.00	0.8254	71.062
1963	9.000	4.000	2.250	9.0000	0.7938	0.8485	0.9249	0.30	0.8487	69.162
1964	9.000	4.000	2.250	9.0000	0.8143	0.8732	0.9471	1.60	0.8744	69.463
1965	9.000	4.000	2.250	9.0000	0.8486	0.8993	0.9670	0.50	0.8996	68.577
1966	9.000	4.000	2.250	9.0000	0.9021	0.9317	0.9931	0.70	0.9321	66.840
1967	9.000	4.000	2.250	9.0000	0.9622	0.9615	0.9921	0.70	0.9617	64.652
1968	9.000	4.000	2.250	9.0000	1.0000	1.0000	1.0000	1.70	1.0000	64.686
1969	9.000	3.943	2.282	9.0324	1.0533	1.0500	1.0073	2.50	1.0489	64.647
1970	11.500	3.660	3.142	11.7671	1.1738	1.1130	1.1395	2.30	1.1136	80.237
1971	14.920	3.491	4.274	15.4641	1.3843	1.1787	1.2056	2.10	1.1793	94.682
1972	14.150	3.189	4.438	15.0502	1.6112	1.2411	1.2599	5.90	1.2422	83.397
1973	14.150	2.673	5.294	15.9070	1.9644	1.3342	1.4060	4.84	1.3377	77.853
1974	13.930	2.588	5.383	15.8305	2.5101	1.4930	1.6479	6.80	1.5035	68.152
1975	14.440	2.460	5.869	16.6992	2.9206	1.6587	1.9741	11.31	1.6944	69.630
1976	16.050	2.518	6.374	18.4116	3.4364	1.7864	2.3097	8.80	1.8325	70.564
1977	18.000	2.322	7.751	21.2513	4.2811	1.9222	2.6446	11.48	2.0051	71.539
1978	24.280	2.009	12.088	30.2980	6.1490	2.0664	2.9276	13.41	2.1819	77.269
1979	31.080	1.833	16.957	40.2667	10.4917	2.2337	3.1794	15.84	2.3835	65.748
1980	76.040	1.818	41.833	98.8631	21.2201	2.4415	3.5546	22.30	2.6897	90.066

1981	111.220	2.260	49.212	132.6274	30.1334	2.6563	3.9704	41.10	3.1964	101.114
1982	162.550	2.427	66.987	188.8992	38.5755	2.8476	4.3119	45.00	3.5065	123.414
1983	225.460	2.553	88.301	257.3964	49.7612	2.9871	4.6482	41.10	3.6698	136.434
1984	366.680	2.846	128.845	403.8550	74.3234	3.1126	4.9178	42.00	3.8708	151.170
1985	518.340	2.944	176.067	564.8220	106.9784	3.2309	5.0654	42.00	4.0014	151.842
1986	669.390	2.172	308.262	810.3045	140.8393	3.3408	5.4909	35.00	4.0933	169.266
1987	857.210	1.797	476.071	1118.9785	194.5983	3.4410	6.1937	30.30	4.2751	176.682
1988	1422.350	1.756	808.997	1875.7595	323.7451	3.5545	7.2714	30.30	4.6807	194.919
1989	2121.680	1.880	1128.074	2719.3340	533.9499	3.6932	8.2676	24.70	4.8231	176.544
1990	2608.640	1.616	1620.640	3577.1200	817.0131	3.8372	9.4250	19.30	4.9156	154.686

SOURCE:

[a] Various issues of *International Financial Statistics Yearbook*, line 'rf'.

[b] Various issues of *International Financial Statistics Yearbook*, line 'rf'.

[c] The exchange rate has been obtained using the information given in the first two columns.

[d] Effective exchange rate is given by the relation $EE = 0.75$ (TL/$\$$) $+ 0.25$ (TL/DM) (68DM/$\$$). where (68DM/$\$$) refers to the price of US dollars in terms of German marks in 1968.

[e] *Statistical Yearbook*, State Institute of Statistics, Turkey.

[f] Various issues of *International Financial Statistics Yearbook*, GDP deflator of industrial countries.

[g] Various issues of *International Financial Statistics Yearbook*, GDP deflator of middle eastern countries.

[h] *Statistical Yearbook*, State Institute of Statistics, Turkey.

[i] Foreign price is determined by the relation $p_f = A\, p_{isl} + (1-A)\, p_{ind}$ where A denotes the share of Islamic countries in Turkish exports, p_{isl} the price level of Islamic countries, and p_{ind} the price level of industrial countries.

[j] Real exchange rate equals $RE = (EE\, p_f)/p_{Turkey}$ where p_{Turkey} denotes the Turkish GDP deflator.

TABLE 2.8 Anti-export bias

I-O code	Sector name	Using nominal rates				Development over time	Using effective rates			Development over time
		AEB83	AEB84	AEB88	AEB90		AEB83	AEB84	AEB90	
1	Agriculture	0.861	0.791	0.803	0.961	+	0.856	0.776	0.903	+
2	Animal husbandry	0.903	0.866	0.873	0.934	+	0.988	0.960	0.859	−
3	Forestry	0.795	0.765	0.878	0.951	+	0.738	0.711	0.866	+
4	Fishery	0.834	0.802	0.613	0.671	−	0.839	0.803	0.621	−
5	Coal mining	0.620	0.595	0.858	0.933	+	0.562	0.533	0.832	+
6	Crude petroleum	0.898	0.848	0.889	0.817	−	0.791	0.745	0.738	−
7	Iron ore mining	1.045	0.989	1.045	1.060	+	1.091	1.022	0.983	−
8	Other met. ore mining	1.061	0.998	0.863	1.051	−	1.084	1.010	0.959	−
9	Non-metallic mining	0.594	0.568	0.675	0.910	+	0.548	0.519	0.823	+
10	Stone quarrying	1.059	1.007	0.958	1.012	−	1.107	1.042	0.922	−
11	Slaughtering & meat	0.766	0.713	0.805	1.023	+	0.662	0.578	1.077	+
12	Fruits & vegetables	0.524	0.486	0.597	0.639	+	0.219	0.004	0.264	+
13	Vegetable & animal oil	0.811	0.758	1.038	0.961	+	0.818	0.738	0.964	+
14	Grain mill products	0.792	0.736	0.683	0.825	+	0.618	0.610	0.342	−
15	Sugar refining	0.540	0.502	0.574	0.806	+	1.815	1.720	0.596	−
16	Other food processing	0.584	0.500	0.481	0.718	+	0.113	0.067	0.445	+
17	Alcoholic beverages	0.689	0.635	0.373	0.324	−	0.254	0.202	0.154	−
18	Non-alcoholic beverages	0.792	0.730	0.444	0.429	−	0.699	0.596	0.125	−
19	Processed tobacco	0.227	0.211	0.626	0.605	+	−0.046	−0.038	0.450	+
20	Ginning	0.965	0.936	0.723	1.029	−	1.158	1.175	1.007	−
21	Textiles	0.638	0.613	0.675	0.809	+	0.444	0.404	0.625	+
22	Clothing	0.568	0.520	0.412	0.487	−	0.571	0.462	0.024	−
23	Leather & fur products	0.574	0.532	0.883	1.041	+	0.403	0.313	1.044	+
24	Footwear	0.549	0.503	0.839	0.820	+	0.553	0.492	0.733	+
25	Wood products	0.943	0.696	1.010	0.765	−	1.290	0.726	0.536	−

#	Industry									
26	Wood furniture	0.743	0.554	0.479	0.591	−	0.848	0.520	0.454	−
27	Paper & paper products	1.061	0.812	1.096	1.039	+	1.240	0.750	1.022	+
28	Printing & publishing	1.375	1.044	1.019	0.821	−	1.837	1.248	0.728	−
29	Fertilizers	1.073	0.982	1.002	1.005	−	1.351	1.171	0.942	−
30	Pharmaceutical products	1.066	0.980	1.005	0.798	−	1.227	1.093	0.732	−
31	Other chemical products	0.897	0.896	0.859	0.900	+	0.948	0.928	0.780	+
32	Petroleum refining	0.900	0.855	0.965	1.017	+	0.868	0.750	0.889	+
33	Petroleum & coal products	0.881	0.838	1.202	0.988	−	0.885	0.780	0.852	−
34	Rubber products	0.905	0.842	0.875	0.866	+	0.981	0.873	0.758	+
35	Plastic products	0.400	0.382	0.613	0.727	−	0.035	−0.014	0.483	−
36	Glass & glass products	0.798	0.713	0.489	0.610	−	0.754	0.639	0.478	−
37	Cement	0.910	1.193	1.114	0.828	+	0.838	1.268	0.598	+
38	Non-metallic minerals	0.893	0.808	0.905	0.823	−	0.889	0.734	0.688	−
39	Iron & steel	1.106	0.980	1.106	1.254	+	1.475	1.149	1.531	+
40	Non-ferrous metals	0.972	0.921	0.972	1.023	+	1.122	0.950	0.937	−
41	Fabricated metal products	1.104	0.829	0.670	0.820	−	1.562	0.901	0.584	−
42	Non-electrical machinery	0.936	0.896	0.727	0.930	−	1.110	1.038	0.865	−
43	Agricultural machinery	1.003	0.909	0.779	0.955	−	1.323	1.111	0.934	−
44	Electrical machinery	1.065	0.835	0.726	0.896	−	1.391	0.926	0.865	−
45	Shipbuilding & repairing	0.818	0.760	0.590	0.706	−	0.830	0.753	0.585	−
46	Railroad equipment	0.964	0.911	0.747	0.804	−	1.067	0.971	0.644	−
47	Motor vehicles	0.853	0.789	0.665	0.653	−	0.888	0.772	0.421	−
48	Other transport equipment	1.138	1.039	0.926	0.901	−	1.192	1.067	0.787	−
49	Other manufact. industries	0.829	0.588	0.772	0.925	+	0.931	0.545	0.831	+
	Mean	0.864	0.792	0.830	0.914		0.896	0.790	0.840	
	Standard deviation	0.213	0.195	0.201	0.178		0.409	0.354	0.275	

SOURCE: Author's calculations.

1990, the ordering had changed and five industries had π values greater than unity, while 44 industries had π values less than unity. During 1990, the highest π figures applied to the iron and steel (1.531), slaughtering and meat (1.077), and leather and fur products (1.044) sectors. The clothing (0.024), non-alcoholic beverages (0.125), and alcoholic beverages (0.154) sectors were receiving the lowest π figures.

In Table 2.8, the columns showing the development of π values over time have been obtained by regressing the π value on time (t)

$$\pi = \alpha + \beta\, t.$$

In the table, the sectors for which β is positive (negative) are shown with a '+' ('−') sign. The table indicates that when anti-export bias is estimated by using nominal effective subsidy and protection rates, anti-export bias has been decreasing for 23 (18) sectors and increasing for 26 (31) sectors. For the economy as a whole, anti-export bias has been decreasing (constant) over time.

Table 2.9 shows the sectoral profitabilities of producing for exporting relative to home production, measured by he relation $\upsilon_i = (E\, p_i^\$ (1 + s_i)\, /\, p)$ where s_i denotes the nominal subsidy rate of sector i. From the table, it follows that the economy-wide υ increased over the period 1983–8, but decreased substantially over 1988–90. Thus, the incentives provided to production of exportables relative to domestic production decreased substantially over the period 1988–90.

3   COMPARATIVE ADVANTAGE

It has been shown by various economists that free trade policy is the optimal policy for a small country in the world economy. Under free trade, the country will produce and export (import) the commodities in which it has comparative advantage (disadvantage). Theoretically, comparative advantage can be determined by comparing the autarkic equilibrium price vector with the free trade price vector. But difficulties are encountered when trying to evaluate the autarkic equilibrium price vector empirically. For the determination of the sectors with comparative advantage, we first consider domestic resource costs and then revealed comparative advantage. As is well known, empirical measures of comparative advantage can help to identify the overall direction and thrust which a country's investment and trade should take in order to exploit international differences in product and factor supply and demand.

TABLE *2.9* *Sectoral real effective exchange rates*

I–O code	Sector name	1983	1984	1986	1988	1990
1	Agriculture	1.000	1.050	1.079	1.278	0.830
2	Animal husbandry	1.000	1.042	1.074	1.082	0.802
3	Forestry	1.000	1.046	1.096	1.067	0.777
4	Fishery	1.000	1.041	1.066	1.070	0.754
5	Coal mining	1.000	1.033	1.088	1.107	0.828
6	Crude petroleum	1.000	1.032	1.088	1.108	0.830
7	Iron ore mining	1.000	1.031	1.079	1.086	0.773
8	Other metallic ore mining	1.000	1.026	1.066	1.076	0.756
9	Non-metallic mining	1.000	1.030	1.070	1.077	0.774
10	Stone quarrying	1.000	1.013	1.033	0.946	0.695
11	Slaughtering & meat	1.000	0.981	0.979	0.925	0.698
12	Fruits & vegetables	1.000	0.993	1.003	1.032	0.729
13	Vegetable & animal oil	1.000	1.010	1.041	1.063	0.755
14	Grain mill products	1.000	1.005	1.060	1.346	0.832
15	Sugar refining	1.000	0.997	1.016	1.010	0.763
16	Other food processing	1.000	1.002	0.897	0.906	0.699
17	Alcoholic beverages	1.000	0.991	1.004	1.035	0.694
18	Non-alcoholic beverages	1.000	0.995	1.015	1.045	0.705
19	Processed tobacco	1.000	0.989	1.157	1.163	0.894
20	Ginning	1.000	1.040	1.121	0.957	0.877
21	Textiles	1.000	0.986	0.935	0.931	0.689
22	Clothing	1.000	0.982	0.886	0.857	0.631
23	Leather & fur products	1.000	0.992	1.669	0.962	0.705
24	Footwear	1.000	0.980	0.991	1.050	0.760
25	Wood products	1.000	0.799	0.798	0.816	0.533
26	Wood furniture	1.000	0.798	0.818	0.829	0.542
27	Paper & paper products	1.000	0.807	0.816	0.849	0.643
28	Printing & publishing	1.000	0.803	0.808	0.801	0.542
29	Fertilizers	1.000	0.994	1.010	0.963	0.680
30	Pharmaceutical products	1.000	0.993	1.008	1.060	0.688
31	Other chemical products	1.000	1.006	1.039	1.045	0.723
32	Petroleum refining	1.000	1.031	1.073	1.077	0.766
33	Petroleum & coal products	1.000	1.027	1.069	1.031	0.711
34	Rubber products	1.000	1.028	1.008	1.076	0.726
35	Plastic products	1.000	1.021	1.001	1.003	0.679
36	Glass & glass products	1.000	0.979	1.000	1.014	0.697
37	Cement	1.000	0.984	1.005	1.003	0.689
38	Non-metallic minerals	1.000	0.979	0.994	1.049	0.722
39	Iron & steel	1.000	0.951	0.938	1.056	0.755
40	Non-ferrous metals	1.000	0.944	0.927	0.935	0.620
41	Fabricated metal products	1.000	0.809	0.708	0.731	0.469
42	Non-electrical machinery	1.000	1.029	0.970	0.983	0.677

cont. on page 38

TABLE 2.9   *continued*

I–O code	Sector name	1983	1984	1986	1988	1990
43	Agricultural machinery	1.000	1.037	0.987	1.088	0.696
44	Electrical machinery	1.000	0.876	0.885	0.901	0.635
45	Shipbuilding & repairing	1.000	0.997	0.960	0.942	0.619
46	Railroad equipment	1.000	1.029	1.048	1.046	0.747
47	Motor vehicles	1.000	1.006	0.975	1.094	0.626
48	Other transport equipment	1.000	0.996	0.957	1.066	0.623
49	Other manufact. industries	1.000	0.990	1.060	1.038	0.673
Mean		1.000	0.997	1.011	1.059	0.738

SOURCE: Author's calculations.

3.1   Domestic resources cost

The concept of domestic resource cost was developed during the early 1960s in Israel. It measures the resource cost of earning foreign exchange through exporting commodities or saving foreign exchange through import substitution. The concept is closely related to the concept of effective rate of protection. This relation can be shown using the measure of effective protection coefficient given by

$$VA_d \, / \, VA_w$$

where VA_d denoted valued added at domestic prices and VA_w value added at world prices. Since $VA_w = E \, VA_w^\$$, where $VA_w^\$$ denotes value added at world prices measured in foreign currency and E the exchange rate, we note that the effective protection coefficient is the same thing as the DRC ratio. Hence the DRC coefficient can be calculated as

$$DRC = VA_d \, / \, VA_w^\$ = (1 + EPR/100)) \, E$$

where EPR denote the effective protection rate.

The domestic resources cost (DRC) coefficients for the tradeable sectors are shown in Table 2.10. In the calculation of DRC coefficients, we used the average value of the exchange rate of 521.98 TL/\$ for the year 1985, the year in which the input–output table was prepared and the effective protection coefficients calculated by Togan (1993). The last column of Table 2.1 shows the development of the DRC coefficient over time. For that purpose, we regress the value of the DRC on time (t).

$$DRC = \alpha + \beta \, t,$$

and show the sectors for which β is positive (negative) with a '+' ('−') sign. In Table 2.10 the sectors are divided into four cells. The top two cells contain sectors with decreasing DRC values over time and the lower two cells the sectors with increasing DRC values over time. The top (lower) two cells have been ordered according to their DRC values, and the dividing measure is the average value of DRC for the economy as a whole. The upper (lower) cell contains the sectors with lower (higher) DRC values than the average. The broad mix of goods appearing in the upper cell may be considered as the sectors having comparative advantage. By contrast, we can say that the sectors in the lower cell of Table 2.10 have comparative disadvantage according to the DRC criteria.

3.2   Revealed comparative advantage

It is generally recognized that the disaggregated exports of a country indicate where the domestic industries display international competitiveness, while a country's imports pinpoint where it lacks such competitiveness. Following Volrath (1991), we calculate the 'revealed comparative advantage' by the formula.

$$RCA_i = \ln\left[(X_i/X) \, / \, (X_i^w/X^w)\right]$$

where X_i denotes exports of commodity i by the country, X total exports of the country, X_i^w world exports of commodity i excluding the exports of the country, X^w world exports excluding the exports of the country, and 'ln' the natural logarithm of the variable.

In this study, the RCA indexes were calculated for two digit SITC classification of trade data over the period 1980–8. Turkey's leading export industries are those in the uppermost cell of Table 2.11 – products with high and rising RCAs. A broad mix of goods appear in this cell. By contrast, the lowest cell of Table 2.11 lists products with low and falling RCAs, hence commodities with comparative disadvantage according to RCA criteria. Weak but improving export positions are evident in the cell 'low and rising RCA', which contains commodities with increasing but with negative RCA values greater than −1. In the following, we call the sectors which have RCA values greater than −1

TABLE 2.10   *Comparative advantage according to domestic resource cost (DRC)*

I–O code	Sector name	DRC 1990–1
Low and falling		
7	Iron ore mining	578.0929
8	Other met. ore mining	590.4377
3	Forestry	599.5201
10	Stone quarrying	601.8690
48	Other transport equipment	602.0778
29	Fertilizers	610.2207
13	Vegetable & animal oil	619.0422
1	Agriculture	633.5010
39	Iron & steel	639.2428
33	Petroleum & coal products	640.5478
32	Petroleum refining	663.6454
11	Slaughtering & meat	671.4751
23	Leather & fur products	675.2594
5	Coal mining	683.4023
40	Non-ferrous metals	684.1070
49	Other man. industries	717.8791
42	Non-electrical machinery	718.7404
9	Non-metallic mining	729.1017
43	Agricultural machinery	738.9671
31	Other chemical products	762.2996
High and falling		
27	Paper & paper products	809.3822
45	Shipbuilding & repairing	820.2916
21	Textiles	884.1036
38	Non-metallic minerals	886.0089
37	Cement	900.5199
47	Motor vehicles	990.7963
24	Footwear	993.3540
36	Glass & glass products	1000.2964
41	Fabricated metal products	1012.4324
26	Wood furniture	1098.0632
25	Wood products	1141.7269
12	Fruits & vegetables	2240.5209
17	Alcoholic beverages	3196.1096
Low and rising		
20	Ginning	548.3922
2	Animal husbandry	619.2249
46	Railroad equipment	631.1782

28	Printing & publishing	707.1002
6	Crude petroleum	756.7405
30	Pharmaceutical products	764.3614

High and rising

44	Electrical machinery	810.8176
34	Rubber products	839.5526
4	Fishery	856.8302
16	Other food processing	1046.9353
35	Plastic products	1152.6623
15	Sugar refining	1166.2077
19	Processed tobacco	1405.0136
14	Grain mill products	2541.0

SOURCE: Author's calculations.

TABLE *2.11*   *Comparative advantage according to the values of revealed comparative advantage*

SITC		1989–90
High and rising RCA		
57	Explosives	3.0118
52	Inorganic chemicals	2.7275
84	Clothing	2.0696
42	Fixed vegetable oils and fats	1.1894
67	Iron and steel	1.1450
09	Animal oils and fats	0.8408
56	Fertilizers, manufactured	0.6109
55	Essential oils and perfume materials	0.4640
83	Travel goods	0.3333
43	Animal and vegetable oils and fats, proc.	0.1363
81	Sanitary, plumbing, heating	0.0954
41	Animal oils and fats	0.0906
07	Miscellaneous edible products	0.0680
28	Metalliferous ores and metal scrap	0.0662
Medium and rising RCA		
68	Non-ferrous metals	−0.1639
62	Rubber manufactures	−0.1688
54	Medicinal and pharmaceutical products	−0.4432
69	Manufactures of metal	−0.6177
51	Organic chemicals	−0.7472
85	Footwear	−0.8179
33	Petroleum and petroleum products	−0.8421

cont. on page 42

TABLE *2.11   continued*

SITC		1989–90
Low and rising RCA		
53	Dyeing, tanning, and colouring materials	−1.0306
72	Electrical machinery	−1.1781
64	Paper	−1.5627
59	Chemical materials and products	−1.7483
23	Crude rubber	−1.7498
61	Leather manufactures	−1.8614
08	Feeding stuff for animals	−2.1977
71	Machinery, other than electric	−2.2259
58	Plastic materials	−2.3168
86	Scientific instruments and optical goods	−3.4336
High and falling RCA		
05	Vegetables and sugar preparations	2.1225
12	Tobacco	2.0279
00	Live animals chiefly for food	1.9369
27	Crude fertilizers and crude minerals	1.7021
65	Textiles	1.2806
26	Textile fibres and their wastes	1.1097
29	Crude animal and vegetable materials	0.4641
66	Non-metallic mineral manufactures	0.1273
Medium and falling RCA		
04	Cereals and cereal preparations	−0.5363
03	Fish and fish preparations	−0.5625
06	Coffee, tea, cocoa, spices	−0.5656
Low and falling RCA		
63	Wood manufactures	−1.5015
01	Meat and meat preparations	−1.5302
24	Cork and wood	−1.6937
82	Furniture	−1.6987
22	Oil seeds and oleaginous fruit	−1.7888
89	Miscellaneous manufactured articles	−1.8514
11	Beverages	−1.8658
02	Dairy products	−1.9274
73	Transport equipment	−2.2525
21	Hides, skins and fur-skins, raw	−3.8368
32	Coal	−4.8407
25	Pulp and waste paper	−5.0133

SOURCE: Author's calculations.

TABLE *2.12a*   *Correlation coefficients of Turkish RCA values for the*
period 1986–8 with the RCA values of different countries for the periods
1986–8, 1983–5 and 1980–2

	1986–8	*1983–5*	*1980–2*
Argentina	0.1319	0.1385	0.3344
Brazil	0.2455	0.1697	0.1996
Indonesia	0.2827	0.1118	0.0427
Spain	0.1810	0.2442	0.2959
Korea	0.4484	0.3809	0.4823
Malaysia	0.2983	0.2381	0.2644
Portugal	0.0797	0.1116	0.0908
Thailand	0.2431	0.3072	0.4226
Greece	0.5334	0.4094	0.4281

SOURCE: Author's calculations.

TABLE *2.12b*   *Correlation coefficients of Turkish RCA values for the*
period 1989–90 with the RCA values of different countries for the periods
1989–90, 1986–8, 1983–5 and 1980–2

	1989–90	*1986–8*	*1983–5*
Argentina	0.0806	0.1381	0.1675
Brazil	0.2725	0.2874	0.2261
Indonesia	0.2572	0.1958	0.1404
Spain	0.2828	0.3141	0.3207
Korea	0.2832	0.4235	0.3745
Malaysia	0.2757	0.1126	0.0791
Portugal	0.0210	0.1413	0.2008
Thailand	0.2900	0.0034	0.1081
Greece	0.3820	0.5699	0.3785

SOURCE: Author's calculations.

and which are increasing over time 'industries with comparative advantage according to RCA criteria'.

To see where Turkey's export pattern, evidenced by RCA values, fits among those of other countries, we examine the similarity of Turkish RCA indexes to those calculated for other economies. The results are presented in Table 2.12a and b, in which we have considered the mean RCA values for the periods 1980–2, 1983–5, 1986–8 and 1989–90, and determined in Table 2.12a the correlation coefficients between Turkish RCA values for the period 1986–8 with those for period 1986–8, 1983–5 and 1980–2. Table 2.12b shows the correlation coefficients between

TABLE 2.13 Revealed comparative advantage (RCA) of Greece and Korea, 1989–90

	Greece			Korea	
SITC	Commodity	RCA	SITC	Commodity	RCA
Increasing and high RCA values			**Increasing and high RCA values**		
42	Fixed vegetable oils and fats	2.5843	85	Footwear	2.0466
84	Clothing	1.9187	72	Electrical machinery	0.7226
26	Textile fibres and their wastes	1.0213	89	Miscellaneous manufactured articles	0.6808
04	Cereals and cereal preparations	0.8745	61	Leather manufacture	0.4308
68	Non-ferrous metals	0.7172	52	Inorganic chemicals	0.0170
11	Beverages	0.6637			
67	Iron and steel	0.4715			
33	Petroleum and petroleum products	0.2440	**Increasing and medium RCA values**		
56	Fertilizers, manufactured	0.2366	26	Textile fibres and their wastes	-0.3764
03	Fish and fish preparations	0.1250	58	Plastic materials	-0.3931
02	Dairy products	0.0189	81	Sanitary, plumbing, heating	-0.6154
			71	Machinery, other than electric	-0.6642
Increasing and medium RCA values			82	Furniture	-0.8278
53	Dyeing, tanning, and colouring materials	-0.2541			
06	Sugar and sugar preparations	-0.3247	**Increasing and low RCA values**		
54	Medicinal and pharmaceutical products	-0.3339	53	Dyeing, tanning, and colouring materials	-1.0377
55	Essential oils and perfume materials	-0.4249	68	Non-ferrous metals	-1.1877
62	Rubber manufacture	-0.7232	23	Crude rubber	-1.2795
			33	Petroleum and petroleum products	-1.5715
Increasing and low RCA values			59	Chemical materials and products	-1.7422
07	Coffee, tea, cocoa, spices	-1.1886	54	Medicinal and pharmaceutical products	-1.9690
01	Meat and meat preparations	-1.3962	04	Cereals and cereal preparations	-2.3923
22	Oil seeds and oleaginous fruit	-1.4144	07	Coffee, tea, cocoa, spices	-2.7409
34	Gas, natural and manufactured	-1.4827	21	Hides, skins and fur skins, raw	-3.0893
24	Cork and wood	-1.6269	08	Feeding stuff for animals	-3.1966
71	Machinery, other than electric	-2.2577	41	Animal oils and fats	-4.8938
25	Pulp and waste paper	-3.2300	32	Coal	-5.8073
23	Crude rubber	-4.1863	00	Live animals chiefly for food	-6.5640

Decreasing and high RCA values

05	Vegetables and fruit	2.2411
12	Tobacco and tobacco manufactures	2.0797
27	Crude fertilizers and crude minerals	1.3447
61	Leather manufactures	0.9786
21	Hides, skins and fur skins, raw	0.6818
65	Textiles	0.6488
66	Non-metallic mineral manufactures	0.6215
28	Metalliferous ores and metal scrap	0.0131

Decreasing and medium RCA values

85	Footwear	-0.0438
81	Sanitary, plumbing, heating	-0.2840
09	Miscellaneous edible products	-0.3838
69	Manufactures of metal	-0.5410
63	Cork and wood manufactures	-0.5882
08	Feeding stuff for animals	-0.6331
29	Crude animal and vegetable materials	-0.6838
51	Organic chemicals	-0.8999
64	Paper	-0.9883
59	Chemical materials and products	-0.9974

Decreasing and low RCA values

89	Miscellaneous manufactured articles	-1.1151
43	Animal and vegetable oils and fats	-1.3214
57	Explosives	-1.3460
83	Travel goods	-1.4749
58	Plastic materials	-1.5490
72	Electrical machinery	-1.6385
82	Furniture	-2.3885
00	Live animals chiefly for food	-2.5636
73	Transport equipment	-3.4663
41	Animal oils and fats	-5.5222
52	Inorganic chemicals	-5.5625
32	Coal	-7.8328

Decreasing and high RCA values

83	Travel goods	2.2525
84	Clothing	1.4786
65	Textiles	1.0629
03	Fish and fish preparations	0.8564
62	Rubber manufactures	0.6028
67	Iron and steel	0.5076
69	Manufactures of metal	0.2673
29	Crude animal and vegetable materials	0.2096

Decreasing and medium RCA values

56	Fertilizers, manufactured	-0.2423
06	Sugar and sugar preparations	-0.3322
73	Transport equipment	-0.3482
66	Non-metallic mineral manufactures	-0.6343
27	Crude fertilizers and crude minerals	-0.7975

Decreasing and low RCA values

51	Organic chemicals	-1.0375
64	Paper	-1.1432
05	Vegetables and fruit	-1.2123
09	Miscellaneous edible products	-1.3400
63	Cork and wood manufactures	-1.3848
12	Tobacco and tobacco manufactures	-1.4353
57	Explosives	-1.8756
55	Essential oils and perfume materials	-1.8805
24	Cork and wood	-2.1347
11	Beverages	-2.2822
01	Meat and meat preparations	-2.3445
28	Metalliferous ores and metal scrap	-2.5260
34	Gas, natural and manufactured	-3.9006
43	Animal and vegetable oils and fat	-3.9538
22	Oil seeds and oleaginous fruit	-6.3042
02	Dairy products	-6.5227
42	Fixed vegetable oils and fats	-6.6314
25	Pulp and waste paper	-7.0263

SOURCE: Author's calculations.

Turkish RCA values for the period 1989–90, with RCA values for other countries for the periods 1989–90, 1986–8, 1983–5 and 1980–2. From the table, it follows that Turkish exports are similar to Greek and Korean exports with a mean lag of two years. Table 2.13 shows the RCA values for Greece and Korea.

In the following, we consider the sectors which satisfy the criteria for having comparative advantage according to at least two of the three criteria (DRC, RCA and locomotive sector for either Greece or Korea) as the industries in which the country has comparative advantage. The approach leads to the conclusion that Turkey has comparative advantage in the production of the following sectors:

   (i)   agriculture (I–O code 1);
   (ii)   iron ore mining (I–O code 7);
  (iii)   vegetable and animal oils and fats (I–O code 13);
  (iv)   other food processing (I–O code 16);
   (v)   clothing (I–O code 22);
  (vi)   leather and fur products (I–O code 23);
 (vii)   footwear (I–O code 24);
(viii)   fertilizers (I–O code 29);
  (ix)   pharmaceutical products (I–O code 30);
   (x)   other chemical products (I–O code 31);
  (xi)   petroleum refinery (I–O code 32);
 (xii)   iron and steel (I–O code 39);
(xiii)   non-ferrous metals (I–O code 40);
 (xiv)   non-electrical machinery (I–O code 42);
 (xv)   agricultural machinery (I–O code 43).

4   CONCLUSION

During the 1980s, Turkey successfully liberalized its import and export regimes. The economy-wide average level of nominal and effective protection and subsidy rates were reduced substantially over the period. However, the rates are still high – as evidenced by the nominal and effective protection rates for some of the industrial and developing countries shown in Table 2.14a–d. Furthermore, there exists considerable variation in the inter-industry distribution of incentives. The EPRs are far from being equalized among the industries. It is well known that for maximization of consumption possibilities, the EPRs must be equalized among the industries, and if some sectors are

TABLE 2.14a *Nominal and effective protection rates in selected developed countries (1962)*

	USA		United Kingdom		EEC		Japan	
	Nominal	Effective	Nominal	Effective	Nominal	Effective	Nominal	Effective
Intermediate goods I	8.8	17.6	11.1	23.1	7.6	12	11.4	23.8
Intermediate goods II	15.2	28.6	17.2	34.3	13.3	28.3	16.6	34.5
Consumer goods	17.5	25.9	23.8	40.4	17.8	30.9	27.5	50.5
Investment goods	10.3	13.9	17	23	11.7	15	17.1	22
Mean	11.6	20	15.5	27.8	11.9	18.6	16.2	29.5

SOURCE: Balassa (1967).

TABLE *2.14b* *Nominal protection rates in manufacturing sectors of selected developed countries*

	1925	1950	1976	1987
Germany[a]	20	26	–	7
UK[a]	5	23	–	7
USA[a]	37	14	–	7
Greece[b]	–	–	22	–
Portugal[b]	–	–	13.4	–
Spain[b]	–	–	16.2	–

SOURCE: [a]World Bank (1991).
[b]Donges *et al.* (1982).

TABLE *2.14c* *Nominal and effective protection rates in Germany (1970)*

Sector name	Nominal protection	Effective protection
Mining	0.3	–1.1
Textiles & clothing	11.0	21.2
Chemicals	11.4	13.3
Rubber & plastic	10.3	13.6
Hides & leather	12.3	15.5
Wood products	11.0	15.0
Glass, ceramics and cement	12.6	14.9
Metals	5.5	20.6
Metal products	6.0	25.2
Machinery other than electrical	7.9	3.3
Electrical machinery	9.5	6.8
Transportation equipment	11.2	8.3
Other manufacturing products		

SOURCE: Donges *et al.* (1973).

TABLE 2.14d *Nominal and effective rates in selected developing countries*

Sector name	Korea, 1968		Singapore, 1967		Taiwan, 1969		Argentina, 1969	
	Nominal protection	*Effective protection*	*Nominal protection*	*Effective protection*	*Nominal protection*	*Effective protection*	*Nominal protection*	*Effective protection*
Agriculture	17	18	–	–	2	–4	–10	–13
Mining	7	3	–	–	0	–7	30	32
Intermediate goods I	10	14	2	3	11	10	27	142
Intermediate goods II	19	24	5	10	12	16	67	122
Non-durable consumer goods	9	–9	2	0	10	8	56	48
Durable consumer goods	31	51	7	10	14	29	88	144
Machinery	28	43	5	6	9	1	87	117
Transport equipment	54	164	1	–1	27	55	109	207
Mean	13	11	5	6	10	6	55	96

SOURCE: Balassa *et al.* (1982).

to be given priority, there must be a common difference in the EPRs of priority and non-priority sectors. There also still exists anti-export bias in the economy, and the real exchange rate must depreciate over time in order to reduce the trade deficit in the long run. Finally, the sectoral effective real exchange rates fluctuated considerably over the period, and decreased substantially over the period 1988–90. Thus, there still remains considerable room for improvement. Finally, it should be emphasized that the tariff and subsidy system prevailing in Turkey is too complicated and is not transparent. A simplification of the system is desirable. The protection and subsidy rates could be further lowered and the inter-industry dispersion of protection and subsidy rates could be further narrowed down. Such attempts should also note that frequent alterations in tariff and subsidy rates cause uncertainty for importers and exporters, creating unnecessary difficulties in planning for future production.

REFERENCES

Balassa, B. (1967), *Trade Liberalization Among Industrial Countries: Objectives and Alternatives* (New York: McGraw Hill).
Balassa, B. (1981), 'The Policy Experience of Newly Industrializing Economies after 1973 and the Case of Turkey', in *The Role of Exchange Rate Policy in Achieving Outward Orientation of the Turkish Economy*, proceedings of a conference held in Istanbul, Turkey, in July 1981, Istanbul, Meban Securities.
Balassa, B. *et al.* (1982), *Development Strategies in Semi-Industrial Economies* (Baltimore, MD: The Johns Hopkins University Press).
Baysan, Tercan and Blitzer, Charles (1988), 'Liberalizing Foreign Trade: The Experience of Turkey, Statistical Appendices' (Washington, DC: Brazil Department, World Bank).
Baysan, Tercan and Blitzer, Charles (1991), 'Turkey', in D. Papageorgiou *et al.* (eds), *The Experience of New Zealand, Spain and Turkey*, vol. 6 of *Liberalizing Foreign Trade* (Cambridge, Mass.: Blackwells).
Donges, Juergen B., *et al.* (1973), *Protektion und Branchenstruktur der Westdeutschen Wirtschaft* (Tubingen: J. C. B. Mohr).
Donges, J. B. *et al.* (1982), *The Second Enlargement of the European Community: Adjustment Requirements and Challenges for Policy Reform* (Tubingen: J. C. B. Mohr, Paul Siebeck).
Krueger, A. O. (1974), *Foreign Trade Regimes and Economic Development: Turkey* (New York: Columbia University Press).
Krueger, A. O. and Aktan, O. H. (1992), *Swimming Against the Tide: Turkish Trade Reform in the 1980s* (San Francisco, CA: International Center for Economic Growth, ICS Press).

Togan, S. (1993), *1980'li Yillarda Türk Dis Ticaret Rejimi ve Dis Ticaretin Liberalizasyonu* (Ankara: Turkish Eximbank).

Vollrath, T. J. (1991), 'A Theoretical Evaluation of Alternative Trade Intensity Measures of Revealed Comparative Advantage', *Weltwirtschaftliches Archiv*, vol. 127, pp. 265–79.

World Bank (1991), *World Development Report 1991* (Oxford: Oxford University Press).

3 Trade Reform and Changes in the Terms of Trade in Turkey

David Greenaway and David Sapsford

1 INTRODUCTION

The last decade has seen unprecedented liberalization in developing countries. Some liberalizations have been unilateral, others have been initiated as part of the conditions associated with World Bank structural adjustment lending (SAL) programmes. The extent of these liberalizations has been well documented (see, for example, Greenaway and Morrissey, 1993a; Whalley, 1989) and the economic impact of some of the earlier ones has been subject to some scrutiny, especially those with a SAL connection, (e.g. Mosley *et al.*, 1991; Thomas *et al.*, 1991), as also have those which predated SALs (e.g. Papageorgiou *et al.*, 1991). As a result we now know quite a lot about timing, sequencing and economic effects (see Greenaway and Morrissey, 1993b for a review).

Turkey has undergone a staged liberalization over quite a long period, culminating in the changes implemented in the 1980s. The background to the implementation and economic effects of the programme have been evaluated by Baysan and Blitzer (1991), Celasun (1992) and Olgun and Togan (1991). It is not our intention to duplicate this work. Rather, we focus on a particular aspect of the liberalization experience in Turkey, namely the relationship between trade reforms and the terms of trade. Put simply, have movements in the terms of trade affected, or been affected by liberalization? As we shall see, on theoretical grounds we can make a case both for terms of trade shocks leading to liberalization, and vice versa. Our intention is to see what the evidence suggests, and evaluate the implications for policy.

The remainder of the paper is organized as follows. Section 2 briefly reviews the Turkish experience of liberalization over the post war period. Section 3 looks at what theory suggests about the interaction between trade reforms and the terms of trade. Broadly speaking there are two competing paradigms. One derives from the Singer–Prebisch view of

52

the world and sees terms of trade shocks as an endogenous response to liberalization. The other sees liberalization as a by-product of a trade shock. In Section 4 we report the results of a model developed to discriminate between these competing hypotheses to see which best fits the Turkish experience. Finally, in Section 5 we offer some concluding comments.

2   TRADE REFORMS IN TURKEY: AN OVERVIEW

As noted in the Introduction, there have been several attempts at trade liberalization in Turkey over the post-war period. The experiences are well documented and have been extensively evaluated by, *inter alia*, Baysan and Blitzer (1991), Olgun and Togan (1991) and Celasun (1992). By way of providing appropriate background to what follows, we briefly review this experience.

Baysan and Blitzer (1991) focus on developments in the foreign trade sector between 1950 and 1984. They identify four distinct episodes – 1950, 1958, 1970 and 1980. The first three are seen as 'one shot', the last one as broader and deeper liberalization. In fact, the first three are essentially little more than exchange-rate devaluations, with few alterations to border measures. By contrast, the 1980 liberalization represents a more fundamental attempt by the government to commit to a more open trade regime. Underlying this attempt were several objectives: stabilization of the balance of payments; rationalization of the foreign exchange system; improved efficiency of state enterprises; a boost to the private sector; and encouragement of worker remittances and foreign direct investment. The episode began with a devaluation of almost 50 per cent, followed by several further devaluations. To stimulate exports, tax rebates and discriminatory allocation of foreign exchange were introduced. Baysan and Blitzer argue that the export subsidy equivalent of these measures was 20 per cent. Initially there were limited changes to the import regime. The key binding constraint here was quantitative restrictions (QRs), and these only began to be reformed in 1983. In 1983 and 1984, quota liberalization was initiated together with some tariff cuts. Baysan and Blitzer estimate that, for a sample of 23 consumer, intermediate and capital goods industries, the average nominal tariff fell from 38.8 to 2.3 per cent between December 1983 and January 1984.

A fall in average tariffs of 36 percentage points would appear to be very dramatic. There are, however, several problems in interpreting this. First, the data only applies to a (non-random) sub-set of industries; second, one often finds instrumental substitution, i.e. reductions in nominal tariffs are offset by increases in other restraints; third, the data reported applies to nominal and not effective tariffs. Olgun and Togan (1991) address these deficiencies by calculating nominal and effective protection, and providing an audit of all non-tariff-barriers and their tariff equivalents. This is then combined with data on nominal tariffs and input–output information to calculate nominal and effective protection rates for some 49 industries, for 1983, 1984, 1988 and 1989. They show that although there was some quota liberalization over the period 1980–3, and although customs duty was reduced for a number of commodities, average nominal protection actually increased between 1983 and 1984, from 65 to 70 per cent. It then subsequently declined to 55 per cent in 1988 and 41 per cent in 1989. This implies that some instrument substitution did actually occur early on in the liberalization. To some extent changes in effective protection mirror these changes in nominal protection. The average effective rate increased from 59 per cent in 1983 to 79 per cent in 1984, remaining at this level in 1988. In 1989 it then showed a sharp drop to 54 per cent.

Two other features of the Olgun–Togan results are notable. First, as the average effective protection rate fell, so too did its dispersion. From a resource allocation standpoint this is desirable, and would be regarded by most analysts as one objective of liberalization. Second, they show that the export sector benefited from significant protection.

In sum, then, over the period since 1950 there have been several attempts at trade liberalization in Turkey. Some of these attempts have been one-shot affairs, the more recent experience has been of a broader and deeper reform of trade restraints. There is evidence to suggest that the recent liberalization has cut into average rates of nominal and effective protection. Having established the basic facts, our task is now to see whether the liberalization process has been affected by, or affects, movement in terms of trade.

3   TRADE REFORM AND THE TERMS OF TRADE

3.1   Trade shocks and liberalization

Bevan *et al.* (1987, 1989, 1991a, b), Collier (1991) and Collier and Gunning (1994) investigated in detail the consequences of the 1976 coffee boom in Kenya. Their enquires have caused some rethinking on macroeconomic management in less developed countries (LDCs). Their work also resulted in some revision of ideas on the links between terms of trade shocks and trade liberalization. Specifically they argue that favourable shocks lead to liberalization, whilst unfavourable shocks lead to retrenchment. To understand why, we need to briefly review their findings for Kenya.

In 1976, world coffee prices increased dramatically as a consequence of a supply-side shock. From the Kenyan standpoint, the shock was clearly exogenous; according to Bevan *et al.*, it was equally clearly temporary. Conventional wisdom suggested that the government's optimal response was stabilizing taxation – the windfall should be taxed to ameliorate the effects of the boom. In fact, the Kenyan government made no special fiscal provisions – despite advice from the World Bank to do so. Interestingly, however, the boom was correctly interpreted by coffee farmers as transitory and, as permanent income theory would predict, a large part of the windfall was saved. The marginal propensity to save out of the windfall gain on the part of the coffee farmers was around 90 per cent.

Although the government did not make special fiscal provisions, tax revenues did increase, partly due to an increased yield on coffee taxes, partly due to an increase in expenditure taxes. In contrast to the private sector, the public sector's marginal propensity to save out of windfall income was very low, and an increase in government expenditure followed. However, most of this increased expenditure was in the non-tradeables sector, in particular government capital programmes, fuelling an increase in construction activity.

What of the private sector savings 'boom'? Domestic financial markets were thin and, moreover, rates of return were, in the main, controlled. In addition, access to international capital markets was tightly constrained. Consequently, a large part of the windfall savings found its way into the market for land and property, thereby exacerbating the construction boom. There then followed further feedback effects of the construction boom on trade policy and financial markets. In order to widen the range of assets and consumer goods available, the government liberalized financial markets to reduce financial repression, and liberalized imports to widen the consumption set. The rationale behind the moves was twofold. First, the boom was treated by the government as if it were permanent rather than temporary. Second, because the boom had occurred against the backcloth of pervasive controls, their impact on the economy was clearly distortionary. Given a wider menu of portfolio choices, both for assets and durables, as Bevan *et al.* argued, the construction boom would not have been so marked. Recognition of this, combined with a belief that the original trade shock had increased the permanent income of (public and private) agents in the economy led to liberalization.

3.2   The Singer Hypothesis

According to the preceding hypothesis, it is improvements in the terms of trade which give rise, after some time lag, to increased trade liberalization. There is, however, a contrary hypothesis which has been put forward by Hans Singer. According to this, it is changes in the orientation of a country's trade policy which lead, eventually, to changes in its terms of trade. The basic idea here is easily understood with reference to the import supply and export demand functions faced by the country in question. In the small open-economy model both of these functions will be perfectly elastic at the prevailing level of world prices for the commodities in question. Under such conditions the export and import prices faced by the country are fixed, with the consequence that its terms of trade will remain unchanged if it embarks on a policy of trade liberalization. However, the small open-economy model with its assumption of parametric prices of tradeable goods may be inappropriate for certain countries, especially those who trade in markets characterized by differentiated products.

More importantly, there is a potential problem resulting from what Singer (1991) sees as a case of the fallacy of composition. While the small open-economy argument sketched out above may provide a reasonable description of the conditions faced by some economies, it rests heavily on the *ceteris paribus* assumption, which takes the behaviour of other relevant economies as given. However, in practice it may prove to be the case that while a particular economy is embarking on its policy of trade liberalization, so too are others who export the same or similar products, with the consequence that its export price may no longer be taken as given. Although Singer (1991) concentrates on the export side of the picture, analogous forces may be at work on the import side. If the other liberalizing countries are also increasing their demands for the goods and services imported by the country in question, this will mean that its import prices can no longer be taken as given. Thus such economies are subject to downward-sloping demand curves for their exports, accompanied by upward-sloping import supply functions. This scenario may be particularly appropriate in respect of the experience of certain developing countries which are subject, along with others, to structural adjustment programmes. The case which Singer (1991) cites in support is the first phase of the World Bank's Special Programme for Africa (SPA) which covered the calendar years 1988–90. The SPA involved structural adjustment programmes in a number of sub-Saharan African economies and the evidence cited by Singer showed that the terms of trade of the SPA core countries deteriorated by some 6 per cent during 1988–90 relative to a 1987 base, whereas the terms of trade of the non-SPA countries had improved by 2.5 per cent. To quote Singer's own conclusion, 'Presumably the deterioration of the terms of trade of SPA core countries has something to do with their greater expansion of export volume and indicates the fallacy of composition involved in pushing sub-Saharan African countries simultaneously into "outward orientation"' (1991, p. 3).

In summary, Singer sees causation as running in the opposite direction to that suggested by the trade shocks hypothesis – from trade liberalization to the terms of trade, with increased liberalization leading eventually to a worsening in the terms of trade. (For a more formal analysis of this relationship, see Bleaney (1993).)

4 STATISTICAL ANALYSIS

These alternative hypotheses differ in terms of both the posited direction and temporal sequencing of the two variables in question. The purpose of this section is to investigate, using causality analysis, the relationship which exists between trade orientation and the terms of trade in the Turkish economy in order to discriminate between these competing hypotheses.

4.1 Data issues

The terms of trade series employed in the following analysis is the IMF's index of Turkey's terms of trade.[1] The problems encountered when attempting to construct measures of trade orientation, suitable for either cross-section or time-series analysis, are both formidable and well known (see, for example, Leamer, 1988; Edwards, 1992). We do not in this paper seek to develop yet further quantitative measures of trade liberalization. Instead, we rely in the following analysis on one of the simplest measures suggested in the literature, namely the extent of openness of the economy as proxied by the sum of exports and imports expressed as a percentage of GDP. This simple measure is by no means new, but it has proved useful in a variety of earlier studies as a proxy of outward orientation in trading relations (e.g. Greenaway and Sapsford, 1987; Greenaway and Milner, 1991).

Data relating to this index of trade orientation were constructed for the period 1956–68 through to 1986 as the sum of the import and export to GDP ratios published in IMF (1988).[2]

Given the conceptual and measurement difficulties attached to measures of trade orientation, it seemed sensible to compare the openness index described above with the *Trade Liberalisation Index* constructed for Turkey by Baysan and Blitzer (1991). This index, like those presented by the World Bank (1987), Papageorgiou *et al.* (1991) and others, is essentially a *subjective* index of trade orientation. The Baysan–Blitzer (B–B) index is designed to represent Turkey's foreign trade policy seen in terms of the degree of liberalization of the economy and the extent of the government's commitment to such policies. It is constructed on a scale of 1 to 20, where 1 corresponds to the most highly controlled and restrictionist trade regime and 20 corresponds to completely free trade policies. Scores in the range 1 through to 9 are seen as identifying restrictionist trade regimes, scores in the 10–20 range are achieved by outward-oriented trade regimes. Although such subjective indices create problems where used comparatively (see Greenaway, 1993) the B–B index provides a useful cross-check on the validity of our own, openness-based, index of trade orientation. The B–B index covers the period up to 1985 and Figure 3.1 plots this index along with ours. It is clear from Figure 3.1 that the two indices move very closely together over the period 1968–85, with the correlation coefficient between them being 0.887.

4.2 Causality analysis

The concept of causality we adopt is *Granger causality*. The idea lying behind Granger's (1969) notion of causality is simply that if some variable (say x) causes some other variable (say y), changes in x should precede changes in y. Given that this concept of causality rests upon the temporal precedence, or sequencing, of movements in the two series in question, the term precedence is sometimes used in preference to the term 'Granger causality' (e.g. Leamer, 1985; Maddala, 1992).

Granger (1969) proposed the following procedure for testing the hypothesis that x causes y in the sense discussed above. Consider the following model:

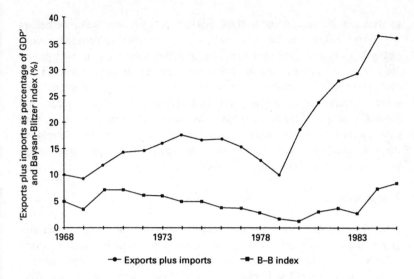

FIGURE *3.1* *Turkey's trade orientation, 1968–85*

$$y_t = \sum_{i=1}^{p} \alpha_i y_{t-i} + \sum_{j=1}^{q} \beta_j x_{t-j} + u_t \qquad (3.1)$$

where x and y are expressed as deviations about their respective means, and u_t is a disturbance term which is assumed to possess white-noise properties. Equation (3.1) may be estimated by regression techniques, given assumed values of the lag orders p and q. The null-hypothesis that x does not Granger-cause y is that $\beta_j = 0$ for all values of $j = 1,2,\ldots,q$. This null-hypothesis that the β_j coefficients are jointly zero may straightforwardly be put to the test by the use of either a standard F or Lagrange multiplier test.

Having performed this test, it is necessary to allow for the possibility that causation may be running in the other direction, in the sense that y might also (or instead) Granger-cause x. To test for this it is simply necessary to interchange the variables x and y in equation (4.1) above and repeat the test procedure described already. In the context of this second, or reverse, causality test the null-hypothesis that y does not Granger-cause x is tested by testing the restriction that the coefficients of the lagged y variables in this second regression equation are jointly zero. If both of these tests reject the null, then we may conclude that causation runs in both directions and that we have a *feedback system*.

Although the Granger concept of causation and its associated testing procedures are not without their critics (see, for example, Jacobi *et al.*, 1979; Feige and Pearce, 1979) they nevertheless provide a convenient framework for analysing the question addressed in this paper. Notice, in particular, that the above procedure allows us to discriminate, in principle, between four possible outcomes regarding Turkey's terms of trade–trade liberalization relationship. First, causality may run from the terms of trade to trade orientation; second, it might run in the opposite direction; third, it may run in both directions (implying the existence of a feedback system) and fourth, there may turn out to be no evidence of causality in either direction.

4.3   Evidence

Since both of the above test procedures are based on regression analysis, it is necessary prior to estimation to ensure that the series satisfy the required stationarity conditions. Application of the usual Dickey–Fuller and Augmented Dickey–Fuller unit-root tests shows that Turkey's terms of trade series, as well as our openness index (and indeed also the B–B trade liberalization index) are all $I(1)$, or possibly $I(2)$, variables when expressed in logarithms. Accordingly, particular emphasis is placed in the following statistical analysis on specifications in which variables are expressed as suitable differences of natural logarithms.

The results which were obtained when Granger's test procedure was applied are summarized in Table 3.1 In applying Granger's test, the choice of lag length is usually seen as essentially arbitrary. The results reported in Table 3.1 were obtained with the maximum lag lengths, p and q in equation (3.1), both set equal to 4, which seems reasonable given the degrees of freedom at our disposal. However, experimentation with a range of alternative values of p and q showed the overall results to be insensitive to the choice of lag lengths.

The results reported in rows 1 and 2 of Table 3.1 suggest the existence of unidirectional causality. The results set out in row 1 are such that we are led to reject the null hypothesis that Turkey's terms of trade do not Granger-cause her trade orientation. To test for the possibility that causation also flows in the opposite direction (thereby giving rise to a feedback system), we performed the reversed Granger test, the results of which are summarized in row 2 of Table 3.1. As can be seen, the results of this test are such that we are unable to reject the null-hypothesis that Turkey's trade orientation does not Granger-cause her terms of trade. Taken together, these results would seem to indicate

TABLE 3.1 *Turkey's trade orientation and terms of trade, 1968–91: causality analysis*[a]

Test no.	Granger tests dependent variable	Independent variables[b]	Tests of exclusion restrictions[c]	
			LM	LR
1	Openness	Lagged openness, lagged terms of trade	7.2331	9.2501
2	Terms of trade	Lagged terms of trade, lagged openness	2.6048	2.8137

NOTES [a] All variables were logged and pre-filtered prior to OLS estimation according to Sims's suggested filter given by expression (3.2) in the text.

[b] In the above tests $p = q = m = n = 4$ (see equation (3.1) in text).

[c] LM and LR denote, respectively, the Lagrange multiplier and likelihood ratio test statistics of the null hypothesis that the coefficients of the relevant set of excluded variables are jointly zero. Both test statistics are distributed as χ^2 with 4 degrees of freedom.

that over the period in question, the outwardness of Turkey's trade orientation was caused by her terms of trade, while the reverse was not true.

Sims (1972) proposes that series be filtered prior to analysis in order to ensure the whiteness of regression residuals. The 'pre-whitening' procedure which he proposes involves application of the following filter to all variables expressed in natural logs prior to regression:[3]

$$1 - 1.5\ L + 0.5625\ L^2 \qquad (3.2)$$

where L denotes the lag operator defined such that for any variable (say x_t) $L^j = x_{t-j}$.

Taken as a whole, the results reported in Table 3.1 are consistent with the hypothesis that over the period in question, the outwardness of Turkey's trade orientation was caused (in the Granger sense) by her terms of trade, while the reverse was not true. In summary, the results of the preceding causality analysis find support for the trade shocks hypothesis in Turkey's post-1968 experiences, but reveal no support for the alternative hypothesis put forward by Singer.

4.4 Distributed Lag Representation

Since the above analysis reveals the presence of *unidirectional causality* running from Turkey's terms of trade to the outwardness of her trade orientation, they suggest that it is appropriate to model the relationship between these two variables as a distributed lag formulation in which current trade orientation is specified as a distributed lag function of previous values of the terms of trade. In econometric terms, what the results of the suggest is that it is appropriate to treat the terms of trade as exogenous in a regression of trade orientation on current and past terms of trade (Sims, 1972, p. 550).

Letting y denote the outwardness of Turkey's trade orientation and x her terms of trade, we accordingly fitted the following general model to the data:

$$y_t = \sum_{i=0}^{m} \gamma_i x_{t-i} + u_t. \qquad (3.3)$$

Experimentation with alternative values of m indicated that various lags up to and including order eight achieved significance in this regression. Table 3.2 summarizes the ordinary least squares results thus obtained.

TABLE 3.2 *Turkey's trade orientation, 1968–91: a distributed lag model*

| Dependent variable | Estimated coefficients | | | R^2 | D-W | χ^2_1 | χ^2_2 |
	a_1	a_2	a_3				
Openness	−0.588 (1.8162)	1.3016* (2.0792)	1.5671* (2.3446)	0.3726	2.8	2.5982	1.0232

NOTES: Estimated parameters of model: openness$_t$ = a_1 + a_2 terms of trade$_{t-4}$ + a_3 terms of trade$_{t-8}$ + u_t.

Figures in parenthesis are absolute t values and an asterisk denotes significance at the 5 per cent level or above. χ^2_1 is the test statistic for the Lagrange multiplier test for serial correlation, while χ^2_2 is the Jarque Bera test statistic for the normality of regression residuals. Both statistics are distributed as χ^2, with one and two degrees of freedom respectively. The former test provides no evidence of serial correlation, while the latter is such that we are unable to reject the null hypothesis of normally distributed errors. All variables are expressed as natural logs and were filtered prior to ordinary least squares estimation using the Sims filter (3.2).

As may be seen from Table 3.2, significant effects exist at both 4 and 8 year lags (with all other lag coefficients having turned out to be insignificantly different from zero). In addition, all lag coefficients are positively signed, in accordance with the trade-shocks hypothesis described above. In short, not only do these results provide support for the trade-shocks hypothesis, but they also suggest that the full effects of terms of trade fluctuations could take up to 8 years to filter through to trade orientation.

5   CONCLUDING REMARKS

This paper has used Turkish data in an investigation of the relationship between the outwardness of trade orientation and changes in the terms of trade. There are two alternative hypotheses relating to this relationship; first, the trade shocks hypothesis and second, the Singer hypothesis. Causality analysis of the Granger variety provides evidence of *unidirectional* causality consistent with the trade-shocks hypothesis, and suggests the existence of fairly long lags in the system. It would seem, therefore, that changes in the terms of trade have led to trade reform in Turkey, rather than the other way around.

NOTES

1. Terms of trade data covering the period through to 1984 were obtained from IMF (1988). The IMF does not publish data for the post-1984 period (see the most recent issues of both its monthly *International Financial Statistics* and the *International Financial Statistics Yearbook*). However, it was possible to extend the IMF's terms of trade series to cover the period up to and including 1991 by utilizing the OECD's published data relating to year-on-year changes in Turkey's export and import unit values (see *OECD Economic Survey, Turkey*, 1989/90 and 1991/92, Tables 9 and 7 respectively). Regrettably, no data for the pre-1968 period are available from the usual internationally published sources.
2. This series was subsequently extended forward to 1990 using data published in *International Financial Statistics* (August 1992). The observation for 1991 is the authors' own estimate, based on data reported in *OECD Survey, Turkey* (1991–2) relating to the year-on-year growth in Turkey's imports, exports and GDP.
3. It is important from an econometric standpoint to notice that the application of Sims's filter prior to estimation removes the above-mentioned unit-root problems associated with the raw data series. This follows from the

application of both the Dickey–Fuller and Augmented Dickey–Fuller tests to the filtered series, the results of which lead us in every case to decisive rejection of the null-hypothesis of the presence of a unit root. It is an interesting aside to note that, although Sims's work pre-dated the publication of the influential Dickey–Fuller unit-root paper by some seven years, his suggested filter appears to work extremely well, not only in the sense of pre-whitening the regression residuals, but also in the sense of providing a fractional difference operator to remove unit-root problems.

REFERENCES

Baysan, T. and Blitzer, C. (1991), 'Turkey', in D. Papageorgiou, M. Michaely and A. Choksi (eds), *Liberalizing Foreign Trade*, vol. 6 (Oxford: Basil Blackwell), pp. 263–405.

Bevan, D., Collier, P. and Gunning, J. (1987), 'Consequences of a Commodity Boom in a Controlled Economy: Accumulation and Redistribution in Kenya, 1975–1983', *World Bank Economic Review*, vol. 1, pp. 489–513.

Bevan, D., Collier, P. and Gunning, J. (1989), 'Fiscal Response to a Temporary Trade Shock: The Aftermath of the Kenyan Coffee Boom', *World Bank Economic Review*, vol. 3, pp. 359–78.

Bevan, D., Collier, P. and Gunning, J. (1991a), 'Consequences of External Shocks in African Type Economies', in C. Milner and A. J. Rayner (eds), *Policy Adjustment in Africa* (London: Macmillan).

Bevan, D., Collier, P. and Gunning, J. (1991b), 'The Kenyan Coffee Boom of 1976–79', Centre for the Study of African Economies, University of Oxford (mimeo).

Bleaney, M. (1993), 'Liberalisation and the Terms of Trade of Developing Countries: A Cause for Concern?', *The World Economy*, vol. 16, pp. 453–66.

Celasun, M. (1992), 'Trade and Industrialisation in Turkey', METU, Ankara (mimeo).

Collier, P. (1991), 'Public Policy Towards External Shocks in Developing Countries', Centre for the Study of African Economies, University of Oxford (mimeo).

Collier, P. and Gunning, J. (1994), 'Trade and Development: Protection, Shocks and Liberalisation', in D. Greenaway and L. A. Winters (eds), *Surveys in International Trade* (Oxford: Basil Blackwell).

Edwards, S. (1992), 'Trade Orientation, Distortions and Growth in Developing Countries', *Journal of Development Economics*, vol. 39, pp. 31–57.

Feige, E. and Pearce, D. (1979), 'The Causal Relationship Between Money and Income: Some Caveats for Time Series Analysis', *Review of Economics and Statistics*, vol. 61, pp. 521–33.

Granger, C. (1969), 'Investigating Causal Relationships by Econometric Models and Cross-Spectral Methods', *Econometrica*, vol. 37, pp. 424–38.

Greenaway, D. (1993), 'Liberalizing Foreign Trade Through Rose-Tinted Glasses', *Economic Journal*, vol. 103, pp. 208–23.

Greenaway, D. and Milner, C. (1991), 'Fiscal Dependence on Trade Taxes and Trade Policy Reform', *Journal of Development Studies*, vol. 27, pp. 95–132.

Greenaway, D. and Morrissey, W. O. (1993a), 'Structural Adjustment and Liberalisation: What Have We Learned?', *Kyklos*, vol. 46, pp. 241–61.

Greenaway, D. and Morrissey, W. O. (1993b), 'Trade Liberalisation in Developing Countries', in M. Murshed and K. Raffer (eds), *Trade Problems and the World Economy* (Aldershot: Edward Elgar).

Greenaway, D. and Sapsford, D. (1987), 'Fiscal Dependence on Trade Taxes: A Further Econometric Investigation', *Public Finance*, vol. 42, pp. 309–19.

IMF (1988), *International Financial Statistics: Supplement on Trade Statistics*, Supplement Series no. 12 (Washington, DC: International Monetary Fund).

Jacobi, R. L., Leamer, E. and Ward, M. (1979), 'The Difficulties with Testing for Causation', *Economic Enquiry*, vol. 17, pp. 401–13.

Leamer, E. (1985), 'Vector Autoregressions for Causal Inference', in K. Brunner and A. Meltzer (eds), *Understanding Monetary Regimes* (supplement to *Journal of Monetary Economics*), pp. 255–304.

Leamer, E. (1988), 'Measures of Openness', in R. Baldwin (ed.), *Trade Policy and Empirical Analysis* (Chicago, IL: University of Chicago Press).

Maddala, G. S. (1992), *Introduction to Econometrics*, 2nd edn (New York: Macmillan).

Mosley, P., Harrigan, J. and Toye, J. (1991), *Aid and Power*, 2 vols (London: Routledge).

Olgun, H. and Togan, S. (1991), 'Trade Liberalization and the Structure of Protection in Turkey in the 1980s: A Quantitative Analysis', *Weltwirtschaftliches Archiv*, vol. 127, pp. 152–70.

Papageorgiou, D., Michaely, M. and Choksi, A. (1991), *Liberalizing Foreign Trade* (Oxford: Basil Blackwell).

Sims, C. A. (1972), 'Money, Income and Causality', *American Economic Review*, vol. 62, pp. 540–52.

Singer, H. W. (1991), 'Does the World Bank Structural Adjustment Programme in Sub-Saharan Africa Work? A Troubling Doubt', Institute of Development Studies at the University of Sussex (mimeo).

Thomas, V. *et al.* (eds) (1991), *Restructuring Economies in Distress* (Oxford: Oxford University Press).

Whalley, J. (ed.) (1989), *Developing Countries in the Uruguay Round* (London: Macmillan).

World Bank (1987), *World Development Report* (Washington, DC: World Bank).

4 Financial Reform in Turkey since 1980: Liberalization without Stabilization

P. N. Snowden

1 INTRODUCTION

Bank time deposit interest rates in Turkey were first deregulated in July 1980 as part of an overall programme of economic liberalization. Although early difficulties led to the reintroduction of controls in 1982, the Central Bank usually set deposit rates above the rate of inflation after 1984 (when non-preferential loan rates were also liberalized). The re-introduction of deposit rate competition in the late 1980s subsequently stimulated intense competition in the Turkish financial sector as commercial banks sought to secure funds.

While a substantial academic literature supports the view that financial sector liberalization is conducive to an increase in both the quantity of investible funds, and in the efficiency with which they are allocated, results in Turkey have been somewhat mixed. Financial assets have increased as a fraction of GDP and a wider range of instruments has been made available to savers. This enhanced supply of intermediated funds has not, however, stimulated private sector investment spending which was the key objective of the reforms (OECD, 1990, pp. 92–3).

Following a brief review of the theoretical justification for financial sector liberalization, Sections 3 and 4 of this paper examine two of the key complications which have arisen in its application to the Turkish economy since 1980; the continuing demands of the public sector for credit and the impact on intermediation costs of prudential regulations. Recognizing the negative consequences of these factors for the funding of private sector investment, Section 5 discusses the possible contribution of the encouragement of equity finance as a supplement to bank intermediation.

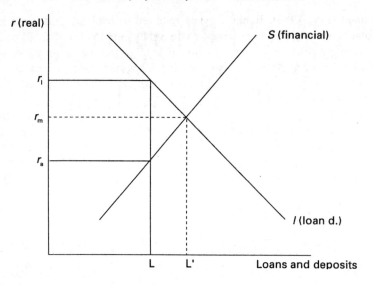

FIGURE *4.1   Disequilibrium in the market for bank credit*

2   THE CASE FOR FINANCIAL SECTOR REFORMS IN THE CONTEXT OF ECONOMIC LIBERALIZATION

Initiated by the highly influential studies of McKinnon (1973) and Shaw (1973), a large literature has advanced the case for liberalizing the financial sector as part of a programme of reforms in developing economies. The key arguments focus on the banking system as the dominant element of the organized financial sector and are easily summarized. Pre-reform economies are characterized in this literature as being 'financially repressed' with interest rates being administered on either or both the loans and deposits of the banking system. For varying reasons, such as a belief that 'low' interest rates stimulate investment spending or objections to 'usury', market rates are held below the market clearing price of credit. The consequences of this practice may be shown in Figure 4.1 (see, for example, Fry 1982).

Bank deposit interest rates are held at the administered level r_a leaving the credit market in disequilibrium with the quantity of bank loans (L) determined by the availability of deposits to the banks at that rate. While banks may be able to evade regulation of their effective loan rates over the range r_l–r_a by requiring the holding of minimum deposits by borrowers, some constraint on the lending rate is often assumed (Fry, 1982). Banks may be required to lend to 'priority' bor-rowers, or may choose to lend to safe established (and probably large) borrowers because of the impediment to charging a risk premium on their loans. Thus safe but low yielding loans may be favoured at the expense of higher yielding activities to the detriment of longer run economic performance.

In the disequilibrium conditions described, the diagram suggests the counter-intuitive argument of the financial liberalization literature that a rise in deposit rates towards r_m (together with associated loan rates) will *increase* bank lending. The two sections of the paper which fol-low may be seen as modifications and extensions of this simple dia-grammatic analysis to allow for the public sector deficits and the cost influences in bank intermediation which have been important in Tur-key during the 1980s. Before turning to these applications an impor-tant implicit assumption of the model should be stressed for its importance in the Turkish case.

While it is clear from Figure 4.1 that the supply of deposits (financial saving) needs to be responsive to a rise in interest rates offered, this is not enough to ensure that the reforms will boost overall financial in-termediation and domestic investment spending. The central implicit assumption is that the increased supply of bank deposits is diverted away from other low productivity forms of saving. In the Turkish con-text gold hoarding may provide an appropriate example (Akyuz and Kotte, 1991). If, on the other hand, the diversion is away from loans intermediated through a well-developed curb market, there may be a decline in overall lending if the intermediation costs of banks are higher than those of the unofficial markets (see, for example, Van Wijnbergen, 1982). It has been noted that this argument appears to be relevant to Turkey with the 1982 'broker crisis' cited in evidence (Akyuz and Kotte, 1991). This episode followed the initial deregulation of deposit rates and resulted from the continuing suppression of these rates through the collusive agreement of the major commercial banks. Smaller banks began to sell certificates of deposit to an informal group of brokers who sold them on to the public attracted by interest rates between 2 and 5 percentage points higher than the cartel rate. Mounting claims on brokers contributed to a loss of confidence and collapse of the market in mid-1982 after which deposit rates were again determined by the Central Bank. This was an inauspicious start to the liberalization pro-gramme and the broker crisis indicates that informal financial arrange-ments and expertise are not lacking in Turkey (see also OECD, 1990, esp. p. 93).

If informal markets exist, an important issue in determining the overall success of the financial reforms is the relative intermediation cost position of the formal and informal sectors. Before examining the issue of bank intermediation costs in Turkey, however, the following section assesses what is probably a more fundamental problem confronting the ability of the banking system to fund private investment spending; chronic public sector financial deficits. While advocates of financial liberalization have always stressed that control of these deficits is an essential precondition, others have noted the implication that financial repression (interest rate ceilings) is more appropriate in the event of their continuation (for example, McKinnon, 1982; Dornbusch and Reynoso, 1993, respectively).

3 LIBERALIZATION WITHOUT STABILIZATION: BUDGET DEFICITS AND THE BANKS SINCE 1980

The Turkish reforms have included a series of significant developments in the financing of the public sector with the concentration on personal income taxes evident in 1980 being gradually reduced. Inflation, and the 'fiscal drag' with which it was associated, had made these taxes onerous and inequitable; especially for wage earners (OECD, 1990, p. 96). Indirect taxes were reformed with the introduction of a VAT in 1985 and, reflecting the importance of the Vito Tanzi effect in the high inflation context, a system of advance corporation tax was introduced in 1986 to reduce collection lags (OECD, 1990).

In terms of overall fiscal balances, however, the slight increase in tax revenues as a fraction of GDP which was achieved in the 1980s was nearly offset by an increase in transfers from the government to state enterprises (SEEs), low income groups and exporting enterprises (OECD, 1990, p. 98). The net result has been that sizeable budget deficits have characterized the post-reform period as the figures in Table 4.1 suggest.

The extent to which these public sector deficits have 'crowded out' private investment spending in the context of financial liberalization will be discussed further below. Table 4.1, however, makes clear that financial liberalization can have significant implications for the size of the budget deficit which has to be funded. The most immediate connection, of course, is that financial liberalization requires the government to raise funds at market-related interest rates. The consequences become clear in the years following 1985 when interest payments have

TABLE 4.1 *Central government budget: ratios to total expenditure (percentages)*

Year	1980	1981	1982	1983	1984	1985	1986	1987	1988	1989
Budget deficit	15.4	8.2	9.8	12.0	25.9	15	17.3	20.5	19.0	20.2
Transfers	36.9	37.7	34.2	41.0	42.4	41.2	42.7	46.2	49.6	43.0
Of which interest payments	2.9	5.0	5.5	8.1	11.6	12.7	16.3	17.9	23.7	21.7

SOURCE: OECD (1991, Table L).

been roughly comparable with the budget deficit itself. Although interest payments are the largest component of the item labelled 'transfers' another element of the latter should be noted. In common with many other intermediate economies, the financial structure of Turkish manufacturing firms is characterized by high debt–equity (or 'gearing') ratios (OECD, 1991, pp. 96–101). The strains imposed by rising interest charges on the heavy stock of debt carried by exporting firms has required the provision of preferential credit which impinges on the budget deficit as a transfer component (OECD, 1990, p. 94). In principle, such links between interest rate liberalization and the budget deficit requires a modification in the diagram of Figure 4.1 above.

With government borrowing from the banking system being influenced by the level of interest rates in the market for loans, a rise in administered rates towards the market clearing level implies a *shift* of the overall demand function for loans.

To the extent that budget deficits are aggravated by the impact of liberalization on the burden of public debt servicing, the crowding out of the private sector reflected by the asterisk (*) in Figure 4.2 is a consequence of the decision to liberalize interest rates. This relationship between public sector deficits, the level of interest rates and the availability of credit for the private sector is derived more formally in Appendix 1 which produces the following expression for the evolution of private bank debt (and therefore lending) to GDP:

$$(\overset{o}{D}_p - \overset{o}{GDP}) = -D_g/D_p\{(PBD - dC)/D_g + (i - \overset{o}{GDP})\}. \quad (4.1)$$

With dots indicating proportionate rates of change, the right-hand side therefore determines the ability of private sector bank debt to grow in line with nominal GDP. If, of course, the ratio of private bank debt to GDP were to remain unchanged over time, the left-hand side would be zero. For a given initial ratio of government to private bank debt, (D_g/D_p), the two elements inside the curled brackets determine whether the private claims will grow or decline relative to incomes. The first determinant is the size of the primary (non-interest) budget deficit which is not covered by the non-interest bearing (seignorage) issue of cash or reserves. The greater this net deficit, the stronger the crowding-out pressures on the private sector. The second component in the expression above adds to these pressures when nominal interest rates exceed the growth rate of nominal GDP.

In this simple model where the government only borrows from the banking system, while wishing to exercise some control over the rate

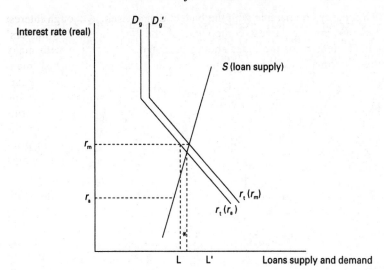

FIGURE *4.2 Interest liberalization with endogenous budget deficits*

of domestic inflation, the effects of interest rate liberalization are highly significant for private sector credit. If control of inflation is to be achieved by control over the growth of the money stock, the growth of high powered money (*dC*) must be constrained. For a given primary budget deficit (PBD), however, this action will force up (liberalized) market interest rates effecting the crowding out of private sector loans. This outcome may be compared with the consequences of budget deficits in the context of financial repression. With inflation and pegged nominal interest rates the debt service element of public sector deficits is partly avoided at the expense of deposit holders (the second element in the curled brackets above is rendered negative). Provided that the inflation 'tax' does not result in a substantial shift out of money balances, more credit may be made available to private investors. The combination of financial liberalization with inflation in Turkey during the 1980s has, on the other hand, eroded the base of the inflation tax as the public has switched out of cash and low-interest-bearing deposits into interest-bearing accounts (OECD, 1990, p. 92 and Table 33). Whereas time (saving) deposits represented 40.4 per cent of the total money stock (M2) in 1981, their share had risen to 56.1 per cent in 1990. In December 1990, nominal interest rates on sight deposits were 12 per cent whereas those on time deposits ranged from 38 to 59 per cent (OECD, 1992, Tables 17 and K). Although the rates just quoted for time deposits ranged from −14 to +0.6 per cent in real terms, the losses on sight deposits were clearly much greater (OECD, 1992). This amelioration in the position of depositors, given the continuing budget deficits, has been partially funded at the expense of private borrowers. For reasons to be discussed in the following section, negative real deposit rates are quite consistent with positive real borrowing rates due to high intermediation costs.

The arguments above over-simplify the relationship between public and private credit in Turkey in at least one respect. Whereas the model in Appendix 1 assumes that the government only borrows from the banking system, an important development in the financing of the public sector has been the growth in the issue of marketable securities to the non-bank public. In addition to the deficits themselves, therefore, the financial conditions facing the private sector have been affected by a change in funding policy. Table 4.2 below reviews the structure of the accumulating debt of the public and private sectors. The data show the proportion of bank and other debt in total financial assets together with the proportion of public debt in total bank assets.

Although there has been a small erosion in its position, Table 4.2 suggests that the banking sector has retained a dominant share in Turkish asset portfolios. Significantly with respect to the earlier discussion, however, the share of the public sector in outstanding bank credit declined over this period with the implication of a corresponding rise in the proportion of bank claims against the private sector.

The continuing budget deficits indicated in Table 4.1 have given rise to a growth in the share of government securities in the hands of the non-bank public; a category including government bonds, treasury bills and income sharing certificates, (issued by certain extra-budgetary funds including the Mass Housing Fund). The growth of these three categories of marketed government debt has clearly been associated with a decline in the share of the private sector in such issues.

In addition to the general pressure which the budget deficit exerts on financial conditions, therefore, the table suggests that there has been a further influence through the structure of claims in the Turkish case. While private sector borrowing has become increasingly concentrated in the banks, the public sector has been tending to increase the marketed element of its liabilities. The wisdom of this trend in funding policy will be discussed further in the context of the development of the capital market in Turkey in the final section below. With private borrowing currently dominated by bank loans, however, the next section is devoted to the cost influences on bank intermediation as an additional factor in the liberalization process.

TABLE 4.2 *The structure of financial claims in Turkey (1981–7) (percentages)*

Year	1980	1981	1982	1983	1984	1985	1986	1987
Bank claims/total assets	82.5	85.8	86.7	84.5	82.8	81.9	81.3	78.7
Government securities/total assets	12.0	9.8	8.9	9.1	11.6	13.8	14.9	17.8
Private securities/total assets	5.5	4.4	4.4	6.4	5.6	4.3	3.8	3.5
Public sector bank debt/total bank claims	48.0	40.2	34.8	31.7	25.2	27.2	27.1	29.0

SOURCE: OECD (1990, Table 33) and OECD (1991, Table K).

4   INTERMEDIATION COSTS AND PRUDENTIAL REGULATION

Although financial liberalization has introduced strong competitive pressures, the Turkish banking industry remains highly concentrated. One estimate is that three banks: Ziraatbank (a state owned agricultural bank); Isbank (also state owned); and the private Akbank, account for more than half the banking sector's assets (Murray Brown, 1991). The large private banks, including the successful Akbank, are frequently affiliated with substantial industrial groupings and cross-shareholdings are common. In some cases equity holdings in related companies exceed the capital base of the banks (Murray Brown, 1991). Following the financial reforms of the 1980s, however, this established structure has been challenged by growing numbers of new entrants attracted by a tradition of high profitability in the sector.

Despite the new competition, however, considerable inefficiency in the sector continues to be noted with operating costs and gross earnings margins being significantly greater than in other OECD economies (OECD, 1990, p. 93 and Diagram 21). The margin between borrowing and lending rates is certainly large. Overnight inter-bank interest rates in April 1992 were quoted at 66.7 per cent with one-year retail deposits attracting 71–3 per cent from the large banks and up to 81 per cent from the smaller institutions. The corresponding borrowing rate for corporate customers was between 100 and 120 per cent compared with an annual inflation rate at the time of roughly 77 per cent. Somewhat extreme real rates are, of course, implied by these figures and help to explain the recent dearth of private sector borrowers (Barchard, 1992).

In terms of the diagram introduced in Figure 4.1 above, the 'wedge' between deposit and loan rates implies a leftward shifted supply schedule of loans (see figure 4.3).

The loan rate (r_l) exceeds the rate of interest offered on deposits (r_d) with the effect of reducing the investment which can be financed by new loans from L^* to L. A number of factors appear to account for these large intermediation spreads in Turkey. With some risk continuing to be attached in the eyes of the public to deposits held at small banks, part of the competitive process has been reflected in the rapid expansion of branch networks, computerization and an associated expansion of customer services at the large institutions (Murray Brown, 1991). In addition to these physical costs, high reserve requirements (roughly 13 per cent of deposits in 1991) add to the wedge between deposit and lending costs. The vice-chairman of Akbank (the most

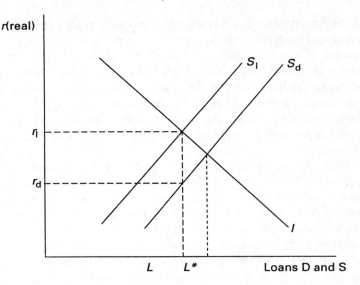

FIGURE *4.3 Intermediation costs and loan supply*

successful private institution) recently claimed that 90 per cent of this wedge was accounted for by required reserves, taxes and staffing costs (reported in Barchard, 1992).

Two further and rather less easily quantifiable factors need to be taken into account. With strongly positive real interest rates being charged on loans to both the private and public sectors, there is some doubt over the extent to which the threat of default is eroding the quality of private loans in bank portfolios (Murray Brown, 1991). The longer that the pressure of the public sector borrowing requirement and excessive costs hold these rates up, the more banks will need to finance loan loss provisions out of current earnings: a further element in the intermediation wedge. An extreme example of this problem is provided by the crisis episode of 1981–2 when real interest rates on non-preferential credits rose to between 25 and 30 per cent per annum. It is possible that between 40 and 60 per cent of nominal credit expansion in these years was used to refinance the interest payments due on non-performing loans (Celâsun and Rodrik, 1989, p. 676).

The second and newer consideration is the further requirement that the banks comply with the internationally agreed BIS rules on capital adequacy. This agreement established various acceptable forms of bank capital and the constraint that these should not fall below 8 per cent of total assets on a risk-weighted basis. While Turkish banks are attempting to comply with the target, one concern is that a significant fraction of their capital is made up of real estate and equity investments of uncertain marketable value (Barchard, 1992). The high cost of capital funds is therefore likely to constrain the expansion of bank loan books in favour of high lending margins. The effect of these various influences on private sector lending by the banks in the presence of government loan demand is examined in a formal model in Appendix 2.

Reflecting the situation described above, it is assumed that the representative bank is imperfectly competitive and decides the interest rates it will offer on deposits and loans. While this is consistent with varying deposit rates in a competitive environment, it is also consistent with the weekly treasury auctions in Turkey where banks bid to replenish their holdings of government securities. With these securities currently representing about one-third of bank assets, the yield implied by their auction bid determines the volume of securities they attract. Given the interest elasticity of deposit supply to the bank, these purchases of government debt must reduce the amount made available to private borrowers. The model also attempts to reflect the sensitivity of private loan losses to rising interest rates as well as the resource costs of maintaining the deposit base.

Assuming profit maximization, the first order conditions of the model yield a solution value for the level of lending to the private sector as follows:

$$L_p = c_{i3}'/\{(1 + e_{1p}) + e_{1p}/[i_3(\pi/\theta)]\} \qquad (4.2)$$

where:

$$\pi = -r(1 + 1/e_d) - c_d' + i_1 \text{MIN} - \rho[\text{BIS}/(1 - \text{BIS})]$$

and

$$\theta = 1 - \text{MIN} - \text{BIS}/(1 - \text{BIS}).$$

The numerator in the main expression (c_{i3}') represents the marginal increment in loan losses (default) as interest rates charged on private sector loans (i_3) are increased. Intuitively, the more significant these costs are, the more reluctant the bank will be to raise loan rates; loans will thus be higher than otherwise. This theoretical result reflects a serious practical difficulty for new borrowers which has been widely recognized and was indicated above. Typically, such extra lending will involve discrimination *between* borrowers in that sector. Large individual loans, which may be at risk of default in the climate of high interest rates, will tend to attract further loans to forestall the effects on the bank. Viable new borrowers are further crowded out by this mechanism (for example, World Bank, 1989, pp. 70–4).

With the interest elasticity of demand for private bank loans (e_{lp}) negative by assumption, the magnitude of lending is strongly influenced (given demand conditions) by the values taken by π and θ. Other than the small value i_l MIN which reflects the interest earned by the bank on minimum reserve asset holdings, all other components of π are unambiguously negative. Since θ is certainly positive, a *large* numerical value for π is associated with a *smaller* equilibrium value of private loans. Thus a high interest rate on minimum reserve holdings, (i_l), by reducing the implicit 'tax' on intermediation reflected by such requirements, is a positive influence on the volume of loans.

The first expression in π concerns the (assumed positive) interest elasticity of supply of bank deposits (e_d). Private lending volumes clearly benefit from a high responsiveness of deposit supply to interest rates offered. Equally unsurprisingly, a high marginal real resource cost of deposit funds (c_d') depresses private lending. The impact of prudential requirements is captured in the final element of π where BIS indicates the capital adequacy ratio guidelines and ρ the opportunity cost of capital funds to the bank. The greater the value of these two components the less will the bank be inclined to make private loans. The two prudential ratios appear again in θ above confirming further the depressing effects of BIS and of a high minimum reserve requirement (MIN). The implication that lower reserve requirements imply more lending in this model (and the attraction of more deposits to fund it) is consistent with recent experience. Between December 1990 and September 1991, legal reserve ratios were reduced from 19 to 16 per cent on sight deposits and from 9 to 7.5 per cent for time deposits. The ratio of M2 to the reserve money base has risen strongly in consequence (OECD, 1992, pp. 55–6). It appears that these measures were intended to reduce bank intermediation costs (OECD, 1992, p. 55).

While the model serves to confirm that the various institutional factors identified will act to shift the supply schedule of private loans to the left in Figure 4.3, other factors not explicitly considered will tend to have the same effect by biasing the banks in favour of lending to the government. At least up to 1991, for instance, government securities formed the basis of an *overall* liquidity requirement which stood at 30 per cent of deposit liabilities (Murray Brown, 1991). Moreover, government bond holdings attract tax exemptions not available on private sector claims (Murray Brown, 1991). The gross terms on these bonds will therefore help to determine the minimum, net of taxation, return on private loans. In addition, if 30 per cent of deposits must be maintained in the form of government debt, the bank must raise 143 in deposits for every 100 of private loans it wishes to make. If there are significant real resource costs in raising these funds a further constraint on private lending is implied.

The discussion in this and the preceding section has concerned the impact on the availability of bank loans to the private sector of financial liberalization in Turkey's context of continuing public-sector deficits and high costs of bank intermediation. In summary, the unavoidable crowding out implied by the deficits appears to be exacerbated by the high resource costs of maintaining deposits in the ratio to private loans which official reserve requirements necessitate.

Given that there is likely to be a continuing public-sector-deficit, the next section asks if the funding position of the private sector could be improved by the development of Turkey's non-bank capital markets paying particular attention to equity finance.

5   EQUITY FINANCE IN THE DEVELOPMENT OF TURKEY'S FINANCIAL STRUCTURE

Continuing budget deficits in the context of market-determined interest rates inevitably imply a higher real cost of finance for the private sector. If, moreover, conditions are such that nominal interest rates exceed nominal growth of GDP, private investment spending is likely to be discouraged by an additional consideration implicit in equation (4.1) above. The need to finance service payments becomes an increasingly important part of the public deficit raising the probability that inflationary liquidation of the public debt will eventually take place (Sargent and Wallace, 1986). The prospect of further financial instability is likely to have a damaging effect on private sector expectations.

If control of the deficit is, therefore, a primary requirement, the question remains whether any developments could improve funding for the private sector given the budget position of the authorities. The analysis of the previous section is relevant in this respect. By circumventing the high physical resource costs of bank intermediation, an expansion in the issue of 'primary' marketable securities, (bonds and shares), could raise the aggregate quantity of investible resources. Moreover, serious recourse to such issues by the private sector would encourage the banks to lower their operating costs.

Since equity holdings also offer substantial protection against inflation (as real claims), it is possible that inflation 'hedges' such as gold and capital exports could be more productively re-deployed through equity investment. Despite high interest on bank deposits, there is little sign that any substantial shift from gold holdings has taken place in recent years (Akyuz and Kotte, 1991). Moreover, one of the most dynamic elements in the balance sheet of the banking system has been the rapid increase in deposits denominated in foreign currency (OECD, 1990, p. 92). A broader and more liquid market in equities could offer an attractive substitute thereby releasing investible resources for the domestic economy.

While the development of markets in primary securities may be valuable in easing the availability of finance to the private sector, there are other reasons for believing that such a development away from bank intermediation would be desirable. It has been noted that complete dependence on loan finance with its implication of contractual interest obligations probably implies a sub-optimally low level of investment financing (Cho, 1986). The contractual interest obligation means that money cannot be raised against the 'upper tail' of the probability distribution of returns to the enterprise to be financed. Equity issues in which the holder shares in both the good and bad returns can therefore increase the amount of financing available (Cho, 1986).

This observation suggests an important, although not widely acknowledged, connection between financial development and changes in industrialization strategy of the type experienced by Turkey in January 1980. The subsequent shift from a protected to a more trade-oriented economy has implications for appropriate financial structure. In a heavily protected economy, investment projects are typically intended to serve the domestic market by replacing imports. With data on previous import trends beforehand and a frequently monopolistic position in the market afterwards, the riskiness of such investments is relatively low. Cash flows are stable enough to justify a large proportion of (bank) loans in overall financing; gearing ratios can be quite high. The financial structure of Turkish manufacturing firms continues to reflect this legacy (OECD, 1991, pp. 96–101).

The cost of this predictability of returns is that *mean* returns tend to decline as the inefficiency associated with inward-looking industrialization increasingly makes itself felt. From the financial view-point, the outward-looking strategy has the opposite characteristics. Mean returns rise reflecting the (comparative advantage) based effi-ciency gains and the scale economies which exporting makes possi-ble. At the same time, *enterprise* risk is increased. Foreign markets are less predictable and certainly a lot more competitive. While mean returns increase, therefore, the same is probably true for their vari-ance. High enterprise gearing ratios are clearly less appropriate in these circumstances suggesting an increasing need for risk bearing finance. Equity investors are able to spread their investments between differ-ing enterprises with the 'upper tail' of returns on some investments compensating returns in the 'lower tail' on others. In this way, diver-sified equity portfolios can provide the improved average returns which the efficient industrialization strategy permits, while avoiding the higher variance associated with the fortunes individual enterprises.

Some evidence for this hypothesized relationship between financial and economic structure is offered by the following simple regression results. Using the World Bank International Finance Corporation Emerg-ing Markets data base for the two years 1986 and 1987, national mar-ket capitalization as a fraction of GDP was regressed against two explanatory variables on a pure cross-section basis. Exports as a frac-tion of GDP were taken as an indication of openness in the economy and the ratio of M3 to GDP was used to represent relative national financial wealth. The 18 countries involved are taken from the 20 which comprise the IFC composite index and include Turkey.[1]

$$CAP86 = -0.087 + 0.0047 \ XGDP + 0.0016 \ M3GDP$$
$$(-1.77) \quad (2.02) \quad (1.67)$$

$$R^2 = 0.56, \ F(2,15) = 12.0$$

$$CAP87 = -0.096 + 0.0061 \ XGDP + 0.0017 \ M3GDP$$
$$(-3.21) \quad (4.29) \quad (2.82)$$

$$R^2 = 0.83, \ F(2,15) = 45.0.$$

(All data from *Emerging Stock Markets Factbook 1991 (IFC)* and *World Development Report 1989* (World Bank appendix tables).)

While these results are highly tentative, they do suggest that more open economies (with their relative money holdings constant) will tend to have more fully developed stock markets. If this cross-national relationship has validity, it is worth noting that in both years the *predicted* value for the capitalization of the Turkish market at Istanbul was considerably greater than its *actual* capitalization as a fraction of GDP. Thus, in 1986, the actual ratio was 1.6 per cent of GDP compared with a predicted value of 5.3 per cent. Using 1986 $ values, the discrepancy suggests that market capitalization could have been $2.1 billion higher than its actual $935 million. Conducting the same calculation for 1987, when actual capitalization was at the higher level of 4.8 per cent of GDP, the predicted value was 7.4 per cent. On the basis of 1987 $ values, this was equivalent to a shortfall in capitalization of $1.78 billion compared with the actual $3.22 billion.

Despite their crude basis, these estimates support the general impression that the Turkish capital market is underdeveloped (for example, OECD, 1990, p. 94). A number of reasons have been suggested above as to why a correction of this situation may be desirable. As the OECD report makes clear, however, formidable obstacles exist in the form of family-based ownership anxious to avoid the dilution of control. The concluding section addresses the possible policy options in the light of such difficulties.

6 POLICY CONCLUSIONS

While recognizing the fundamental need for the government's financial deficits to be brought under control, further policy measures aimed at expanding the market in equities and bonds appear worthy of consideration in light of the above analysis. In assessing them, however, a potential danger in seeking to provide the private sector with an alternative to bank finance must be acknowledged.

It was noted in connection with expression (4.2) above that a fraction of bank credit extended to the private sector is at risk of being preempted to defend those loans where serious risk of default exists. Essentially, new loans are being used to finance the interest due on old debt and solvent borrowers may thus be inadequately supplied with credit. If such borrowers are to be offered an alternative means of raising finance the risk of a further deterioration in the quality of bank loan portfolios arises. Policy measures must therefore avoid the unintended effect of further undermining the stability of the monetary sector.

If the fundamental insolvency of certain existing bank borrowers is to be recognized, the losses which the economy has already incurred in supporting them must be allocated explicitly. Two possibilities arise which would probably both be involved in any programme of reform. Loan losses could be written off against the funds of bank shareholders and the government may accept responsibility for some of the bad loans. Whereas the latter implies that tax payers in general would be obliged to accept the losses, it would also complicate the budgetary problems discussed in the Section 3 above. Cancellation against bank capital, especially in light of the Basle requirements discussed in Section 4, would slow the growth of bank lending and the banks themselves would have to raise new equity. How might alternative channels of finance be encouraged to counter any curtailment in the supply of bank credit without exacerbating the problems of that sector?

Firstly, the trend noted earlier for the government to increase the issue of marketed bonds to the public could be ended in favour of sales to the banking system. This change in funding policy would add relatively secure assets to bank balance sheets and help to make way for private sector security issues. Secondly, an accelerated programme of privatization sales could be used to fund the repurchase of domestic government debt, thereby cutting service payments to the benefit of future budgets. The new shares would also serve to expand the securities available for private investors seeking to diversify their asset portfolios. While there may well be efficiency gains from privatization sales, the benefits indicated here for the development of Turkey's financial structure do not depend on them.

APPENDIX 4.1

Private sector credit growth budget deficits and interest rate liberalization

The expression in the text is derived from the following simplified relationship starting with the balance sheet of the banking system:

$$M = D_p + D_g + eF. \tag{A.1}$$

Neglecting minor components, the money stock (M) reflects the stock of domestic private and government debt owed to the banks (D_p and Dg respectively) and the net foreign exchange reserves (F) expressed in domestic currency through the exchange rate (e).

Expressing both sides as a fraction of GDP and assuming that the ratio of M/GDP remains constant in the long run, differentiation of the corresponding asset ratio produces the following requirement when divided through by M:

$$\overset{0}{D}_p(D_p/M) + \overset{0}{D}_g(D_g/M) + \overset{0}{e}F(eF/M) - \overset{0}{\text{GDP}} = 0. \tag{A.2}$$

Assuming that the (domestic currency) value of net foreign exchange assets grows over time at the same rate as nominal GDP (reflecting both real accumulation and exchange rate depreciation):

$$\overset{0}{e}F = \overset{0}{\text{GDP}} \tag{A.3}$$

(A.2) above may be simplified as follows:

$$\overset{0}{D}_p - \overset{0}{\text{GDP}} = -(D_g/D_p)[\overset{0}{D}_g - \overset{0}{\text{GDP}}]. \tag{A.4}$$

If it is assumed that the government *only* borrows from the banks the evolution of the government's debt will be:

$$\delta D_g = \text{PBD} + iD_g - \delta C. \tag{A.5}$$

The change in the debt is therefore equal to the primary deficit (PBD), plus the service burden on the existing debt (iD_g) minus the issue of currency (δC). Dividing (A.5) through by D_g produces the growth rate of the public debt:

$$\overset{0}{D}_g = \text{PBD}/D_g + i - \delta C/D_g. \tag{A.5a}$$

Insertion of this equation in (A.4) above results in the expression in the text:

$$(\overset{0}{D}_p - \overset{0}{\text{GDP}}) = -D_g/D_p\{(\text{PBD} - \delta C)/D_g + (i - \overset{0}{\text{GDP}})\}. \tag{A.6}$$

APPENDIX 4.2

Model of bank lending to the private sector

As noted in the text, the bank maximizes profits by varying interest rates offered and charged on deposits and loans. Its simplified balance sheet is composed as follows:

$$R + L_g + L_p \equiv \text{Assets} \equiv K + D. \tag{A.i}$$

Thus reserves (R) plus (other) loans to the government (L_p) plus loans to the private sector (L_p) are equal to the sum of capital funds (K) and deposits (D).

The bank maximizes its profit function:

$$\eta = i_1 R + i_2 L_g + i_3 L_p - \rho K - rD - C(D, i_3), \tag{A.ii}$$

where i_1, i_2, i_3 and r are the appropriate interest rates, r is the cost of equity and the final term reflects a cost function which rises with the volume of deposits (D) attracted by the bank and with the rate of interest charged on private loans (i_3). The latter is intended to reflect the cost of mounting defaults as interest rates rise. The constraints which must be satisfied concern the balance sheet and its structure:

$$\lambda_1 (R + L_g + L_p - K - D) = 0, \tag{A.iii}$$

$$\lambda_2 (\text{BIS} - K/(K + D)) = 0, \tag{A.iv}$$

$$\lambda_3 (\text{MIN} - R/D) = 0. \tag{A.v}$$

Thus, the balance sheet constraint, the capital adequacy requirement, (BIS), and the minimum reserve ratio, (MIN), are all assumed to be met continuously. The bank maximizes its profits by choosing i_2, i_3, r, R and K (with i_1 and ρ assumed given from the viewpoint of the bank). Manipulation of the first order conditions of this constrained maximization problem yields the solution value for private lending reported in the text.

NOTE

1. The 20 are Argentina, Brazil, Chile, Colombia, Greece, India, Indonesia, Jordan, Korea, Malaysia, Mexico, Nigeria, Pakistan, the Philippines, Portugal, Taiwan, Thailand, Turkey, Venezuela, and Zimbabwe. Incomplete data caused Indonesia and Taiwan to be excluded from the regression exercise.

REFERENCES

Akyuz, Y. and Kotte, D. J. (1991), 'Financial Policies in Developing Countries: Issues and Experience', UNCTAD Discussion Paper no. 40.

Barchard, D. (1992), 'Banks Start to Catch up', in 'Turkey FT Survey', *Financial Times*, London, 21 May.

Celâsun, M. and Rodrik, D. (1989) 'Debt, Adjustment and Growth: Turkey' in J. D. Sachs, and S. M. Collins (eds), *Developing Country Debt & Economic Performance*, vol. 3 (Chicago, IL: Chicago University Press for NBER).

Cho, Y. J. (1986), 'Inefficiencies from Financial Liberalisation in the Absence of Well-Functioning Equity Markets', *Journal of Money, Credit, & Banking*, vol. 18, pp. 191–9.

Dornbusch, R. and Reynoso, A. (1993), 'Financial Factors in Economic Development', in R. Dornbusch (ed.), *Policy Making in the Open Economy: Concepts and Case Studies in Economic Performance* (Oxford: Oxford University Press for the World Bank).

Fry, M. J. (1982), 'Models of Financially Repressed Developing Economies', *World Development*, vol. 10, pp. 731–50.

McKinnon, R. I. (1973), *Money and Capital in Economic Development* (Washington, DC: The Brookings Institution).

McKinnon, R. I. (1982), 'The Order of Economic Liberalisation: Lessons from Chile and Argentina', in K. Brunner and A. Meltzer (eds), *Carnegie Rochester Conference Series on Public Policy*, 17 (Amsterdam: North Holland) pp. 159–96.

Murray Brown, J. (1991), 'Leaner Times Ahead' in 'Turkish Finance, Investment & Industry Survey 2', *Financial Times* (London, 17 January).

OECD (1990), *Economic Survey: Turkey 1989–90* (Paris: OECD).

OECD (1991), *Economic Survey: Turkey 1990–91* (Paris: OECD).

OECD (1992), *Economic Survey: Turkey 1991–92* (Paris: OECD).

Sargent, T. and Wallace, N. (1986), 'Some Unpleasant Monetarist Arithmetic' in T. Sargent (ed.), *Rational Expectations & Inflation* (New York: Harper & Row).

Shaw, E. S. (1973), *Financial Deepening in Economic Development* (New York: Oxford University Press).

Van Wijnbergen, S. (1982), 'Stagflationary Effects of Monetary Stabilisation Policies: A Quantitative Analysis of South Korea', *Journal of Development Economics*, vol. 10, pp. 133–69.

World Bank (1989), *World Development Report 1989* (Oxford: Oxford University Press for World Bank).

5 Foreign Aid and Adjustment in Turkey

Oliver Morrissey

1 INTRODUCTION

Aid has played a prominent role in the Turkish economy at various stages in the post-war period. In the immediate post-war period, US aid was an important source of funds for investment in agriculture and infrastructure (Krueger, 1974). Turkey was land-abundant and relatively well endowed with resources; it was more 'dualistic' than the average middle income country, the share of agriculture in GDP being close to the norm for all developing countries (Baysan and Blitzer, 1991). It was well placed to be a major exporter of agricultural commodities from the 1950s. However, the exchange rate was fixed at 2.8 Turkish Lira (TL) to the dollar from 1946 to 1958. While aid flows were able to sustain this initially, relatively high inflation (fuelled by a large budget deficit due to agricultural price support and the favourable position of State Economic Enterprises (SEEs)) lead to real overvaluation. Exports were discriminated against while the import-competing sector was protected. An inability to finance necessary imports led Turkey to accept an IMF stabilization programme in 1958 and a substantial devaluation in 1960. While IMF credits helped to finance imports, the principle of government intervention, the favourable position of SEEs and protection for the import-substitution (IS) sector remained unquestioned and unchanged (Krueger, 1987).

In the 1960s, Turkey adopted a clear IS strategy and aid support amounted to 2–3 per cent of GNP throughout the decade. Export growth slowed as the decade progressed and high inflation again led to overvaluation. There was another major devaluation in 1970 (Krueger, 1987). Despite high inflation during the 1973–4 oil crisis, the nominal exchange rate adjusted slowly. By the end of the decade, the TL was again overvalued and the country had an unsustainable current account deficit. In January 1980, the government announced major reforms: a devaluation of almost 50 per cent and a promise to maintain the real exchange rate, supported by an IMF stand-by agreement and a programme of five structural adjustment loans SALs worth some $1.5

billion over 1980–4 (Kirkpatrick and Önis, 1991). Turkish adjustment in the 1980s appears to have been a success. Why was this the case in the 1980s when previous reforms had not been sustained? This is the question we address, in the context of evaluating Turkish reforms against lessons that can be derived from the experiences of other reforming countries.

We begin by noting that Turkey in 1980 exhibited all the economic policy failures of typical less developed countries (LDCs) which precipitated the need for structural adjustment (Krueger, 1992). Typical macroeconomic failures have been observed in the budget deficit and exchange rate. The budget deficits fuel inflation. As interest rates are typically less than inflation, credit rationing is introduced (in the Turkish case SEEs had preferential access, see Baysan and Blitzer, 1991). Numerous LDCs have tried to sustain overvalued exchange rates, which reduce the domestic cost of debt-servicing but discriminate against exports (and reduce the foreign exchange earnings which can be used to meet debt interest payments). Economic crises frequently begin with a balance of payments crisis and the recommended solution is stabilization, as imposed by the IMF: devaluation and reducing the budget deficit.

The second area of failure is government intervention. LDCs have generally failed to provide adequate social and physical infrastructure, imposing costs on business and slowing growth. The proliferation of controlled prices, import licences, foreign exchange and credit controls give rise to distortions (such as reflected in relatively high effective protection and relatively high domestic resource costs; see Krueger (1974) for evidence on Turkey), rent-seeking and rationing. Public enterprises, such as SEEs, account for large shares of investment, output and employment, with favourable access to scarce resources. These tend to be relatively inefficient and have low factor productivity (Baysan and Blitzer, 1991) and create vested interests which subsequently oppose economic reform. The low return on public investment precipitates debt-servicing crises and contributes to the ineffectiveness of aid.

Inappropriate policies generated a wide variety of distortions throughout the economy. Consequently, to facilitate growth required wide-ranging economic reform. We appraise the way in which Turkey embarked on such reform in the 1980s and evaluate its success in a manner that allows us to derive lessons for other reformers. Section 2 presents an overview of the role of aid, excluding SALs, in Turkey over the last decade. Section 3 addresses Turkish structural adjustment: how did the Turkish package compare to other SAL recipients, how

well did Turkey comply with the conditions and how successful was
it. Section 4 broadens this discussion to consider, in particular, credibility
and sequencing issues. Section 5 presents the conclusion.

2   AID TO TURKEY IN THE 1980s

In both 1970–1 and 1980–1, Turkey received the fifth largest share of
aid from OECD countries, accounting for 2.5 per cent of the total. By
1989–90, Turkey's share ranked 14th and it accounted for 1.3 per
cent of the total (Development Assistance Committee (DAC), 1991,
p. 226). This was a very high position for a middle-income country
(MIC). Clearly, even through a period of relatively successful adjustment, Turkey has remained a major aid recipient although, as we will
show, the nature of this aid has changed somewhat. We begin this
section by reviewing the pattern of Turkish receipts of official development assistance (oda, the DAC term for aid) and then consider some
probable effects.

2.1   An overview of turkey's aid receipts

Some important features of Turkish aid receipts are given in Table
5.1. Total net oda receipts fell during the 1980s, reflecting the increased cost of servicing aid that was received in the form of loans.
Although low relative to the MIC average, with the possible exception
of 1987, per capita oda and aid as a share of GNP were quite high
considering that Turkey became a relatively rich MIC during the period.
We are most concerned with the period 1980–6 surrounding the
adjustment programme. Capital flows to Turkey remained substantial
throughout the period and the increasing share attributable to multilateral agencies, a third of the total in the mid-1980s, reflects the SALs.
The economic growth in Turkey is reflected in the changing pattern
of bilateral financial flows from DAC donors. Although variable, the
share of grants declined while that of loans more than halved. Export
credits, of which more in Section 2.2, accounted for over half of bilateral flows by the mid-1980s.

The sources of aid also changed. The US share fell consistently
from 23 to 6 per cent in 1986, while Japan's share rose steadily from
2.0 to 5.6 per cent (and exceeded that of the US in the late 1980s). It
is notable that the subsidy element in US aid also declined (but the
data for Japan are patchy). There was a dramatic drop in German aid

TABLE 5.1 *Patterns of Turkish aid receipts*

	1980	1985	1987	1989
Total net oda receipts ($m)[a]	952.0	179.0	376.0	122.0
$ per capita oda receipts[a]	n.a.	3.5	7.9	2.2
MIC average	n.a.	11.4	13.4	12.0
oda as % GNP[a]	n.a.	0.3	0.6	0.2
MIC average	n.a.	0.9	0.8	0.6
	1980	**1982**	**1984**	**1986**
Capital flows ($m)[b]	2068.2	1956.5	1953.9	2865.6
Multilateral (%)	18.8	28.7	34.8	34.1
DAC financial flows (composition of)[b]				
oda grants (%)	12.3	23.4	9.3	10.2[c]
oda loans (%)	36.7	24.6	23.1	15.9[c]
Export credits (%)	28.9	14.6	48.6	87.2[c]
Shares of total financial flows[b]				
USA (%)	22.5	30.8	16.3	5.9
Germany (%)	26.9	8.8	7.0	12.2
Japan (%)	1.8	3.9	4.0	5.6
Rest of world (%)[d]	42.5	43.6	66.1	68.4
Subsidy rates of project credits[b]				
USA (%)	26.0	−0.2	10.0	1.4
Germany (%)	53.4	46.3	6.8	9.0
Japan (%)	n.a.	33.1	n.a.	−5.1
Multilateral (%)	23.6	11.6	8.1	4.7

NOTES AND SOURCES: [a] Data from *World Development Report*, various years.
[b] Data from Önis and Özmucur (1991), various tables.
[c] Figures refer to 1985.
[d] Includes multilateral agencies.
n.a. indicates not available.

in the early 1980s, but this was partially restored and it regained its place as the largest single bilateral donor by 1986; the subsidy element was also slashed but remained relatively high. The dominant trends were that multilaterals increased their share of financial flows, although the subsidy element fell steadily, while export credits displaced normal aid in bilateral flows. We now turn to the effects of aid.

2.2 Some salient effects of aid

The primary objective of aid is to support economic growth in recipients, but the aggregate effect of aid on growth presents a complex problem because the two variables are inter-related: it may be as easy to claim that slow economic growth attracts increased aid as it is to argue that high levels of aid promote growth. Also, the linkage between aid and growth is indirect; for example, aid may affect the level of private investment and/or relative prices, especially the exchange rate, which in turn can constrain any beneficial impact on the growth rate. Three critical parameters determine the effectiveness of aid: the productivity of (public and private) capital should be high; the proportion of aid diverted to recurrent budgets should be minimized, as should the potential distortionary effects of aid, whether on relative prices or crowding-out private investment (Mosley *et al.*, 1987). Tied aid, with its emphasis on capital goods, often imposes a burden on future recurrent expenditure, while capital projects are more likely than poverty-focused projects to substitute for domestic private investment.

US aid to Turkey in the immediate post-war period was concentrated on agriculture and infrastructure (Krueger, 1974). Such aid was consistent with an inward-oriented view of development and would have contributed to Turkish reliance on capital imports, the more so if the aid was tied to US goods. The investment in agriculture and the subsequent reliance on price support for the sector did pose an unbearable burden for recurrent expenditure. Domestic investment was directed towards the IS sector and Turkey remained relatively reliant on capital imports. Furthermore, the productivity of public capital, at least, was relatively low. Many of the problems associated with aid, especially tied aid, were experienced by Turkey in the 1950s and possibly the 1960s. They were also evident in the 1980s (Önis and Özmucur (1991) see below).

Tying imposes a cost on recipients, the greater to the extent that it causes them to purchase more goods from the donor, and at a higher price, than would otherwise be the case. If all aid were untied so that the recipient could choose how to spend it, each would have the opportunity (whether or not they fully avail of it) to determine its own investment projects, to determine the technology appropriate to its long term interests and to purchase exports at world prices. Tying restricts competition to the donor industries so the potential for excess profits increases: studies suggest that tied prices could include 33 to 50 per cent 'excess costs' to recipients (Bhagwati, 1967). Tying also increases the likelihood that the goods offered are not those that would be chosen in a perfect world and therefore represent an inefficient allocation of resources (Johnson, 1967). Tied aid reflects donor technology and the specifications create a dependency, for maintenance and spare-parts, which is rarely accounted for in the aid award. In general, 'the goods and services offered are of low priority to the recipient, are excessively capital-intensive, are highly dependent on Western technologies and are import-biased' (Jepma, 1989, p. 10).

Mixed (or export) credits, a form of aid in which the donor offers a subsidy to one of its companies seeking a contract in an LDC, exacerbates these problems. First, contracts which receive the support of mixed credits are normally initiated by companies as commercial orders. Second, the motivation behind mixed credits is to favour the donor firm in winning the order against competition from firms of other donors, they are thus equivalent to export subsidies. Third, the aid element is only a portion of the contract value, normally between a quarter and a third, the remainder of which has to be financed by the LDC government, normally through commercial export credits (hence the term mixed credits) though occasionally with conventional (tied) aid. For these reasons, mixed credits have a strong commercial orientation, are favoured by donor firms and often justified by donors because of the commercial benefits to donor firms; it is assumed that the recipients desire the project, hence it contributes to development, and that the subsidy element implies that goods are being provided to the LDC at a reduced price. Neither assumption need hold (see Morrissey, 1993).

The relatively rich LDCs that win mixed credits may benefit if they can successfully play one donor off against the other(s); while donors play 'beggar-thy-neighbour' the recipient might get cheap imports. Turkey has been a prominent recipient of aid in the form of mixed credits, a notable case being the Bosphorus projects. Önis and Özmucur (1991) show that subsidized capital flows facilitated the increase in capital imports that helped Turkey recover from an acute balance of payments crisis in the late 1970s. On the plus side, subsidy rates were high in the early 1980s and facilitated economic growth in certain sectors. On the negative side, the subsidies encouraged over-borrowing and were directed at infrastructure rather than manufacturing investment, hence did not assist the expansion of exports required to ease the burden of debt servicing. There was evidence that credits were used to support donor exports and that they increased the capital–output ratio in infrastructure and Turkish dependency on imports of capital goods. Aid may have conferred benefits to Turkey in the post-war period, but it also imposed costs.

In this brief sketch we hope to have offered enough evidence to suggest that the benefits of bilateral aid to Turkey are questionable. The manner in which aid can support capital imports would have reinforced some of the imbalances in Turkey. There is clear evidence, at least for the late 1960s and early 1970s, that agricultural sectors in Turkey (potentially strong exporters) faced negative protection while IS sectors were heavily protected and this imposed high domestic resource costs (Baysan and Blitzer, 1991, pp. 309–11). Aid policies would have done little to improve the relative position of agriculture while at the same time providing an avenue for donor exporters to circumvent protection against imports.

3   TURKEY'S STRUCTURAL ADJUSTMENT PROGRAMME

While aid in general has been of dubious benefit to Turkey, the large volumes of aid associated with the SAL packages seem to have precipitated a beneficial transformation of the Turkish economy in the 1980s (Baysan and Blitzer, 1991; Kirkpatrick and Önis, 1991). The clear advantage of SAL-type aid is its fungibility: it is not tied to donor exports but can be used, with relative discretion, to support adjustment and alleviate payments crises. The importance of SAL packages, however, is the conditions attached to them: to a greater or lesser extent, recipients are required to alter the structure of their economy. What alterations was Turkey asked to make, to what extent did it make them and did they contribute to economic growth? These questions are addressed in successive sections.

3.1   The nature of SALs

According to a World Bank appraisal, the SAL programme was initiated in response to fundamental disequilibrium in developing countries – disequilibrium which resulted from the second oil shock and domestic policy weakness (World Bank, 1988). Crises were attributed also to microeconomic distortions and the bank advocated SALs to reform the underlying structure. The bank wishes to influence the economic policies of recipients, but does not wish to be portrayed as 'buying' reform, so the conditionality underpinning SALs evolves in a process of negotiation and bargaining. Recommendations are made for reforms and disbursement of SAL funds is conditional upon the acceptance of these reform proposals. The process can be thought of as a stick and carrot mechanism. The carrot comes in several forms, notably quickly disbursed finance on concessional terms, but occasionally funds that can be used to compensate losers. The stick takes the form of a threat by the bank not to offer further finance if the recipient reneges (slips) on the conditions. Often loans are tranched, providing the opportunity for periodic appraisal of the extent to which loan conditions are being met. In the event that non-compliance occurs, the bank can suspend the loan. *Ceteris paribus*, slippage will be greater the less dependent is the recipient on a future loan. The recipient has a likelihood of wanting future loans and will not wish to slip sufficiently to be in-eligible for future loans (as happened to Bolivia, which had about 80 per cent slippage on its SAL). Then there is partial slippage and a probability of still receiving future loans, e.g. Kenya and the Philip-pines got second SALs despite slippage on the first. The implication is that recipients did not see slippage leading to punishment as a credible threat because the bank needs to lend, many conditions are vague and some slippage can be blamed on external factors (Mosley *et al.*, 1991a).

Table 5.2 provides details of the policy areas where conditionality is most frequently applied in connection with SALs. Some nine dif-ferent areas of policy have been affected. The area which has been least subject to conditionality is exchange rate policy, which accounted for only 2 per cent of all conditions attached. This does not reflect a view that the exchange rate is an unimportant policy variable. Rather, it reflects the fact that the exchange rate is traditionally in the sphere of influence of the IMF. Recipients of SALs are usually recipients of stabilization loans from the IMF in which the exchange rate is a major target of conditionality. This was clearly the case for Turkey where an IMF stabilization programme preceded the first SAL (Table 5.5 below). The single area most frequently subject to conditionality is trade policy: this accounted for 28 per cent of all conditions and tended to figure more prominently in the conditions imposed on richer recip-ients. Turkey is notable in this respect, where almost half the condi-tions applied to trade, which is to be expected given the principal objective of removing the anti-export bias and protection of IS sectors.

The prominence of trade is attributable largely to the belief that outward-orientation facilitates more rapid economic growth (for which there is empirical support). More generally, liberal trade policies minimize price distortions and facilitate a more efficient allocation of resources. Furthermore, protectionist trade policies, particularly those grounded in direct controls, encourage rent seeking. Finally, many of the instruments of trade policy are readily identifiable and compliance with particular conditions is relatively easily monitored. Techniques of policy analysis are fairly well-developed for trade issues, such as incidence and effective protection, which facilitates the design, negotiation and implementation

TABLE 5.2   *Conditionality content of SALs*

	Various policy areas as a percentage of all conditions			
Item	*SSAs*[b] *(13)*[a]	*HIC*[c] *(22)*	*All (51)*	*Turkey (5)*
1. Exchange rate	4.2	1.9	1.9	2.0
2. Trade policies	25.0	32.0	28.1	44.9
3. Fiscal policy	8.3	10.8	11.4	12.2
4. Budget/public spending	11.8	8.9	9.9	26.5
5. Public enterprises	19.4	16.6	15.5	12.2
6. Financial sector	3.5	13.1	10.9	18.4
7. Industrial policy	6.9	2.3	3.3	0.0
8. Energy policy	1.4	3.1	6.0	6.1
9. Agricultural policy	17.4	10.0	11.3	0.0
10. Other	2.1	1.3	1.7	0.0
Total	**100.0**	**100.0**	**100.0**	**100.0**

NOTES: [a] Numbers in parenthesis are total numbers of loans; 'All' refers to all SAL recipients over the period 1980–7 inclusive.
   [b] SSA, sub-Saharan Africa.
   [c] HICs, highly indebted countries.

SOURCE: World Bank (1988, Table 4.2); estimates for Turkey are derived from Kirkpatrick and Önis (1991, Table 11.2).

of policy. In the latter respect, the first Turkish SAL included the condition that a detailed study of protection be undertaken.

Liberalization of import policy may in itself have a beneficial impact on incentives to export. Arguably, complete import liberalization would obviate the need for any positive export promotion policies, since complete liberalization will, *ceteris paribus*, result in neutrality in the structure of relative prices. However, in SAL programmes, complete liberalization is not typical, either because reforms are gradually phased in or because a certain 'core' level of protection is conceded. Thus, positive export policy is frequently recommended, as it was in the first two Turkish SALs. This may take the form of understandings on the exchange rate with a view to reducing the extent of overvaluation. An exchange rate which is overvalued distorts the price of tradeables relative to non-tradeables to the disadvantage of the former. Moreover, as the costs and risks associated with exporting tend to be greater than those of competing on the home market, it is often argued that an overvalued exchange rate disadvantages the export sector in particular (which appears to apply to Turkey).

The other most important areas are the public sector (fiscal policy, public expenditure and the budget deficit and parastatals), agricultural policy, and financial sector reform. It is curious that agriculture did not feature directly in any of the conditions attached to Turkish SALs. The public sector, especially expenditure, did feature prominently for Turkey. 'Arguably the most important government interventions are through the public investment budget' (Baysan and Blitzer, 1991, p. 276). Many of the conditions imposed on Turkey in this area did relate to public investment, which was to be reduced in scale and redirected towards infrastructure and away from SEEs. Interestingly, Önis and Özmucur (1991, p. 31) observe the trend in public investment after 1980 as being away from manufacturing and towards infrastructure, which they criticise as a 'tendency towards disequilibrium' (in terms of future debt-servicing). However, the trend in consistent with implementation of SAL conditions, infrastructure is an appropriate area for public investment and may not crowd-out private investment.

Another significant area for Turkish conditions was SEEs because the public sector 'dominates heavy industry, receives the lion's share of investment, and pays the highest wages while accounting for the smallest share of employment' (Baysan and Blitzer, 1991, p. 278). The conditions were intended to reduce the prices, wages and favourable access to credit of SEEs and increase their efficiency. This is an area were success was limited (see 3.2 below). The final area of note is the financial sector which featured more prominently for Turkey than for SALs in general. This is partly because Turkey is relatively developed and most of these conditions related to the provision of credit and establishing a stock exchange, and featured in the fifth SAL.

The range of policy instruments affected by SAL programmes makes them difficult to negotiate and agree for two main reasons. First, there are problems of policy interdependence. Thus, for example, tariff reductions may impact on government fiscal constraints. When changes are taking place across a range of areas simultaneously it may be extremely difficult to predict *a priori* quite how these changes will ultimately affect economic activity. Turkish conditions were relatively well integrated. For example, the reforms of SEEs would also reduce public expenditure and the budget deficit while facilitating private sector expansion. Second, the greater the number of policy areas involved in a particular reform package, the greater the number of government agencies involved in the negotiation of the package. As the number of interested parties increases, the potential trade-offs between agencies increases. This also in unlikely to have been a critical problem for

Turkey as it was rarely the case that any one SAL related to a large number of conditions, while Turkey had a relatively skilled and capable bureaucracy. In conclusion, Turkey's conditions were more focused on trade and public investment and better integrated, than for most SALs.

3.2   Compliance with conditionality

In assessing the effects of SALs an important distinction can be made between the 'success' of the Bank in obtaining compliance with proposed conditions, and the effects of the reforms that were implemented. Countries that did not comply with the conditions imposed would not be expected to achieve the expected gains. In fact, if slippage undermines credibility, countries with high slippage could be worse off after the reforms than before (Rodrik, 1989). Assessing compliance with conditionality appears to be a relatively simple exercise. We take the information on conditionality, and assess the degree to which this was adhered to. Any such assessment would necessarily be qualitative in making judgements on when a condition was 'fully implemented', and when 'substantial progress' had been made. The World Bank (1988) assessment is summarised in Table 5.3 with a comparable exercise for Turkey (our difficulty of assigning percentages for Turkey calls into question the process of assigning values, although the relative magnitudes are remarkably similar). For the 40 countries in the World Bank sample, 70 per cent of all conditions were assessed as fully implemented in the period concerned. In our judgement, Turkey made somewhat less progress largely because of dubious compliance with conditions on import liberalization and SEE reform (our total is the sum of the figures in each area weighted by the share of that area in total conditions).

This approach avoids the fact that not only is slippage difficult to measure, being a subjective judgement, but it is also difficult to interpret. Simple figures for percentage slippage are unable to distinguish cases where recipients did not implement conditions they had never, at the negotiating stage, intended to implement from cases where slippage occurred because recipients were unable to implement the conditions (either because they were too ambiguous or too ambitious). For Turkey, the trade policy conditions in SAL III were vague ('further progress to be made on import liberalisation'). There were further cases where conditions were met but their effects undermined by subsequent policies, such as in Turkey where the 'ambiguous' moves towards

TABLE 5.3   *Compliance with conditionality, 1980–7*

| | *Percentage of SAL conditions implemented during the loan period* | | | |
| | All SALs[a] | | Turkey[b] | |
Item	(1)	(2)	(1)	(2)
1. Exchange rate	70	90	80	100
2. Trade policies	55	84	40	80
Import QRs	63	93	40	50
Import duties	62	77	50	60
Import/export finance	20	80	60	80
Export incentives	61	82	60	80
3. Fiscal policy	53	78	50	80
4. Budget/public expenditures	68	78	40	80
5. Parastatals	61	87	50	60
6. Financial sector	71	86	60	90
7. Industrial policy	53	93	–	–
8. Energy policy	79	83	60	90
9. Agriculture policy	57	82	–	–
All conditions	68	84	48	83

NOTES AND SOURCES: [a] Data on all SALs from World Bank (1988, Table 4.3); percentage shares refer to (1) 'fully implemented' and (2) fully plus 'substantial progress'. Original source gives figures to one decimal place but this would appear to be spurious accuracy (all values should be interpreted as relative).
[b] Estimates for Turkey derived from Kirkpatrick and Önis (1991, Table 11.2); percentages are judgements for all SALs. We do not classify any of the Turkish conditions as relating to industrial or agricultural policy.

import liberalization were partially offset by increased use of the import levy scheme from 1984. The evidence in Table 5.3 indicates that, overall, most conditions were met. It does not, however, indicate if the conditions were sustained.

The evidence in Table 5.3 indicates differences in implementation by policy instrument; the percentage of trade policy conditions fully implemented was relatively low, whilst for energy policy it was relatively high. This may have something to do with the nature of the reforms involved: if those for energy involve price changes but those for trade policy involve reductions in effective tariffs, one can see how the greater complexity of the latter could make for greater difficulty of compliance. Another possibility is that greater political interests may be at stake with trade policy than with, say, energy policy. A further issue is sequencing. It may be appropriate to implement some conditions before others so that compliance increases over time (Section 4.2).

It may be the least important conditions which are adhered to, and the most important which are resisted. This problem has been acknowledged but should not be serious if 'on balance, the performance on key conditions is better than the performance on all conditions' (World Bank, 1988, p. 62). There is a distinct possibility that this does not hold for Turkey. Three important areas of conditions were complied with to a high degree, namely exchange rates, export promotion and public investment. While there was initial compliance with the demands to reduce the budget deficit, public investment grew after the restoration of parliamentary democracy in 1983 and this condition may not be sustainable (Önis and Özmucur, 1991, p. 20). Two important areas were not convincingly complied with: while quota lists and tariffs were reduced, many imports remain subject to restrictions; while SEE's staffing levels and access to credit were reduced, SEE legislative reforms were delayed (and the second tranche of SAL II was delayed in response) while internal reforms to increase productivity were never implemented (Kirkpatrick and Önis, 1991).

3.3 Performance under adjustment programmes

Evaluating the effects of a reform programme is a difficult exercise. First, there is no way of accounting for the counterfactual, what would have occurred without reform, nor are there reliable means of accommodating the effects of exogenous shocks. Consequently, evaluation is frequently by reference to the achievement of targets. Second, many of the SAL reforms are supply-side, directed at altering relative incentives in the medium to long run. It may, therefore, take some time for the reforms to have an impact on economic activity. Third, other lending programmes could interact with a SAL, notably IMF stabilization loans; how does one disentangle the effects of the two programmes? Fourth, in any cross-section study different countries start from different positions, they face different conditionality, the sequencing of programmes may be different, and so on. Finally, as already discussed, the conditions of a given SAL may not have been fully adhered to. Notwithstanding these difficulties, there have been several attempts to evaluate the impact of SALs (e.g. World Bank, 1988, 1990; Mosley *et al.*, 1991a, b).

To assess SALs, one must first select the relevant targets, then choose the methodology to evaluate the success of the SAL in achieving these. Medium-term growth, the sustainability of the balance of payments and export growth are seen as key objectives. These are obvious indicators. Methodologically there are two approaches one can take; 'before and after', and 'with–without' SALs. The former traces the path of, for example, export growth before the SAL and compares it with post-SAL performance, the difference being attributed to the impact of the lending programme. There are two major shortcomings with this. First, it presupposes sustainability of pre-existing policies, as the implied counterfactual, whereas most recipients are facing a crisis brought on by unsustainable policies (Krueger, 1992, p. 43). The other problem is that it is difficult to control for exogenous shocks like commodity price changes. 'With–without' compares the performance of SAL countries (the 'with' group) against that of non-SAL countries. Differences are then attributed to the impact of adjustment lending. The principal problem here is in the choice of 'control' and the impact of 'other factors' on the control. This, however, is the approach used by World Bank (1988, 1990) and Mosley *et al.* (1991a). One can note that, in effect, this approach compares the 'with' and 'without' groups both 'before' (when they are expected to be similar) and 'after' (when they are expected to differ).

Before commenting on the results, summarized in Table 5.4, one methodological observation is in order regarding the SAL/non-SAL comparisons. In the World Bank studies the data were pooled, i.e. all SAL countries were treated as one discrete sub-sample and all non-SAL countries as a separate sub-sample. Mosley *et al.* (1991a) regard this as flawed because the countries in each sub-sample may be unrepresentative. They match with and without countries on a pairwise basis using information on, *inter alia*, economic structure, income per capita, and growth of GDP. This is defended as allowing for the non-randomness of the two sample groups and the degrees of slippage. Despite this difference, one is struck by the similarity of outcomes (Table 5.4). Mosley *et al.* (1991a) are more favourable on exports and the current account, slightly less favourable on GDP growth, and almost identical on investment. Overall, both studies appear to suggest that adjustment lending might encourage real export growth and might contribute to improvements in the current account of the balance of payments. On the other hand, they imply that the impact on real GDP growth is neutral, whilst the effect on investment is negative (which could undermine future growth).

TABLE 5.4 *Comparison of results of effectiveness of SALs*

| | % SAL countries which outperformed non-SAL countries | | | |
	Growth of real GDP	Investment % GDP	Growth real exports	Current account % of GDP
World Bank (1988)	53	37	57	70
Mosley *et al.* (1991a)	50	36	65	79

Performance[a]	Ave annual 1980–9	Gross domestic 1985	1989	Ave Annual 1980–9	Net balance 1985	1989
Turkey	5.1%	20	22	11.4%	–2.1	1.3
Greece	1.6%	21	18	4.1%	–11.2	–6.4

| | Effect of SAL on variable[b] | | Effect of compliance[b] | |
	Growth of real GDP	Growth real exports	Growth of real GDP	Growth real exports
All (19)	–ive	–ive	+	+
MIC (14)	–ive		+	+

NOTES AND SOURCES: From Greenaway and Morrissey (1993, Table II), except:
  [a] Greece was paired with Turkey in Mosley *et al.* (1991a); data reported here are from *World Development Report* (1987, 1991). Current account balance is after official transfers.
  [b] Summary of econometric results in Mosley *et al.* (1991a, pp. 212–14); only those coefficients estimated as statistically significant are reported. Numbers in parentheses are number of countries in sample and middle-income countries (MIC). Both SAL and compliance variables were lagged.

These results can be compared with the econometric estimates of Mosley *et al.* (1991a), summarized in the lower part of Table 5.4. They found that SALs, even accounting for lags of up to two periods, tended to have a negative effect on growth, largely because they initially tended to retard the growth of real exports. They also found that when the degree of compliance was accounted for, the effects on growth of GDP and exports were more likely to be positive. Countries that adhered to the conditions of SALs, which tended to be those countries with more favourable initial conditions, were more likely to reap the benefits of increased real growth rates. Countries with high slippage rates, however, were more likely to face even lower growth rates.

Turkey's performance was relatively good on all criteria, notably a significant increase in exports which contributed to more rapid economic growth. Exports nearly trebled in real terms between 1980 and 1985 and such growth was 'promoted by explicit incentives to manufacturers to compensate them for reduced domestic demand' (Baysan and Blitzer, 1991, p. 281). Table 5.4 also includes a limited comparison of Turkey and Greece, which essentially relates to after the SALs and therefore addresses an element of sustainability as well as the effects. The rapid economic and export growth compares very favourably with Greece and can be attributed substantially to high compliance with export promotion. Import growth in Turkey remained substantial over 1980–5, especially for iron and steel, machinery and transport equipment (Baysan and Blitzer, 1991, p. 280), but Turkey reduced the current account deficit throughout the late 1980s and actually attained a surplus by 1989 whereas Greece still faced a substantial deficit. Unlike adjusting countries in general, Turkish gross domestic investment actually increased following the SALs whereas Greece's declined.

It appears that adjustment lending is associated with investment slumps (Mosley *et al.*, 1991a). As investment is directly related to growth this does not augur well for the future. World Bank (1990) argues that since an integral aim of adjustment lending is to curtail private and public sector investment whose efficiency is low, some reduction was to be expected. This is not a convincing explanation, if only because proponents of adjustment lending would also argue that reduction of the public sector should have 'crowded in' private sector investment. This may have been the case for Turkey (although we noted that public investment increased again after 1983). A convincing explanation for the failure of private investment to increase relates to the role of credibility (Rodrik, 1989). In the early stages of a SAL, the private sector has doubts with respect to its sustainability and holds off from making investments until it is clear whether or not the regime change is permanent. This is an appealing explanation and is certainly consistent with the facts.

4   POLICY REFORM IN TURKEY

It is difficult to specify the range of reforms necessary and in what order they should be implemented. Also, there is little agreement on the appropriate speed of reform. These two issues are linked to administrative capacity and credibility. A competent and credible administration can implement more reforms, more quickly and more successfully. We now address some important issues in regard to policy reform in

Turkey within the context of credibility. Section 4.1 considers the initial economic and political conditions which play such an important role in determining the success of any attempt at reform. Section 4.2 addresses sequencing, in what order should reforms be attempted? and timing, how quickly should sequenced reforms be implemented?

4.1 Credibility and political economy

The principal objective of trade liberalization is to facilitate the growth of real exports. A realistic exchange rate is a first step as it increases the relative returns to exporters. Reducing protection, and so removing many price distortions, will encourage exports as it reduces the input costs facing exporters and discourages resources from going into import-competing industries. For reform to succeed, however, it is important that exporting becomes attractive so that resources are released by import-competing sectors and are absorbed by exporting industries. Many reform programmes will include export promotion measures to facilitate this transition. But, if agents are to respond to reform, they must believe the reforms are permanent. The single most important feature of any reform programme is that it be credible. The government's commitment to the reforms and its ability to signal commitment will depend on pre-reform conditions, notably political stability of the state of the macroeconomy.

LDCs seek adjustment at times of crisis and it is rarely the first time they have faced such crises. By implication, previous attempts at resolving such crises have failed and/or been unsustainable, which is a bad augur for the credibility of present reforms. This scenario applied to Turkey in 1980. 'Turkey has experienced considerable instability during the past 25 years. There have been numerous changes in the ruling coalitions, three constitutions, and three episodes of military intervention' (Baysan and Blitzer, 1991, p. 272). The Ecevit administration of 1978–9 sought agreement with the IMF but viewed this 'as a short-run expediency to deal with the immediate balance of payment crisis' (Kirkpatrick and Önis, 1991, p. 11). This would not have instilled credibility. However, Turgut Ozal, who had been at the World Bank, was prominent in the Demirel government that resumed power in 1979, was supported by technocrats, was in touch with the IMF and was appointed deputy Prime Minister in charge of economic policy when the military assumed power in September 1980 (Kirkpatrick and Önis, 1991, p. 14). He became the elected Prime Minister in 1983. His commitment to economic reform did serve to instill credibility and, no less important, was an important factor ensuring external (IMF and World Bank) commitment to Turkish reform.

It is clear that 'new' governments have an advantage (see Papageorgiou *et al.*, 1991). They are not tarnished with the failures of previous governments. Strong new governments are more likely to be able to enforce credibility. They are also better able to withstand the opposition to reforms, from bureaucrats and public employees who are losing influence, if not their jobs, and from those who had earned rents in protected activities. This was made easier for the Ozal government by the military clampdown on trade unions from 1980: real wages, and sectoral differentials, declined in Turkey in the 1980s (Baysan and Blitzer, 1991, p. 286). Committed governments are better equipped to comply with an adjustment programme and 'a dedicated and competent local technocracy is clearly a more effective vehicle for reform' (Mosley *et al.*, 1991a, p. 161). External and internal commitment, a strong technocracy and weakened unions all rendered it easier for Turkey to implement a successful reform package (even then, the strength of vested interests in SEEs is reflected in the high slippage in that area).

Given the existence of political and administrative constraints, programme design is of vital importance. Policy reforms should reinforce each other. In practice this is not always the case. For instance, incentives may be given to exporters to reduce anti-export bias. If, at the same time, protection to producers of intermediate goods is raised, then exporters are disadvantaged. As a result, a potentially vocal lobby in support of reforms is alienated. Related to this, where lending programmes from more than one agency are simultaneously in place, it is crucially important to ensure that they are consistent. In the Turkish case the aid policies of major donors, towards export credits, were consistent with the import liberalization conditions of SALs, while the redirection of public investment towards infrastructure was consistent with the aid objectives of donors. Much was in place to virtually ensure that the government would be able to implement reform. Success, then, depended on an appropriately designed adjustment package. It is to such concerns that we now turn.

4.2 Sequencing and timing

Having taken a decision to liberalize, a major question is timing: should the programme be implemented rapidly or gradually? There are two general arguments for rapid reform: it gives strong signals to economic agents who will respond quickly and it does not provide the political opposition with time to mobilize. Economic theory would suggest that, in the absence of distortions, and with full factor mobility, liberalization should be rapid – the 'big bang' approach. In such circumstances, adjustment would be smooth. Michaely *et al.* (1991) argue that the evidence favours abrupt liberalizations, although the length of an abrupt episode is not well defined (and seems to extend up to a few years!). Even where adjustment is not smooth, one could take the view that adjustment costs are the price we pay for change and are simply a short-run phenomenon. Since the discounted value of the benefits from liberalization will typically exceed to a significant degree the discounted value of any adjustment costs, we should still go ahead and implement reforms quickly, in order to realise the benefits quickly.

A number of arguments can be raised to favour gradualism. First, adjustment costs, notably unemployment, are likely to be higher if reform is rapid (Thomas and Nash, 1991). Theory also shows that even without distortions, adjustment might be sticky if some factors are sector-specific. As a result, sector-specific unemployment follows liberalization. Second, gradualism can be defended on grounds of income distribution (Falvey and Kim, 1992). This relates to adjustment in that one slows down the rate at which rents to factors in the unfavoured (post-reform) sector are reduced, providing more time for them to move into alternative uses. This argument has a political dimension as opposition may be less vociferous if adjustment costs are mitigated.

Finally, there is a credibility argument for gradualism. If a government does not have a reputation for credible reform, then introducing a series of gradual reforms to which it demonstrates commitment can allow that government to build up a reputation for credibility. Being implemented through five SALs over 6 years, the Turkish adjustment should be deemed gradual. In conjunction with the favourable initial conditions, this would contribute to the potential success of the programme.

Linked to timing is the question of sequencing – whether we are dealing with partial or complete liberalization, should all sectors be liberalized together or in order? There is fairly broad agreement on some principles of sequencing (Greenaway and Morrissey, 1993). The abolition of capital controls should follow trade liberalization. If financial markets are reformed and capital controls are abolished prior to trade liberalization, there will be capital inflows to the reforming economy. In turn, these lead to real exchange rate appreciation which erodes the competitiveness of industries producing tradeables. This would then make trade liberalization much more difficult. Clearly, if reform of policy in traded goods sectors precedes the abolition of capital con-

TABLE 5.5 *Sequencing in Turkish adjustment programme*

Loan ($m)		Major conditions	Implementation
IMF (June 1980)	**SDR1.25b**	**Devaluation**	**Full**
SAL I (25 March 1980)	**250.0**	**5 conditions** Export promotion	**Fair** Good
SAL II (15 May 1981)	**300.0**	**17 conditions** Exchange rate Export promotion Reduce quota list Budget deficit SEEs	**Good** Full Good Fair Good Fair
SAL III (16 July 1982)	**304.5**	**8 conditions** Public investment SEEs	**Good** Good Good
SAL IV (23 May 1983)	**300.8**	**5 conditions** Reduce QRs Public investment	**Weak** Fair Weak
SAL V (14 June 1984)	**376.0**	**12 conditions** QRs and tariffs Public investment Financial sector Energy sector	**Good** Fair Fair Good Good

SOURCE: Derived from Kirkpatrick and Önis (1991, Table 11.2); evaluation of degree of compliance in personal and subjective. Dates in parentheses relate to when loan programme was agreed.

trols, the problem simply does not arise. Furthermore, asset markets clear more quickly than goods and labour markets, and therefore need a shorter time to adjust.

Macroeconomic stabilization, in particular devaluation to a realistic (and maintained) exchange rate and control of the fiscal deficit, should be the first element of reform. Trade liberalization can then take place. This will normally comprise a conversion of quantitative restrictions (QRs) to tariffs, which contributes to tax revenues as tariffs are reduced, and a staged reduction of tariffs. The provision of export incentives is optional. Liberalization of the domestic financial market can commence once trade liberalization is well underway. The last stage should be relaxation of capital controls. The sequencing of Turkish adjustment is summarized in Table 5.5 and can be related to these general principles.

We have already indicated that favourable initial conditions were in place – the creation of political commitment and laying support for reform by facilitating political stability (Ozal represented continuity even if regimes changed). The government was also in a position to resist one group of potential losers, namely labour. It is also important that the lending agencies offer support. Strong support can obviously come via conditional finance with regular and efficient monitoring to minimize slippage. The SALs to Turkey were very substantial, amounting to almost a third of all SAL disbursements between 1980 and 1986! Slippage was fairly carefully monitored and generally minimized: the World Bank would have expected Ozal to be reliable, but had invested so much in Turkey that they needed to ensure its success. The principal macroeconomic condition of a realistic exchange rate was also in place (although the IMF agreement in Table 5.5 is dated after SAL I the devaluation preceded implementation of the SAL). A remarkably auspicious beginning to an adjustment programme.

Once the political and economic foundations have been laid, a country should find it easier to liberalize its trade regime. Converting QRs to tariffs is a useful first move, both because tariffs are generally less distortionary and because this can generate tax revenue for the government. Turkey followed a rather different sequence. SAL I emphasized a variety of export promotion measures and control of the budget deficit via restricting public investment. The latter is suitably sequenced as reducing the deficit is an initial macroeconomic target. The former makes sense for credibility reasons: as potential exporters have always experienced relative discrimination, offering real incentives will encourage the shift of resources to exporting sectors.

The full range of trade policy conditions were introduced in SAL II. Again, exchange rate and budget deficit conditions were there to sustain macroeconomic stability, and further export promotion to encourage adjustment. However, implementation on reducing the quota list (effectively transforming QRs to tariffs) was slow and/or ambiguous, as was progress on SEE reform. It is not inconceivable that the whole programme could have come unstuck were it not for the fairly quick export response to the devaluations and promotion measures. This is a lesson for other reformers: early export incentives not only encourage adjustment but can compensate for slow import liberalization. The export incentives were put in place in SALs I and II which was fortuitous as import liberalization did not really occur until SALs III and IV.

Good overall compliance on SALs II and III ensured that SAL IV was forthcoming and, by then, the World Bank was heavily committed and sufficient momentum had been generated so that, despite poor performance on IV, SAL V was released. This is, perhaps, a lesson to recipients on how to sequence implementation so as to avoid the threat of a tranche or loan being suspended! By SAL IV, there is evidence that parts of the programme were coming unstuck and Turkey may not have been the success so frequently portrayed. It is at least questionable whether significant import liberalization actually occurred and was sustained. Quotas were certainly reduced as were effective tariffs, but many restrictions remained. It is clear that SEE reform was incomplete. It is also apparent that the cuts in public investment were reversed from 1983: while this may have avoided the investment slump experienced by many adjusters, it represents notable slippage. The good overall performance on SAL V is attributable to reforms in the financial and energy sectors. Desirable as these may be, their effect and sustainability is undermined by the slippages noted above. In conclusion, Turkey's apparent success is attributable to early export promotion measures and slippage on public investment conditions, and not to strong compliance with the conditions laid down by the World Bank.

5 LESSONS FROM TURKEY'S EXPERIENCE?

The first SAL was equivalent to over a quarter of net aid to Turkey in 1980 and subsequent SALs accounted for about 15 per cent of capital inflows to Turkey in each of the four subsequent years. Aid, both bilateral and SALs, was clearly very important. The manner in which aid can support capital imports, given the increased emphasis on mixed credits, would have reinforced some of the imbalances in Turkey by favouring non-tradeables and imports rather than export sectors. On the other hand, the availability of aid may have made it easier (and cheaper in the short-run) for Turkey to restore public sector investment in infrastructure. There is a potential cost if the investments generate insufficient returns to meet future debt-servicing but this can be offset, and more than offset if the adjustment programme is successful, by the contribution of infrastructure to industrial development. On balance, aid and adjustment may have interwoven beneficially for Turkey.

There are a number of lessons for countries attempting adjustment. First, gradualism makes sense because it eases adjustment of factors, allows governments to alter some conditions if it sees a need and, if slippage is 'optimally sequenced', it allows a recipient to obtain sub-sequent loans without fully complying with conditions. The latter two points are not necessarily disadvantageous to the adjustment process. The World Bank does not always impose the most appropriate conditions and a government should have some flexibility if circumstances change. The lesson for the World Bank is that it too should exercise flexibility. It may be appropriate to let some conditions slip, and Turkey probably benefited by restoring public investment (which was tolerated immediately following democratic elections in 1983), while it is inappropriate to let others slip. Thus, Turkey appears to have got away with slippage on import liberalization, which should have come earlier and been enforced, and SEE reform, which was appropriately sequenced but never enforced. Second, and following these points, the World Bank must learn to see its role as a facilitator more than an enforcer, but here decisions on how rigorously to monitor slippage on different conditions will require political and economic judgements. Third, and perhaps foremost, initial political commitment and capacity is essential to ensure that any adjustment programme can be adhered to, it may even be essential to ensure that a programme can begin. This, with programme design, sequencing and monitoring, is essential for success.

REFERENCES

Baysan, T. and Blitzer, C. (1991), 'Turkey' in D. Papageorgiou, M. Michaely and A. Choksi (eds), *Liberalizing Foreign Trade*, vol. 6 (Oxford: Basil Blackwell), pp. 263–405.

Bhagwati, J. (1967), 'The Tying of Aid', in J. Bhagwati and R. Eckhaus (eds), *Foreign Aid* (London: Penguin), pp. 235–93.

DAC (1991), *Development Co-operation – 1991 Report of the Development Assistance Committee* (Paris: OECD, Development Assistance Committee).

Falvey, R. and Kim, C. (1992), 'Timing and Sequencing Issues in Trade Liberalisation', *Economic Journal*, vol. 102, no. 413, pp. 908–24.

Greenaway, D. and Morrissey, O. (1993), 'Structural Adjustment and Liberalisation in Developing Countries: What Lessons Have We Learned?', *Kyklos*, vol. 46, pp. 241–61.

Jepma, C. (1989), *The Tying of Aid* (International Foundation for Development Economics, University of Groningen; Paris: OECD, 1991).

Johnson, H. (1967), *Economic Policies Towards Less Developed Countries* (London: Allen & Unwin).

Kirkpatrick, C. and Önis, Z. (1991), 'Turkey', in Mosley *et al.* (1991b), pp. 9–38.

Krueger, A. (1974), *Foreign Trade Regimes and Economic Development: Turkey*, (New York: Columbia University Press for the NBER).

Krueger, A. (1987), 'The Importance of Economic Policy in Development: Contrasts between Korea and Turkey' in H. Kierzkowski (ed.), *Protection and Competition in International Trade* (Oxford: Basil Blackwell), pp. 172–203.

Krueger, A. (1992), *Economic Policy Reform in Developing Countries* (Cambridge, MA: Blackwells).

Michaely, M., Papageorgiou, D. and Choksi, A. (1991), *Liberalizing Foreign Trade: Lessons of Experience in the Developing World*, vol. 7 of Papageorgiou *et al.* (1991).

Morrissey, O. (1993), 'The Mixing of Aid and Trade Policies', *The World Economy*, vol. 16, pp. 69–84.

Mosley, P., Hudson, J. and Horrell, S. (1987), 'Aid, the Public Sector and the Market in Less Developed Countries', *Economic Journal*, vol. 97, pp. 616–41.

Mosley, P., Harrigan, J. and Toye, J. (1991a), *Aid and Power: The World Bank and Policy-based Lending*, Volume 1: *Analysis and Policy Proposals* (London: Routledge).

Mosley, P., Harrigan, J. and Toye, J. (1991b), *Aid and Power: The World Bank and Policy-based Lending*, Volume 2: *Case Studies* (London: Routledge).

Önis, Z. and Özmucur, S. (1991), 'Capital Flows and the External Financing of Turkey's Imports', Technical Paper no. 36, OECD Development Centre, Paris.

Papageorgiou, D., Michaely, M. and Choksi, A. (eds) (1991), *Liberalizing Foreign Trade* (Oxford: Basil Blackwell).

Rodrik, D. (1989), 'Credibility of Trade Reform – a Policy Maker's Guide', *The World Economy*, vol. 12, no. 1, pp. 1–16.

Thomas, V. and Nash, J. (1991), 'Reform of Trade Policy: Recent Evidence from Theory and Practice', *World Bank Research Observer*, vol. 6, no. 2, pp. 219–40.

World Bank (1988), *Report on Adjustment Lending*, Document R88–199 (Washington, DC: Country Economics Department, World Bank).

World Bank (1990), *Report on Adjustment Lending II: Policies for the Recovery of Growth*, Document R90–99 (Washington, DC: World Bank).

6 Foreign Direct Investment in Turkey

V. N. Balasubramanyam*

1 INTRODUCTION

Turkey is often referred to as a typical middle income developing country. This judgement is based on the level of her per capita income, growth rate, population size and literacy rate which all lie near to the average for the middle income developing countries as a group. Turkey, however, differs markedly from other middle income developing countries in the relatively low volume of foreign direct investment (FDI) she harbours. Turkey is not idealogically hostile to the participation of foreign capital and enterprise in her economy. Indeed, one of the major objectives of the economic liberalization programme Turkey embarked upon in 1980 is the encouragement of inflows of FDI and workers' remittances. Both for reasons of balance of payments, which in fact provided the impetus for the liberalization programme, and requirements of technology and know-how, FDI is crucial for the development of the Turkish economy. There are signs that foreign investors have responded to the liberalization policies, and inflows of FDI into Turkey have increased in recent years. It is, however, arguable if Turkey is poised to be a major recipient of FDI in the near future. Although, since the beginning of this decade, the world supply of FDI has increased appreciably and several countries including Japan have joined the ranks of suppliers of FDI, demand for FDI has also increased. There are a number of reasons for the observed growth in demand for FDI. First is the search for alternative sources of capital to bank credit on the part of developing countries in the wake of the debt crisis and its aftermath. Second is the entry of the newly liberated Eastern European countries into the market for FDI. Third is the diversion of FDI from other regions in the world into the EC and North America in response to the formation of the Single Market and the North American Free Trade Area. These developments put most developing countries, such as Turkey, which do not have a proven track record in attracting

---

* I am grateful to Mohammed Salisu and Ziya Onis for comments.

TABLE 6.1 Stock of foreign direct investment in Turkey, 1970–91

Year	(1) Stock of FDI in Turkey (US$m)	(2) Stock of FDI in LDCs (US$m)	(1) as percentage of (2)	(3) World stock of FDI (US$m)	(1) as percentage of (3)
1971	300	45 299	0.66	183 586	0.16
1972	343	48 618	0.71	197 219	0.17
1973	421	52 789	0.80	213 460	0.20
1974	509	54 381	0.94	232 983	0.22
1975	662	64 725	1.02	255 269	0.26
1976	690	72 339	0.95	274 121	0.25
1977	872	81 700	1.07	299 219	0.29
1978	967	92 009	1.05	331 954	0.29
1979	1096	103 688	1.06	371 426	0.30
1980	1185	111 420	1.06	406 653	0.29
1981	1326	114 681	1.16	451 714	0.29
1982	1429	128 135	1.12	496 186	0.29
1983	1516	138 400	1.10	540 279	0.28
1984	1678	148 900	1.13	589 263	0.28
1985	1836	160 375	1.14	638 575	0.29
1986	2006	169 343	1.18	710 927	0.28
1987	2177	179 669	1.21	815 543	0.26
1988	2583	192 919	1.34	947 167	0.27
1989	3321	290 010	1.15	1 442 000	0.23
1990	4110	330 000	1.25	1 705 000	0.24
1991	5020	369 000	1.36	1 856 000	0.27

SOURCE: UNCTC (1988) *Multinational Corporations in World Development: Trends and Prospects* (New York); UNCTAD (1989), *Handbook of International Trade and Development Statistics* (New York); UN (1994), *World Investment Directory* (New York).

FDI, at a competitive disadvantage in the market for FDI. This is not to say Turkey should refrain from competing for FDI. It is just that her task in attracting FDI is that much more difficult and poses a major challenge to her management of the economy in general and the policies she adopts towards FDI in particular.

This chapter analyses the reasons for the relatively poor record of Turkey in attracting FDI in the recent past and evaluates the likely impact of the programme of economic liberalization on inflows of FDI into Turkey in the future. The paper is organized as follows. Section 2 reviews the extent and nature of FDI in Turkey at the present. Section 3 analyses the reasons for the relatively low magnitude of FDI in Turkey. Section 4 reviews the recent FDI policy framework of Turkey

TABLE 6.2   *Flows of foreign direct investment: selected developing countries, 1970–88*

	Average flows of FDI		Share in total LDCs	
	1970–80 *(US\$m)*	*1981–8* *(US\$m)*	*1970–80* *(%)*	*1981–8* *(%)*
Spain	573	2984	8.7	25.6
Mexico	716	1607	10.9	13.8
Brazil	1366	1644	20.8	14.1
Columbia	71	509	1.1	4.4
Costa Rica	42	63	0.6	0.5
Indonesia	195	303	3.0	2.6
The Philippines	103	211	1.6	1.8
Nigeria	341	452	5.2	3.9
Thailand	90	392	1.4	3.4
Jamaica	42	−1	0.6	−0.002
Turkey	90	127	1.4	1.1
All LDCs	6556	11 657	100	100

SOURCE: UNCTC (1985), *Multinational Corporations in World Development, Third Survey* (New York); UNCTC (1988) *Multinational Corporations in World Development: Trends and Prospects* (New York); UNCTAD (1989), *Handbook of International Trade and Development Statistics* (New York).

including the establishment of a number of free port zones (FPZs) and its likely impact on inflows of FDI. Section 5 discusses the likely impact of Turkey's intended membership of the EC on inflows of FDI into Turkey. The final section sums up the conclusions.

2   MAGNITUDE OF FOREIGN DIRECT INVESTMENT IN TURKEY

The total book value of the stock of FDI in Turkey in 1971, the earliest year for which data are available, was \$300 million. This had increased to a substantial \$5 billion by the end of 1991. But at no time during the 20 year period did the share of Turkey in the stock of FDI in developing countries exceed 1 per cent (Table 6.1). During the period 1970–80, the annual average inflow of FDI into Turkey was as low as \$90 million. This contrasts with a figure of \$716 million for Mexico, \$194 million for Indonesia and \$573 million in the case of Spain (Table 6.2). Inflows of FDI into Turkey increased markedly from 1981. The annual average flow of FDI into Turkey for the period 1981–8 was

TABLE *6.3* *Sectoral distribution of foreign direct investment in Turkey (January – end May 1992)*

Sector	Firms		Total capital	Foreign capital	
	No.	*%*	*(TL billion)*	*(Tl Bn)*	*% Total*
Agriculture	59	2.8	451.6	346	76.7
Mining	36	1.7	215.5	157	72.9
Manufacturing	608	28.7	9204.6	4188	45.5
Of which					
Food	76	3.6	741.6	409	55.2
Beverages	3	0.1	4.5	2	44.4
Tobacco	7	0.3	261.8	197	75.2
Industrial chemicals	16	0.8	167.1	87	52.1
Other chemicals	45	2.1	433.9	331	76.3
Textiles	31	1.5	214.0	79	37.0
Ready-made garments	73	3.4	205.8	94	45.7
Iron & steel	11	0.5	1819.3	291	16.0
Electrical machinery	40	1.9	475.0	173	36.4
Electronics	31	1.5	524.7	339	64.6
Transport & equipment	14	0.7	1528.5	606	39.6
Transport-related ind.	26	1.2	278.8	142	50.9
Services	1419	66.9	6575.9	3181	48.4
Of which					
Restaurants	791	37.3	859.5	496	57.7
Construction	188	8.9	2435.6	1008	41.4
Banking	34	1.6	1481.9	732	49.4
Insurance	30	1.4	356.6	165	46.3
All industries	2122	100.0	16 447.5	7872	47.9

SOURCE: Turkish sources.

$125 million; even so, annual flows of investment into Turkey were substantially lower than for several other developing countries.

Much of FDI in Turkey is concentrated in the manufacturing sector, followed by the services and mining sectors. In the late 1980s, manufacturing accounted for more than 60 per cent of the inflow, with the share of services being around 30 per cent. The total stock of FDI in Turkey at the end of 1992 was $5 billion of which the manufacturing sector accounted for 53 per cent and services for 40 per cent (Table 6.3). Transport equipment, food industries, electronics, chemicals and textiles account for the bulk of FDI in manufacturing. Construction, banking and restaurants account for a substantial proportion of FDI in services.

The principal investors in Turkey are France (14.5 per cent), the

TABLE 6.4   *Geographical distribution of foreign direct investment in Turkey (January – end May 1992)*

Region	No. of firms	Percentage of total	Share of foreign capital in total capital (%)
Total OECD	1326	62.5	88.1
EC	904	42.6	57.9
Belgium	29	1.6	0.8
Denmark	17	0.8	0.7
Germany	378	17.8	10.4
France	107	5.0	14.5
Netherlands	88	4.1	9.7
UK	170	8.0	12.5
Spain	12	0.6	0.6
Italy	71	3.3	7.5
Luxembourg	15	0.7	1.2
Greece	14	0.6	0.1
Other OECD countries			
USA	155	7.3	11.1
Japan	33	1.6	6.4
Austria	42	2.0	0.6
Switzerland	140	6.6	10.1
South-East Asia	31	1.5	1.5
Singapore	6	0.3	1.0
Korea	6	0.3	0.3
Taiwan	3	0.1	0.3
Middle East	491	23.1	5.6
Eastern Europe	29	1.4	0.2
Other	241	11.4	4.5
Total world	2122	100.0	100.0 (Tl 7872.4 bn)

SOURCE: Turkish sources.

UK (12.5 per cent), Germany (12.4 per cent) and the Netherlands (9.7 per cent) from the EC, and the US (11 per cent), Switzerland (10 per cent), and Japan (6.4 per cent) (Table 6.4).

Like most other developing countries, Turkey too has established a number of Free Port Zones (FPZs). At the end of 1992, there were four FPZs operating in Turkey. Together they accounted for 4 billion Turkish lira of FDI or, at the then prevailing exchange rate, for $0.6 million.

3 WHY THE RELATIVELY LOW MAGNITUDE OF FDI IN TURKEY?

As stated earlier, Turkey is a middle income developing country. She has a fairly well developed infrastructure including transportation, finance and banking. Geographically she is well placed to service a number of markets in the Middle East and Europe. She has also an impressive record of growth, especially so in recent years. These are some of the characteristics recognized in the literature as the major determinants of FDI. Yet, as stated earlier, the volume of FDI in Turkey is low compared with the amount harboured by several other developing countries at a similar stage of development.

In the literature on the economy of Turkey, there are very few references to FDI. Several of the World Bank and OECD reports hardly make a reference to FDI in Turkey. Those studies which do refer to it attribute the relatively low level of FDI in Turkey to sheer neglect and the cumbersome bureaucracy which enforces the policies, rather than the policies themselves. But other developing countries such as Nigeria and Indonesia, which are also known for their cumbersome bureaucratic procedures, have attracted relatively large amounts of FDI.

The reasons for the relatively low level of FDI Turkey has managed to attract have to be sought in the macroeconomic environment for investment in Turkey and the protectionist trade regime she pursued until the end of the 1970s. The literature on the determinants of FDI identifies various location advantages which foreign firms take into account in their investment decisions. These include political stability, price and exchange rate stability, low efficiency wage rates, natural resource endowments, per capita income levels and growth performance. Several studies have attempted to test the impact of these factors on the magnitude of FDI in developing countries (Schneider and Frey, 1985; Root and Ahmed, 1979; Edwards, 1991). In general, relatively low wage rates, exchange rate and price stability appear to exert a strong influence on the relative magnitude of FDI various developing countries have attracted. But the evidence on the influence of political stability on inflow of FDI is inconclusive. Schneider and Frey argue that while neither economic factors nor political factors alone can explain the distribution of FDI between various developing countries, a model which incorporates both factors is able to account for it. But Root and Ahmed's statistical tests of the determinants of FDI in developing countries, based on factor analysis, provide little support for the proposition that political stability of host countries is a major determinant of the magnitude of FDI they attract. The study by Edwards also suggests that economic factors including a reduction in the share of government in economic activity and increased openness of the economy exert a much more significant influence on inflows of FDI than political factors. Admittedly, quantification of political instability for purposes of assessing its influence on capital flows is fraught with problems. Most studies arrive at an index of political instability based on number of changes of government a country has experienced, estimated probability of government changes, and other political events. But none of these may adequately capture the one factor of importance in the decision process of foreign firms – continuity and stability of economic policies. Turkey, for instance, has had several changes of government over the years, and rightist governments have emphasized the role of the private sector in economic activity while leftist governments have placed emphasis on social welfare programmes and economic autarky. But, on balance, most governments have favoured a major role for state enterprises in the economy and until 1983 they adhered to a protectionist foreign trade regime. Available estimates indicate that the average nominal rate of protection for total manufacturing output in 1981 was 32 per cent and the effective rate of protection was around 81 per cent (Celasun, 1992). Furthermore, even after the 1980 liberalization episode, the public sector continues to account for 60 per cent of national investment, owns and operates about 40 per cent of manufacturing enterprises and dominates the mineral sector (Baysan and Blitzer, 1991). This emphasis on state ownership of the means of production and a restrictionist foreign trade regime rather than frequent changes in government may provide a large part of the explanation for the relatively low volume of FDI in Turkey until the beginning of the 1980s.

The impact of protection on inflows of FDI is a much debated issue. It is the received wisdom that import protection induces inflows of FDI. Foreign firms prevented from servicing protected markets through exports, jump tariff and quota walls and establish manufacturing plants in the protected markets. Such protected markets, free of competition from imports, also serve to increase the private rate of return to the foreign investors. The theoretical basis for this line of reasoning is provided by Mundell's (1957) demonstration that international movement of factors of production could be a perfect substitute for free trade in goods. This thesis though, has been challenged in recent years. For instance, Markusen (1983) has demonstrated that international trade and international flows of capital may complement one another and capital movements may not be a substitute for trade.

Much more powerful, and of greater relevance to the determinants of FDI in developing countries, is Bhagwati's thesis that countries pursuing an export promotion (EP) strategy of development are likely to attract relatively larger volumes of FDI than countries pursuing an import-substitution (IS) strategy (Bhagwati, 1978, 1985). The precise hypothesis enunciated by Bhagwati reads 'with due adjustments for differences among countries for their economic size, political attitudes towards FDI and political stability, both the magnitude of FDI inflows and their efficacy in promoting economic growth will be greater over the long haul in countries pursuing the export promotion (EP) strategy than in countries pursuing the import substitution (IS) strategy'.

Several features of this hypothesis are noteworthy. First, it emphasizes the amount of FDI countries are able to attract relative to their size and not the absolute magnitude of FDI. Second, the hypothesis does not emphasize the influence of the type of development policy on FDI to the exclusion of other factors. These include political stability and the attitudes of countries towards foreign enterprise participation in other economies. Third, it emphasizes that it is over the long haul that the EP countries are likely to attract relatively large magnitudes of FDI. It is likely that in the short run the IS strategy with its policy-oriented inducements will attract large volumes of FDI. But these flows may not be sustained over the long run. In contrast, EP countries which adhere to the dictates of comparative advantage and market forces are likely to experience a sustained inflow of FDI over time. Put another way, the incentives provided by an IS strategy are likely to be transient and uncertain, whereas the incentives provided by an EP strategy are likely to be permanent and tangible. In addition, it is to be noted that the EP strategy, as defined by Bhagwati, does not require a country aggressively to promote its exports. Bhagwati defines an EP strategy as one which equates the average effective rate of exchange for exports (EER_x) with the average effective rate of exchange for imports (EER_m). In other words the EP strategy is a trade-neutral or bias-free strategy. In contrast, the IS strategy is one where the EER_m is greater than the EER_x and biases production and resource allocation decisions in favour of import competing industries. In this context, the effective exchange rate is defined as the number of units of local currency units actually received or paid for a dollar's worth of international transactions. If tariffs and quotas on imports, for instance, are not matched by subsidies on exports the EER_m would exceed the EER_x and the country in question is said to pursue an IS strategy.

Bhagwati's hypothesis is difficult to test because of the data problems associated with estimating EER_m and EER_x for a cross-section of developing countries. The required data on tariff rates, quota premiums and subsidies for most developing countries are not readily available. None the less, an attempt has been made to statistically test the hypothesis with various proxies for the type of development strategies pursued by developing countries (Balasubramanyam and Salisu, 1991). These include the distortion indices for various developing countries estimated by the World Bank and the ratio of imports to GNP. The distortion index tends to be relatively high for countries pursuing the IS strategy and the ratio of imports to GNP for these countries also tends to be low. It is the presumption that, in the case of countries with a relatively high ratio of imports to GNP, tariffs and quotas on imports would be low and because they do not provide artificial incentives to import substituting sectors, they do not also need to provide subsidies to export sectors. In other words, countries with a relatively high ratio of imports to GNP would be pursuing an EP strategy. The statistical exercise designed to test Bhagwati's hypothesis included other variables identified in the literature on determinants of FDI, in addition to the proxies for the type of development strategies pursued by a sample of 38 developing countries.

The results of the statistical exercise utilizing regression analysis lend considerable support to Bhagwati's hypothesis. In general, countries pursuing an EP strategy are found to harbour larger volumes of FDI per capita than countries pursuing an IS strategy. The estimated regression equations which provide the basis for this conclusion are shown in Table 6.5. Turkey was included in the sample of 38 countries for which the equation was estimated. The estimated annual average per capita FDI in Turkey at around $1.20 is close to the actual figure of $0.89. This finding lends some support to the proposition that the IS strategy pursued by Turkey is one significant reason for the relatively low magnitude of FDI in Turkey. It is also worth noting that, for a number of years, the EER_m in Turkey exceeded the EER_x by a considerable margin. It is only since 1984, following the liberalization episode which began in 1980, that the EER_x has exceeded the EER_m (Table 6.6). It is worth noting here that the estimates of EER_m and EER_x reported in Table 6.6 may overstate the extent to which Turkey has moved towards an EP regime. These estimates do not take into account the impact of any surviving quotas and other NTBs on the EER_m, and the reported EER_m may understate the incentives for IS that the entire structure of protection continues to provide. It is, however, significant the inflows of FDI appear to have responded to this change in development

TABLE 6.5 *Estimated regression equations (dependent variable – annual average inflows of foreign direct investment per capita for the years 1970– 80)*

Equation	C	GDP/P	GDP_{gr}	A/P	M/GDP	WPI	WR	DI	R^2	N
1	−1.08	0.007*	−0.07	−0.13**	0.12*	−0.05*	−0.02*		0.65	38
	(1.11)	(5.02)	(0.58)	(2.04)	(3.01)	(5.26)	(2.55)			
2	7.17	0.010*	−0.61	0.12***		−0.05*	−0.03*	−2.87*	0.58	38
	(2.08)	(5.35)	(1.40)	(1.85)		(2.98)	(2.59)	(2.11)		

SOURCE: Balasubramanyam and Salisu (1991).

NOTES: ***, **, * denote significance at the 10, 5, and 1 per cent levels, respectively. Figures in parentheses are absolute values of *t*-statistics.
C = intercept term; GDP/P = real per capita GDP; GDP_{gr} = growth rate of real GDP; A/P = aid per capita; M/GDP = ratio of imports to GDP; WPI = rate of inflation; DI = World Bank distortion index; N = number of observations.

TABLE 6.6 *Effective exchange rates for Turkey's exports and imports*

	Inflows of FDI (US $m)	Nominal exchange rate	EER_x	EER_m	EER_m/EER_x
1970	4	12	12.36	22.98	1.86
1973	26	14	15.55	26.01	1.67
1980	35	76	92.81	105.54	1.13
1981	141	111	134.02	154.37	1.15
1982	103	163	196.05	225.62	1.15
1983	87	225	278.20	312.94	1.12
1984	162	367	421.94	375.11	0.89
1985	158	522	623.97	533.99	0.86
1986	170	675	806.02	690.02	0.86
1987	171	857	1024.71	876.93	0.86
1988	406	1422	1700.28	1455.06	0.86
1989	738	2122	2536.28	2170.50	0.86
1990	789	2609	3118.32	2668.60	0.86

SOURCE: IMF (1991) *International Financial Statistics Yearbook*, and S. Togan, *Foreign Trade Regimes and Liberalisation of Foreign Trade in Turkey During the 1980s* (Ankara: EXIM Bank, 1993).

policy towards an EP strategy. There is a recognizable growth inflows of FDI into Turkey since the mid-1980s (Table 6.6).

Apart from the protectionist IS strategy pursued by Turkey, the relatively high rates of inflation, exchange rate instability and relatively high efficiency wage rates have also contributed to the low volume of FDI she has attracted. These factors in the recent economic history of Turkey have been discussed extensively and there is no need to recount them here. It is sufficient to note here that many of these factors may be a consequence of the protectionist trade regime that Turkey pursued until the end of the 1980s. The widespread distortions in factor and product markets engendered by indiscriminate protectionist policies have been extensively analysed, both in the context of Turkey and other developing countries (Krueger and Truncer, 1982; Bhagwati, 1978). In sum, the protectionist trade regime and the emphasis placed by Turkey on state ownership of industry have contributed to the low volume of FDI she has attracted.

4   LIBERALIZATION AND FOREIGN DIRECT INVESTMENT IN TURKEY

The main elements of the programme of economic liberalization initiated by Turkey in the early 1980 are analysed extensively in papers by Togan (1992), Celasun (1992) and others. The principal elements of the programme which impact upon FDI include the move towards an EP regime, the set of incentives offered to prospective foreign firms and the establishment of Free Port Zones (FPZs). The foregoing has referred to the growth in inflows of FDI into Turkey following the adoption of an EP regime. The issue for discussion, though, is whether or not the move towards an EP regime alone will sustain the observed growth in FDI. A point of relevance in this context is the chosen sequence of reforms adopted by Turkey. As Celasun (1992) demonstrates, Turkey has chosen to lead the programme of liberalization with export promotion followed by a gradual move towards fiscal stabilization. This strategy no doubt produced an impressive growth in exports and output, but it also resulted in macroeconomic instability in the late 1980s. To the extent that foreign investors attach importance to macroeconomic stability, characterized by low inflation rates and exchange rate stability, a mere move towards an EP policy centred on export subsidies may not result in a sustained inflow of FDI. It is worth emphasizing here that the virtues of an EP policy do not reside in the incentives for exports it provides, but in its neutrality and the stability of policies it promotes.

As stated earlier, Turkey has never been hostile to FDI. Indeed, her recent policies towards FDI are much more liberal than those of many other developing countries which harbour substantial amounts of FDI. The law relating to foreign capital confers on foreign investors all the rights and obligations afforded to local nationals. Turkey has also entered into several tax agreements which provide for exemption from double taxation, and she is also a signatory to the OECD code on liberalization of capital movements and invisible transactions. In addition, she provides a range of investment incentives to foreign firms. Indeed, Turkey's policies towards FDI contain none of the regulations in force in other developing countries, such as local content requirements and employment regulations. Nor is there any ceiling on the amount of equity foreign firms can own. In recent years she has also streamlined the procedures for approval of FDI proposals and eliminated much of the red tape and bureaucracy which prevailed in the pre-liberalization years.

Has Turkey moved too far in the direction of liberalizing her policies towards FDI? It can be argued that the highly liberal policies of Turkey towards FDI may serve to tilt the distribution of gains from FDI excessively towards foreign firms. It is possible that Turkey may be much too liberal in the incentives she provides to foreign firms. For instance, those foreign firms in possession of investment certificates are eligible for generous exemptions from corporate taxes ranging from 30 to 100 per cent, depending upon the location, sector and the value of investments (General Directorate of Foreign Investment, 1992). There is considerable controversy on the impact of such tax incentives on inflows of FDI. Recent research on Japanese FDI in the EC shows that Japanese firms do respond to regional incentives (Balasubramanyam and Greenaway, 1992). An example of such location decisions based on regional incentives is Japanese investments in Wales in the UK. But several studies on FDI in developing countries produce evidence to show that tax incentives are of little significance in the investment location decisions of foreign firms. In the absence of other location advantages, such as efficient but inexpensive labour, raw material endowments and macroeconomic stability, fiscal incentives play little role in the investment decisions of foreign firms (Lim, 1983; Balasubramanyam, 1986). Although available information does not permit a firm conclusion on the issue of the effectiveness of fiscal incentives in attracting FDI into Turkey, there are grounds for arguing that the incentives she offers foreign firms may be much too generous. Turkey has moved towards an EP policy and is in the process of establishing a stable macroeconomic environment. Foreign firms may place emphasis on the credibility and stability of these policies rather than tax incentives in their investment decision-making process.

Another important element in Turkey's FDI policy framework is the establishment of FPZs referred to earlier. An FPZ is an enclave outside the customs territory of a country. Goods entering the zone can be processed, stored and manufactured without payment of customs duties and local taxes, and exported without payment of duties. Goods imported into, and manufactured in, the zones are liable to the payment of customs duties and local taxes only when sold on the domestic markets of the country. In the case of most FPZs in developing countries, a wide range of fiscal and financial incentives is also provided to firms locating in the zones.

The principal objectives of FPZs are promotion of inward FDI, employment creation, technology transfer and export promotion. Currently there are nearly 500 FPZs in various parts of the world including the UK and the US. In recent years most developing countries have established such zones, with some countries establishing more than one zone. At the end of 1992 Turkey had established four zones and is reported to be planning on establishing five more zones. Turkey's FPZs conform to the classic model of free port zones. They provide several fiscal and financial incentives to firms located in the zones. A feature of the zones is the 100 per cent exemption from corporate and income taxes granted to firms located in the zones for an unlimited period.

Turkey appears to have embraced FPZs with great enthusiasm. But is this enthusiasm justified? There are good reasons for doubting the wisdom of establishing a series of such zones. FPZ's are a classic example of the *Second Best*. They represent a partial movements towards free trade to the extent that tariffs and quotas are imposed on goods imported into regions outside the zone but not on goods entering the zones. In other words, they are islands of free trade surrounded by an economy pursuing an IS policy. This, in fact, has been the case with countries such as India and Indonesia which until recently pursued an IS strategy of development. The cherished belief of policy makers in these countries is that the FPZs would attract FDI and promote exports while the rest of the economy could continue to pursue an IS strategy. Put another way FPZs are a means of having the cake and eating it too. The theory of the second best, however, states that removal of only one of the many distortions in an economy may or may not improve welfare. For instance, in the case of customs unions, which are also in the nature of the second best, welfare of member countries may or may not improve. It all depends on whether or not trade creation effects of the union exceed its trade diversion effects.

Much the same reasoning applies to FPZs. They may merely divert FDI from elsewhere in the economy into the zone without increasing the total volume of such investment. In this case, the country may gain very little from the establishment of FPZs. Indeed, it may incur a loss on account of all the infrastructure costs and incentives it provides for the firms in the zones.

Another reason for doubting the wisdom of establishing FPZs is the record of such zones in other developing countries. Available evidence shows that, with rare exceptions, most of the zones in developing countries such as the Philippines and Indonesia have yielded very little of the hoped for benefits. Peter Warr's (1983, 1984) pioneering social cost–benefit analyses of FPZs in Indonesia and the Philippines show that the social rate of return to public investment in establishing the zones are low or negative in some cases. This is not to say that FPZs have been a failure anywhere and everywhere. In the case of the Massan zone in Korea, the gains to the economy in terms of employment and exports appear to be substantial.

Is it likely Turkey will emulate Korea rather than the Philippines and Indonesia? Available information shows that out of the 1270 applications submitted to the zones by the end of 1992, 155 were foreign companies. But as yet the amount of FDI in the zones is not of an appreciable volume. Admittedly the zones in Turkey are a recent phenomenon and it is too early to pronounce on their performance. But it is arguable if the Turkish zones are likely to be as successful as the Massan zone in Korea. The amount of FDI in Korea as a whole is relatively low. As a matter of policy, Korea has relied on licensing agreements for her requirements of foreign technology rather than on FDI. In the absence of incentives to invest in the domestic sector of the economy foreign firms appear to have invested in the zone. Other factors key to the success of Korea's FPZ are her endowments of an easily trainable resilient labour force and the image of Korea as an economy sympathetic to private enterprise. Admittedly, Turkey is contemplating privatization of her state-owned enterprises and she too is endowed with easily trainable labour. But she is yet to establish an image of a private-enterprise-oriented economy and the productivity of her labour is, at present, relatively low. As stated earlier, available data show that efficiency wage rates in Turkey may be relatively high. In other words, wage rates in relation to labour productivity are high (Figure 6.1).

Another reason for doubting the wisdom of establishing a number of FPZs is the pronounced movement towards the EP strategy of development and the highly liberal policies towards FDI Turkey has adopted.

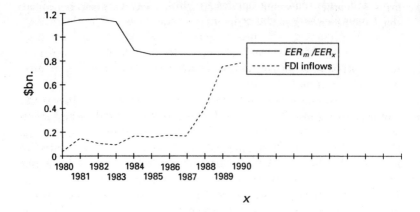

FIGURE 6.1   *Effective exchange rates and inflows of foreign direct investment in Turkey*

FPZs on top of these policies may be largely a luxury and unnecessary. They may only serve to increase the costs of attracting FDI and the share of gains from FDI accruing to foreign firms. Indeed, this is especially so because of the range of tax and depreciation allowances and investment credits Turkey offers firms in the zones. Indeed, the incentives offered to foreign firms on the zones in Turkey appear to be excessively generous. Extolling the attractions of Turkish FPZs to investors, Osman Unsul, an official of the Treasury, writes 'the real 100 per cent tax exemption for an unlimited period including corporate and income taxes, *the possibility of selling merchandise manufactured in free zones to Turkey*, developed infrastructure and superstructure, and the unique non-strike business opportunity, give free zones users enough competitive advantage to perform better in a pleasant climate' (Unsul, 1992). If Turkey were to allow foreign firms to sell goods they manufacture in the zones in the domestic market, albeit with the payment of all local taxes, it would amount to converting the entire economy into a FPZ. Such a policy, though attractive in theory, may defeat the objectives underlying the establishment of FPZs. These include the promotion of exports and transfer of technology. Foreign firms in the zones, however, may find domestic markets much more attractive than export markets and they may also pose a threat to nascent industries in Turkey. In sum, the concessions and incentives offered by Turkish FPZs in particular and Turkey's framework of policies towards FDI may be much too generous. While they may attract foreign firms to Turkey they may also serve to distribute a disproportionate share of the gains from FDI to foreign firms.

5   TURKEY'S MEMBERSHIP OF THE EC AND FDI

Turkey, at present, is an associate member of the EC and is actively seeking full membership. Whether or not Turkey will attain full membership of the EC by the end of this century is a much-discussed issue. Here we focus on the likely impact of full membership on inflows of FDI into Turkey. In broad terms, the issue is would Turkey inside the EC be of greater attraction to foreign firms than Turkey outside the EC? Unfortunately, the theory of integration is of little assistance in discussing the issue. The received wisdom is that regional integration promotes inward FDI, not so much because of the protectionist barriers to imports from third countries it erects, but because of the enlarged markets, growth in incomes and the scope and scale economies it promotes. It is also argued that the distribution of FDI amongst the member countries of an integrated region is determined by the location advantages and regional incentives they offer to foreign firms. These issues are elaborated elsewhere and need no repetition here (Balasubramanyam and Greenaway, 1992).

Few would dispute the proposition that Turkey inside the EC would be a major attraction to foreign firms, rivalling Greece and Portugal. Her geographical location, endowments of relatively cheap labour and a fairly well developed network of transportation and communications should all prove attractive both to firms within the EC and those from Japan and the US. The generous investment incentives she offers would also be an attraction to foreign firms. But once Turkey is admitted to full membership of the EC she may be required to harmonize her investment policies in line with those of other member countries. Admittedly, at present, there is no EC-wide policy towards FDI. But with increasing competition for FDI between member countries it is likely a common policy will be instituted. Such a policy is unlikely to be as generous as the present Turkish policies towards FDI. This may be no bad thing. The principal argument of this paper is that Turkish FDI policy is much too generous. The removal of these policies, however, would require Turkey to compete for FDI on equal terms with the other more developed countries in the EC. This would include not only improved infrastructure and labour productivity but also macroeconomic stability including control of inflation.

Another factor which may work in favour of Turkey inside the EC is in the area of trade policy. Turkey possesses a comparative advantage in the exports of labour intensive goods, especially textiles, clothing and shoes. These and other exports are subject to a number of non-tariff barriers in the EC. Indeed, Turkey is reported to be cited in more anti-dumping cases by the EC than most other countries. Membership of the EC would sweep away these barriers to Turkey's exports and Turkey would prove to be an attractive export location for foreign firms.

Inward FDI into Turkey inside the community may also increase for yet another reason. In the absence of tariff and other barriers to Turkey's exports to the community, it is likely capital will seek labour instead of labour moving to the locale of capital. German firms, for instance, may invest in Turkey to take advantage of her relatively cheap endowments of labour instead of importing Turkish labour into Germany as is the case at present. In sum, Turkey inside the EC is likely to attract relatively larger amounts of FDI than Turkey outside the EC.

6 CONCLUSIONS

This paper has reviewed the reasons for the relatively low volume of FDI in Turkey and the likely impact of the recent programme of liberalization on future flows of FDI into Turkey. The IS strategy of development Turkey pursued until the early 1980s with its attendant distortions and the emphasis she placed on state ownership of manufacturing activity appear to have contributed to the low volume of FDI she has attracted. The programme of liberalization initiated in the early 1980s has served to arouse the interest of foreign firms in Turkey. Whether or not this interest will be sustained and Turkey will be able to attract FDI of a magnitude similar to that in other middle income developing countries will depend largely on her ability to achieve macroeconomic stability and the credibility of the liberalization programme. It is unlikely that a mere reduction tariffs on imports and an array of export subsidies will attract foreign firms to Turkey. The country offers several location advantages to foreign firms, but the absence of exchange-rate and price stability has impeded her efforts to attract FDI. The paper has also argued that, in her enthusiasm for FDI, Turkey appears to be much too generous in the investment incentives she offers foreign firms. These incentives may serve to distribute an excessive amount of the gains from FDI to foreign firms. The FPZs Turkey has established may be largely unnecessary as a method of attracting FDI. In any case the incentives they offer foreign firms are overtly generous. Turkey inside the EC is likely to attract larger volumes of FDI than Turkey outside the EC. These and other observations in the paper are largely in the nature of reasoned speculation rather than conclusions based on an extensive examination of facts and relevant data. Much of the information on FDI in Turkey is not readily available. It is perhaps for this reason, and the fact that Turkey harbours a relatively low volume of FDI, that there is very little discussion of FDI in the literature on Turkey.

REFERENCES

Balasubramanyam, V. N. (1986), 'Incentives and Disincentives for Foreign Direct Investment in Less Developed Countries', in Balassa, B. and Giersch, H. (eds), *Economic Incentives* (London: Macmillan).

Balasubramanyam, V. N. and Greenaway, D. (1992), 'Economic Integration and Foreign Direct Investment: Japanese Investment in the EC', *Journal of Common Market Studies*, vol. 30, no. 2, pp. 175–93.

Balasubramanyam, V. N. and Salisu, M. (1991), 'Export Promotion, Import Substitution and Direct Foreign Investment in Less Developed Countries', in Ad Koekkoek and Mennes, L. B. M. (eds), *International Trade and Global Development – Essays in Honour of Jagdish Bhagwati* (London: Routledge).

Bhagwati, J. N. (1978), *Anatomy and Consequences of Exchange Control Regimes*, vol. 1, Studies in International Economic Relations, no. 10 (New York: National Bureau of Economic Research).

Bhagwati, J. N. (1985), 'Investing Abroad', Esmee Fairbairn Lecture, University of Lancaster.

Baysan, T. and Blitzer, C. (1991), 'Turkey' in Papageorion, Michaely M. and Choksi, A. (eds), *Liberalising Foreign Trade*, vol. 6 (Oxford: Basil Blackwell).

Celasun, M. (1992), 'Trade and Industrialization in Turkey: Initial Conditions, Policy and Performance in the 1980', paper presented at a conference on 'Economy of Turkey since Liberalisation', Bilkent University, Ankara, Turkey, 1992.

Edwards, S. (1991), 'Capital Flows, Foreign Direct Investment, and Debt-Equity Swaps in Developing Countries', in Siebert, H. (ed.) (1991), *Capital Flows in the World Economy: Symposium 1990* (Tubingen: J.C.B. Mohr).

General Directorate of Foreign Investment (GDFI), *Investing in Turkey*, Undersecretariat of the Treasury of Foreign Trade, Government of Turkey, June 1992.

Krueger, A. O. and Tuncer, B. (1982), 'Growth of Factor Productivity in Turkish Manufacturing Industries', *Journal of Development Economics*, vol. 11, no. 3.

Lim, D. (1983), 'Fiscal Incentives and Direct Foreign Investment in Less Developed Countries', *Journal of Development Studies*, vol. 19, pp. 207–12.

Markusen, J. (1983), 'Factor Movements and Commodity Trade as Complements', *Journal of International Economics*, vol. 13, pp. 341–56.

Mundell, R. (1957), 'International Trade and Factor Mobility', *American Economic Review*, vol. 47, pp. 21–35.

Root, F. and Ahmed, A. (1979), 'Empirical Determinants of Manufacturing Direct Foreign Investment in Developing Countries', *Economic Development and Cultural Change*, vol. 27.

Schneider, F. and Frey, B. S. (1985), 'Economic and Political Determinants of Foreign Direct Investment', *World Development* (February).

Togan, S. (1992), 'Trade Liberalization and Competitive Structure in Turkey during 1980s', paper presented at a Conference on 'Economy of Turkey since Liberalisation', Bilkent University, Ankara, Turkey, 1992.

Unsal, O. (1992), 'Investment, Export, Foreign Capital and Free Trade Zone Policies in 1992', in *Turkish Review*.

Warr, P. (1983), 'Jakarta Export Processing Zone: Benefits and Costs', *Bulletin of Indonesia Economic Studies*, vol. 19.

Warr, P. (1984), 'Export Processing Zones in the Philippines', *ASEAN Economic Papers*, no. 2 (School of Pacific Studies, Australian National University).

7 Turkey and the European Community: Regional Integration and Economic Convergence[1]

Robert C. Hine

1 INTRODUCTION

The agreement reached by EC leaders at Maastricht in December 1991 on further steps towards political and economic union represented a high water mark in the evolution of the European Community. It was the culmination of a remarkable period of renewal and development from the doldrums experienced in the early 1980s. The catalyst for this recovery was the drive to create a single European market (SEM) by the end of 1992. The SEM has already had a global impact, causing non-member countries to re-evaluate their relationship with the Community. Fears arose of an inward-looking 'Fortress Europe', increasingly protectionist in its trade policies. Coupled with the political and economic changes arising from the demise of the former USSR, this has led to formal applications for EC membership from a number of neighbouring countries, and expectations of eventual membership in others. However, the partial disintegration of the exchange rate mechanism (ERM) following the crisis of September 1992 and doubts about the desirability of economic and monetary union have placed the debate about the feasibility of simultaneously deepening and widening the Community in a new perspective.

This debate has a particular significance for Turkey, whose special relationship with the EC is a long-standing one, dating back almost to the inception of the Community. The relationship is embodied in the 1963 Association Agreement which has had a rather chequered history. The agreement envisaged that Turkey would eventually become a full member of the EC, and in 1987, following a difficult period in EC–Turkish relations, Turkey made a formal membership application. The Community's response was lukewarm: membership remained the long-term aim, but the immediate proposals were for an interim arrangement of closer co-operation.

From an economic perspective, the critical issue in the EC–Turkey relationship is the disparity in income levels and economic structures. On the one hand, integrationists argue that better access to the EC market and assistance under EC regional policies could help Turkey to close the income gap, and gradually bring Turkish living standards into line with those in the rest of Europe. On the other hand, critics fear that exposure to the full weight of EC competition might lead to a further divergence in economic structures, with Turkish production being confined to low-wage labour-intensive sectors. This paper considers the issue of economic convergence in a regional grouping, and the case of Turkey and the EC in particular. There are three main parts: the first reviews the link between regional economic integration and the convergence/divergence of the member countries' economies (Section 2). Next, the policy measures that might be used to promote integration in a regional economic grouping are outlined (Section 3). In the light of this, thirdly, the experience of Turkey under its Association Agreement with the EC (Section 4) and the economic issues which full membership might entail (Section 5) are examined. The final section of the paper offers some conclusions.

2   REGIONAL ECONOMIC INTEGRATION AND ECONOMIC CONVERGENCE/DIVERGENCE

The term 'economic convergence' is used here to describe a growing similarity over time in the structure and performance of two economies. The concept is clearly mutidimensional but the key features include relative per-capita incomes, inflation/unemployment rates, and production patterns. There are widely differing views among economists on the impact of regional integration on economic convergence. The debate is briefly reviewed below, together with some evidence on economic convergence in the EC.

2.1   The neoclassical view: economic convergence

The simplest forms of regional economic grouping involve measures affecting only trade. Thus a customs union requires the member countries to abolish all tariff and quota restrictions on their mutual trade and to operate a common external tariff on imports from outside the union. A free trade area is even more restricted in scope: there is no common external tariff, and tariffs and quotas are eliminated only on goods produced within the area. More ambitiously, a 'single market' such as the EC's SEM, aims to go beyond a customs union and to get rid of all internal non-tariff barriers such as discriminatory public purchasing policies and national technical standards. The stated aim of these regional groupings is to promote mutual trade, and to reap the benefits of international specialization and the economic stimulus of wider competition. According to standard trade theory, trade acts as a substitute for factor movements. Under certain conditions, including the removal of all obstacles to trade, the result would be factor price equalization: similar factors in different countries would obtain equal returns. Thus, in a labour-abundant country, trade would raise the returns to labour and bring them into line with the (lowered) returns to labour in the capital-abundant country; the changes would be reversed in relation to capital. It is not possible, however, to generalize from this about how the formation of a regional trading group would affect the relative per-capita *incomes* of the member countries. This would depend, *inter alia*, on changes in the terms of trade within and outside the group.

Factor price equalization could come about in a more direct way if the regional group went beyond trade measures and removed all restrictions on the movement of labour and capital, thereby creating a common market. Capital and labour would move to where returns were highest, leading to a convergence of wage and interest rates, as well as raising total output.

As the recent developments in endogenous growth theory have recognized, government policies – in addition to factor endowments – can play an important role in the evolution of trade and the performance of the modern economy. It is, of course, a principal aim of economic policy in countries whose economies are weak to narrow the gap with the stronger economies, i.e. to achieve economic convergence. An important question is whether this convergence can best be achieved by following similar policies or whether the weaker economies need a different set of measures. Membership of a regional grouping highlights this issue because integration generates pressures for policy coordination/harmonization. As customs duties, immigration controls, etc. are eliminated, so the effect on competition of discriminatory government policies in other areas becomes more evident. Thus the completion of the SEM has necessitated agreement on matters like public procurement policies, state aids, indirect taxation, the recognition of national technical standards and regulatory arrangements.

The policy convergence issue can be illustrated by reference to inflation/exchange rate policy. In a regional grouping, the pursuit by national governments of independent monetary and fiscal policies will lead to different national rates of inflation and unemployment. In the absence of policy co-ordination, these policies are unlikely to be consistent with (nominal) exchange rate stability. Fluctuations in exchange rates are a source of uncertainty for business which becomes relatively more important as the degree of integration in a regional grouping increases. In the EC, this has led to a debate between those who argue that exchange rate stabilization measures, and *a fortiori* a single currency, would force economic convergence among the member economies, and those who demand that convergence should take place before fixing exchange rates. The Maastricht Treaty inclines towards the latter in making convergence, particularly in relation to exchange rates, a prerequisite of monetary union. This has important implications for the relationship between rich and poor countries in a regional grouping, since in practice there is typically a divergence in inflation rates according to per-capita incomes, with the richer countries tending to have lower rates (see Appendix Table A.1). In the EC, the poorer countries have successfully demanded assistance in the form of a cohesion fund to help them to achieve economic convergence in preparation for monetary union.

2.2   Economic divergence and the 'cumulative causation' view

The neo-classical convergence view of integration has long been disputed (for example, Myrdal, 1957; Hirschman, 1958; Kaldor, 1970, 1971). Critics argue that the persistence of often severe regional problems within existing nation states[2] cautions against any expectation that economic convergence will be automatic or inevitable. They emphasize the crucial importance in any analysis of taking account of increasing returns. This results in initial differences becoming perpetuated by a cumulative process which is reinforced rather than offset by the movement of factors and trade. Myrdal referred to 'the principle of circular and cumulative causation' whereby the more prosperous areas benefited from increasing returns, taking markets and resources away from the poorer peripheral areas (Myrdal's 'backwash' effect). On this view, the beneficial 'spread' effects of growth at the centre generating demand for the products of the periphery were unlikely to compensate the periphery for the damaging backwash effects. In Kaldor's model, the critical factors determining the relative growth

of regions are the growth of demand for a region's exports (likely to
be more dynamic for the products of the prosperous regions) and embodied technological progress (likely to be faster for countries with a
higher rate of growth of output).[3] These considerations emphasize the
importance for poor countries joining a regional grouping of negotiating appropriate entry conditions.

One can similarly criticize the neo-classical view that removing barriers to factor mobility will lead to a convergence of wage and interest
rates. The important assumption made in this approach is that factors
are homogeneous. In reality this is certainly not the case for labour,
and this raises the possibility that labour movements between countries
may be selective. If the labour which emigrates is the best educated,
skilled and enterprising, then emigration instead of improving the position of the country of emigration by reducing the pool of unemployed
workers, may constitute an economic drain.[4] Correspondingly, the country
of immigration benefits from the influx and the gap between the two
countries could widen.

2.3 Integration and specialization

Although the standard trade theory argues that the removal of trade
barriers will, under certain conditions, lead to factor price equalization, this is shown to take place through specialization. But through
specialization, the creation of a customs union could lead to a divergence in production patterns among the member countries. Trade creation in a customs union, whereby lower-cost partner production displaces
higher-cost home production in home consumption, will tend to be
systematic. Industries which are relatively capital-intensive will tend
to concentrate in countries where capital is abundant – generally the
high income countries – and industries which are labour-intensive will
gravitate towards countries where labour is more plentiful – generally
the low income countries. The process of inter-industry specialization
may be intensified by internal and external economies of scale, leading to an agglomeration of industries in certain countries. Compared
with autarky, production patterns become more, not less, different and
trade would be of an inter-industry kind.

Krugman and Venables (1990) have developed this idea in a recent
paper. In their model, industry in the peripheral countries has the advantage of lower wage costs, but faces shipping costs in supplying the
large central market. Producers in the centre are able to exploit economies of scale and also to avoid shipping costs in supplying their home

market. Several outcomes for production and trade are possible, depending on the magnitude of shipping costs. If shipping costs are sufficiently high, each market will be self-sufficient and there will be no trade. A *partial* reduction in shipping costs would lead to the loss of the industry in the periphery – more transport costs are incurred in transporting the large requirements of the centre from the periphery than in transporting the small requirements of the periphery from the centre. However, if shipping costs could be *entirely* eliminated, the two markets would be fully integrated. The lower production costs in the periphery would lead the industry to be wholly located there, and the central market would be supplied from the periphery. The important conclusion is that integration which only partially removes barriers to trade could lead to de-industrialization in the peripheral, lower income regions. The peripheral regions may then become more specialized in the production of primary products and simple manufacturers whilst the centre dominates the more technology-intensive industries. Dismantling barriers in the periphery through membership of a regional grouping could accelerate this process, unless the grouping takes corrective action.

2.4   Economic convergence in the European Community

There is a wide disparity in living standards among the EC countries; even using international prices, per-capita incomes in Germany were 2.5 times those in Portugal in 1988. There has, however, been some tendency for the income gap to narrow over the postwar period (Molle, 1990). Most of the reduction took place in the first half of this period (see Table 7.1). During this period, Portugal and Greece, currently the two poorest members of the Community, succeeded in considerably reducing the gap in incomes between themselves and their future partners in the Community. The process of convergence was interrupted during the oil shock years of the 1970s and, although there is some evidence of a resumption in the following decade, the pattern of change may have altered. In particular, recent reductions in the variation in per-capita incomes owe more to a convergence among the richer countries than to a catching up process for the poorer ones.

The formation of the EC was expected to lead to inter-industry specialization and there was concern over the adjustment problems that this might provoke. In practice, there has been a movement towards intra-industry trade (IIT) amongst the EC countries (see Table 7.2). This trend has been shared by the Mediterranean countries, including Turkey.

TABLE *7.1* *Variations in per-capita incomes in the EC(12) and Turkey*

(a) At 1980 international prices

| Year | EC(12)[a] | | | Spain | Portugal | Greece | Turkey |
	Mean ($)	Standard deviation ($)	Coefficient of variation	(relative to EC mean)			
1950	2734	923	0.338	0.600	0.343	0.361	0.301
1958	3720	1024	0.275	0.674	0.347	0.385	0.368
1965	4955	1237	0.250	0.698	0.375	0.431	0.284
1972	6479	1424	0.220	0.749	0.458	0.527	0.291
1979	7932	1753	0.221	0.711	0.455	0.551	0.295
1985	11 043	2160	0.219	0.583	0.338	0.404	0.229

SOURCE: *Penn World Tables*: see Summers and Heston (1984, 1988).

Note: [a]EC(12) data weighted by GDPs of member countries.

(b) At current prices and exchange rates

| Year | EC(12)[a] | | | Spain | Portugal | Greece | Turkey |
	Mean ($)	Standard deviation ($)	Coefficient of variation	(relative to EC mean)			
1950	493	206	0.419	0.335	0.337	0.586	0.337
1958	924	332	0.360	0.513	0.267	0.414	0.523
1965	1591	490	0.308	0.471	0.278	0.441	0.170
1972	3059	956	0.312	0.518	0.337	0.463	0.143
1979	8671	2946	0.340	0.616	0.255	0.466	0.183
1985	7864	2229	0.283	0.548	0.273	0.428	0.132

SOURCE: OECD National Account Statistics (1992), and (for years 1950 and 1958) *International Financial Statistics Yearbook* (1986).

NOTE: [a]EC(12) data weighted by GDPs of member countries.

Econometric evidence suggests that EC integration has had a positive influence on the development of IIT; one possible explanation for this is that IIT is concentrated in differentiated products where information flows are important. Integration might then stimulate IIT by reducing barriers to the flow of people and ideas (Greenaway and Hine, 1991).

TABLE 7.2   *The development of intra-industry trade in Europe*

Year	EC(10)	Greece	Portugal	Spain	Turkey
1970	0.659	0.283	0.457	0.570	0.154
1978	0.720	0.415	0.410	0.644	0.120
1980	0.737	0.396	0.453	0.504	0.223
1983	0.766	0.462	0.514	0.677	0.359
1985	0.767	0.463	0.546	0.682	0.468

SOURCE: Greenaway and Hine (1991); Grubel–Lloyd index.

3   POLICY APPROACHES TO PROMOTE CONVERGENCE

Regional integration is pursued for a mixture of political and economic motives, the principal economic aim of integration being to improve the standard of living of people in each of the participating countries. In principle, this could be achieved even though the richer countries raised their per-capita incomes faster than the poorer ones and hence the gap between rich and poor grew. But such a development would probably be politically unacceptable beyond the short-term. Therefore, measures to ensure a degree of economic convergence are politically essential in a grouping of disparate economies.

As the experience of the EC – the most advanced of the regional groupings – demonstrates, the policy measures that may be employed are varied. They will be discussed here under three headings: Transitional Measures; Special Policy Treatment; and Financial Provisions.

3.1   Transitional measures

The aim of transitional measures is to give producers, administrators and others time to adjust to the new circumstances. High cost producers, for example, have a choice between using a transition period to raise their efficiency or, if this is not feasible, to withdraw from production. Either way, the transition period reduces the private costs of adjustment. Two aspects of the transitional arrangements are of particular concern, the *length* of the transition period and the degree of *asymmetry* between the treatment of the partner countries.

By giving enterprises time to assimilate information and to implement changes, a transition period may prevent inefficient producers from being overwhelmed by import competition before they have had an opportunity to reorganize or, alternatively, to withdraw. It also allows for improvements in infrastructure and information flows. However, if the transition period is made very lengthy, the credibility of the process may be undermined, and difficult adjustment decisions put off.

The more prosperous countries could also ease the adjustment process by accepting asymmetrical transition arrangements, for example by dismantling their tariff barriers on mutual trade more rapidly than their poorer partners. In effect, this creates a one-way system of preferences. Given that the production overlap between rich and poor countries will be less than that between the rich countries themselves, the effect of such preferences would be more likely to be trade diverting than trade creating. From a political economy perspective, this would enhance the acceptability of preferences since they would be less likely to damage the interests of politically influential producer pressure groups in the rich countries. Furthermore, continuing tariff barriers in the poor countries may have relatively little effect on imports of sophisticated manufactured products from the more prosperous countries, which sell more on the basis of quality and technical specification than price. Again, the danger of the asymmetrical approach is that it may weaken businesses' belief in their government's over-riding commitment to integration and market opening.

3.2 Special policy treatment

As noted earlier, economic integration, even at the free trade area level,[5] necessitates economic policy co-ordination among the member countries.[6] The Treaty of Rome, the legal basis for the EC, specifically required the member states to establish *common* policies in certain areas including, for example, competition policy dealing not only with collusive business practices but also controls over state aids. Common policies need not mean complete harmonization; some policy differentiation may be seen as necessary in order to achieve economic convergence. This is the case with state aids in the EC, where the degree of state support for investment projects is more strictly limited in the richer countries than in the poorer ones. In principle, special policy treatment of this kind should give the less prosperous countries an advantage in trying to attract new multinational investment projects. In practice, however, the EC restrictions on the prosperous areas have been too weak to have much effect and, in any case, national governments have withheld information where they felt that the assistance they have given might clash with Community guidelines.

Beyond adapting existing measures, a regional group could introduce programmes which are of specific interest to the poorer countries. Until the First Enlargement of the EC, regional policy was almost entirely the responsibility of the member governments. At UK insistence, the EC developed a regional policy programme from which the UK was one of the major beneficiaries. Sectoral policies might similarly be adopted to give particular support for the adaptation of industries in the poorer countries.

3.3 Financial provisions

A regional grouping can assist its poorer members financially, either by lowering their contributions to joint activities or by making special financial transfers from a central budget. With regard to the former, all regional groupings have to find a mutually acceptable method of financing their joint activities and, in general, an element of ability-to-pay enters into the calculation of contributions. As is to some extent the case in the EC, the budgetary burden for the poorer member states can be reduced by adopting a progressive system of contributions reflecting differences in per-capita incomes, and/or giving rebates to the poorer countries.

Within nation states, inter-regional income transfers through national taxation/spending systems offset a major part of regional income disparities (MacDougall Report, 1977). Similarly in a regional integration arrangement income transfers could be used to reduce inter-country differences in living standards. In the EC, the poorer member countries receive assistance from the structural funds, and there are plans to expand these in preparation for possible EMU. But at present the relative magnitude of these transfers does not compare with those occurring inside the member states.

Through transitional arrangements, special policy treatment and financial provisions regional economic groupings can attempt actively to promote economic convergence, or at least to minimize the risk of further divergence. The actions taken depend on a measure of political solidarity: the richer countries have to consider that the long-term gains from the entry of a poorer country to the grouping outweigh any economic burden. For example, an important reason for enlarging the EC to include Greece, Spain and Portugal – all net recipients from the European budget – was the desire to support their new commitment to parliamentary democracy and a market economy. As noted earlier, there is a potential moral hazard problem which should not be overlooked. If the rich countries provide a safety net for the poorer countries, then there is a danger that needed adjustments will be postponed and hard decisions (for example, over the closure of high-cost plants) avoided in the belief that the rich countries will ultimately come to the aid of an ailing partner.

In the following sections, policy measures to promote economic convergence in a regional grouping are considered in relation to Turkey and the EC, first through the 1963 Association Agreement and secondly in the context of Turkey's 1987 bid for full EC membership.

4   TURKEY'S RELATIONSHIP WITH THE EC: THE 1963 ASSOCIATION AGREEMENT[7]

Turkey's commitment to the Western form of development is long-established. Under Ataturk in the 1920s there was a comprehensive and genuine re-orientation towards the West and hence, in view of Turkey's geopolitical situation, towards Europe. This approach was reinforced after the war when Turkey sought membership of the new European/Atlantic institutions being established, such as the OEEC (1948), the Council of Europe (1949) and NATO (1952). Soon after the EC was set up in 1958, Turkey expressed its keen interest in membership, an aspiration which the EC encouraged by signing in 1963 an Association Agreement with a view to ultimate full membership. In EC affairs, 'association' is seen as a form of partial membership, enabling a country to benefit from certain preferential provisions, such as reduced tariffs on its exports, which express a special relationship. Crucially however, association does not confer voting rights in the EC Council, so that it does not give a country a direct influence on EC policy formation. It is true that association agreements provide for consultations through association councils, but given the economic disparity between any individual associate and the EC, the associates have very little policy leverage.

Turkey's application for association with the EC was mainly inspired by political considerations. It was seen as the culmination of Turkey's 'European vocation', confirming Turkey's rightful place amongst the European family of nations. It was also a response to Greece's application for association, made shortly earlier. Little serious thought had been given to the economic consequences of association by either party: the agreement reflected the continuing 'Community tradition of political expediency over-riding economic concerns.'[8]

Those economic concerns arose primarily from the wide disparity in living standards between Turkey in 1958 and the EC. In terms of per-capita GDP converted at purchasing power parity rates, incomes in Turkey were less than 30 per cent of those in Germany. The disparity reflected Turkey's much earlier stage of economic development than most of western Europe. Agriculture was still the backbone of the economy, occupying more than 70 per cent of the population, and accounting for 86 per cent of Turkey's exports at the beginning of the 1960s. By contrast, the corresponding figures for the EC(6) were 16 per cent and 18 per cent, respectively. The social and economic infrastructure of Turkey was backward and the industrial base was weak.

At the time of the EC's formation, Turkey's integration into the world economy was very limited. Whereas exports in the original EEC represented 13.4 per cent of GDP in 1958, in Turkey the share was only 2.0 per cent (Wijkman, 1990). Nevertheless, the orientation of the country's (relatively small) external trade was towards Europe, and hence there was an incentive to ensure that markets were not lost through EC trade policy discrimination, *vis-à-vis* both member countries of the Community and non-member countries like Greece which had secured preferential trade deals. In terms of the share of exports directed to the original six-country EEC, at 34.7 per cent in 1958 Turkey was ahead of France (22.2 per cent), Italy (23.9 per cent) and Germany (27.3 per cent). In short, although Turkey's trade was strongly oriented towards the EC, the disparity between the Turkish economy and those of the EC members was so large that a wide range of measures was called for to promote convergence without excessive adjustment costs.

4.1 Transitional measures

Two stages were envisaged in the agreement: a preparatory stage of at least 5 but up to 9 years, and a transitional stage of 12–22 years. The aim of the preparatory period was to give Turkey the opportunity to strengthen its economy before facing the rigours of intensified competition from EC firms. The transitional period was to phase in Turkey's adaptation to a full customs union with the EC, as well as to align Turkish sectoral and competition policies on those operated by the EC. By any standards, the time-period envisaged for the two stages was very lengthy, at the very least 17 years but possibly extending up to 31 years. The arrangements were also asymmetric. In the **preparatory period** the EC made some tariff concessions on Turkey's four main agricultural exports – tobacco, raisins, dried figs and hazelnuts – accounting for over 40 per cent of Turkey's exports. These concessions, however, were in the form of tariff quotas,[9] not outright tariff cuts. No reciprocal concessions were required of Turkey.

When the arrangements for the **transitional period** were negotiated in 1970, these also were markedly asymmetrical. On *industrial* goods, the EC was to eliminate all customs duties on imports from Turkey with the exception of those on refined petroleum goods (for which tariff quotas were fixed) and on certain textiles. By contrast, the envisaged dismantling of tariff barriers in Turkey was to be much more gradual: for one group of products (55 per cent of the total) this was to be carried out over 12 years, and on the remaining items the phase out was extended to 22 years. Quotas too would gradually be liberalized. Of potentially greater importance, Turkey was committed to align its external tariffs on those of the markedly more liberal EC. The position for *agricultural products* was more complicated because of the Common Agricultural Policy (CAP). Turkey would have to adopt the mechanisms of the CAP over a 22-year period but, more immediately, some 80 per cent of Turkish exports to the EC would benefit from preferential treatment in relation to other non-EC suppliers.

4.2 Special policy treatment

Beyond the CAP arrangements noted, the agreement was vague about policy alignment in areas such as competition and taxation. The most important arrangements concerned factor movements: Turkish workers would be allowed to move freely to jobs in EC countries but this would be phased in between the 12th and 22nd years of the agreement. A similar schedule would be followed for capital movements.

4.3 Financial provisions

In the preparatory period, the EC offered Turkey 175 million ECU in loans to assist the transformation process. A second financial protocol provided loans of ECU 300 million over $5\frac{1}{2}$ years. These were followed by further loans in 1977 and 1980, but the implementation of the latter was blocked initially by the European Parliament (over failure to safeguard human rights) and thereafter by Greece.

In retrospect, the Association Agreement was very inadequate for the task of preparing Turkey for full EC membership, given the wide income disparity that existed between the two parties at the time that the agreement was signed. The strategy was twofold: trade preferences and aid. The tariff preferences for *manufactured* goods appear impressive on paper, but in practice their impact was bound to be limited. Turkey had only a very small manufacturing base and so the initial response in quantitative terms was inevitably small. Furthermore, over whom would Turkey gain a preference? Obviously not the EC members within the customs union. Then, too, the EC extended preferential treatment to a wide range of developing countries under the Generalised System of Preferences from 1971 (the Yaoundé Convention already offered tariff-free access for manufactured goods from the African countries), whilst in the Mediterranean the global policy established in the 1970s offered the same treatment, and from 1973 this was phased in for the EFTA countries as well as the new member countries. Even when Turkey did succeed in developing its exports to the Community, the EC's response in some cases was to bring in measures to restrain them, as with the introduction of import quotas and restrictions in 1977 (especially on cotton yarn and T-shirts). The concessions on *agricultural products* were designed so as not to damage EC farmers – in other words to avoid trade creation. Their ability to divert trade was also weak, the preferences being small and not unique to Turkey. Thus, in a key product like raw tobacco, Turkey failed to increase its share of the EC market in the 1960s, in contrast to rivals Bulgaria and Romania (Yannopoulos, 1988). The other main element in the transitional arrangement – *financial aid* – was very limited, given the size and economic condition of Turkey at the time. Moreover, the bulk of the aid was in the form of loans which had to be repaid, not outright grants.

For its part, Turkey also failed to adopt the necessary measures to make a success of the transitional arrangements and thereby to prepare the country for full EC membership. There was little evidence of the Turkish government acting to strengthen the economy with a view to EC membership: the First and Second Five-Year Development Plans (1963–7 and 1968–72) dealt only in a very general way with the consequences of Association with the EC (Redmond, 1993, p. 27). Moreover, by the time of the negotiations on the transitional stage, no thorough studies of the economic implications of association had been conducted. Turkey's economic policies at this time were the opposite of what was needed to take advantage of preferential access to the EC market. Instead of an export-oriented strategy, Turkey in its Third Five-Year Development Plan adopted a rigid import substitution approach. To minimize the impact of any reduction in trade barriers on EC imports, Turkey raised its tariffs the day before it was due to make tariff cuts in favour of EC products (Birand, 1988).[10]

The inescapable conclusion is that neither the EC nor Turkey took the economic aspects of association – which was supposed to pave the way for full EC membership – sufficiently seriously. EC assistance was inadequate, whilst the economic policy stance of Turkey was inappropriate. Small wonder, then, that the association arrangements foundered in the turbulent years of the mid-1970s. Turkey was concerned over restrictions imposed on the movement of Turkish workers to the EC in the wake of the economic crisis triggered by the 1973 oil price increase, as well as over EC barriers to the growth of competitive Turkish manufactured exports. Furthermore, promised EC financial assistance was seen as insufficient. From the Community's perspective, the problems over Turkey's military intervention in Cyprus were compounded by Turkey's request in 1978 that it be allowed to freeze its dismantling of trade barriers against imports from the EC because of its grave economic difficulties. Turkey had failed to adjust to the oil price shock; it was faced with a large trade deficit, heavy indebtedness and rampant inflation. By the end of 1977 tariff reductions on imports from the EC were 20 or 10 per cent, depending on the industrial product concerned, instead of the 100 and 40 per cent, respectively, envisaged in the agreement. The military coup in 1980 and EC concern over human rights caused further difficulties in EC–Turkey relations, particularly after Greek membership of the EC in 1981.

5 THE 1987 APPLICATION FOR FULL EC MEMBERSHIP

Turkey's formal application for full EC membership in 1987 was a request for a fresh start in EC–Turkey relations – in the Turkish view, the Association Agreement was already dead in the water. The EC, partly because of pre-occupation with the creation of the SEM and the rapidly changing events in Eastern Europe, was slow to respond.

5.1 Turkey's preparedness for closer integration with the EC

Following a radical change of economic policy in 1980, during the 1980s Turkey's economic condition took a turn for the better – this is reflected in the GNP growth figures which show a 5.4 per cent annual increase in 1980–8 compared with 3.3 per cent in 1975–80. The economy is now much more open than it was at the time of the Association Agreement and, indeed, in this respect the gap with the EC is quite small: in Turkey, exports represent 15.0 per cent of GDP, whereas in the EC the proportion averages 17.0 per cent (Wijkman, 1990).

Turkey's relative involvement in trade is greater than that of Spain and Greece, and not far behind that of Italy.

The structure of trade has also been transformed over the last decade. Agriculture's share of exports has fallen from 58 per cent in 1980 to 20 per cent in 1988; meanwhile the share of textiles has almost doubled to 27 per cent, and steel has risen from 1 to 13 per cent. Turkey is now the leading supplier of textiles and clothing to the EC. The trade pattern remains oriented towards the EC: in 1987, 47.8 per cent of exports went to the Community but this is only slightly higher than the figure for 1958 (44.4 per cent) (Wijkman, 1990). In the meantime the EC countries' trade with each other has greatly intensified:

		1958 (%)	1987 (%)
Trade with other	France	31.1	60.4
EC countries as	Germany	37.9	52.8
a percentage of	UK	21.8	49.5
total trade	Italy	34.9	56.1
	Greece	50.9	67.3

These changes may indicate the missed opportunity for Turkey to develop its exports to the EC under the Association Agreement. The Second Enlargement of the Community gave free access to the EC market to some of Turkey's main trade rivals. The product composition of exports to the EC was particularly close to that of Spain in the case of agricultural products and to Greece in the case of manufactures (Yannopoulos, 1988, pp. 76, 86).

Although there were positive developments in the Turkish economy in the 1980s, nevertheless the economic contrast between Turkey and the EC remains large:

- *Per-capita incomes* in purchasing parity terms remain far behind those in the EC – by 1985 per capita incomes had fallen to 24 per cent of those in Germany;
- The *structure of the economy* remains backward, with over 50 per cent of the labour force in agriculture, and productivity is low;
- *Inflation rates* are very high, and the exchange rate correspondingly weak;
- The *foreign debt* is massive – equivalent to 55 per cent of GNP – and debt-servicing takes 8 per cent of GNP;
- *Industrial protection* remains very high;[11]

- There is a low level of *social standards* compared with the EC norms.[12]

How well could Turkey cope with closer integration into, and competition from, the EC market? Turkey has a comparative advantage in labour-intensive,[13] standardized industrial products which it could exploit more fully if it could get unimpeded access to the EC market. At the present time, exports are being harassed by EC measures, such as anti-dumping policies, which have a very doubtful justification in terms of preserving competition in the EC market. Indeed, the reverse may well be true, that EC producers are using the anti-dumping rules to prevent their domestic cartels from being undermined. With the advent of the SEM, EC firms stand to benefit more from the ending of intra-EC border restrictions than Turkish exporters. Hence, Turkish firms may be disadvantaged compared with their rivals in the EC, even though their labour costs may be lower.

Some industries, such as textiles, would clearly benefit from closer integration with the EC involving a mutual reduction of trade barriers. Others might find the going tougher, particularly where they are currently in the protected state sector (State Economic Enterprises). The State Planning Organisation (1988) has expressed confidence about the ability of Turkish firms to compete in the EC market: from a survey it concluded that 40 per cent of Turkish manufacturing industry was already able to compete, and a further 58 per cent could do so if appropriate policies were followed; for only 2 per cent of industry was the position deemed hopeless. A similarly optimistic result emerged from a study by the Foundation for Economic Development, though weaknesses were seen in industries such as chemicals, motor vehicles, pharmaceuticals, cement and mechanical and electrical engineering (IKV, 1988). The European Commission, however, took a more sceptical view in its report: it concluded that the situation was quite mixed even within industries, and a general judgement was difficult because of the many distortions caused by import protection and export incentives (EC Commission, 1989).

Closer integration with the EC could have a large effect both on Turkish agriculture and on the CAP. The budgetary implications for the EC would be potentially massive given the dimensions of Turkish agriculture: a labour force not far short of that in the existing Community as a whole, 40 per cent as many farms as the EC and a usable agricultural area equivalent to a quarter of the EC's. It is difficult to assess with precision how Turkish agriculture might respond to better access to the EC market. Turkey is agriculturally self-sufficient, with a particularly large production of vegetables, which account for two-thirds of farm output (EC Commission, 1989). Prices are substantially below those in the EC, but this exaggerates the benefits that Turkish farmers might get for two reasons. First, the experience with the Second Enlargement of the EC shows that the political strength of EC farmers is sufficient to ensure them a large measure of protection against an influx of agricultural products from new member countries. Secondly, the CAP itself is in the process of major changes in the form and maybe the level of protection. High and open-ended support prices are being phased out in the MacSharry reforms, and it seems unlikely that the new system of compensation would be fully extended to farmers from outside the existing EC who had not benefited from the previous support regime.

5.2 The EC draft proposal

In December 1989, the Commission published its opinion on Turkey's application for full EC membership. A number of considerations weighed against a favourable decision for Turkey. These included: (a) concern over the cost to the EC budget of an extension of agricultural and regional supports; (b) the prospect of an influx of Turkish workers of the Community at a time of high unemployment; (c) the likely shift in the balance of the Community towards the South and the Islamic world; (d) the continuing conflict with Greece, particularly in relation to Cyprus; and (e) the reduction in Turkey's strategic importance to the Community following the end of the Cold War. Against this background, the Commission argued that the time was not right for membership negotiations, a view accepted by the EC Council in February 1990. The Commission proposed instead an alternative arrangement, and detailed suggestions were put forward in June 1990. The main elements of the alternative arrangement, which amounts to a form of association, were as follows.

Transitional measures

The commission proposed the completion of the EC–Turkey customs union by 1995. Since, however, the EC had already eliminated customs duties on all industrial and agricultural products from Turkey by 1 January 1987, the export benefits would largely accrue to the EC. The Commission further proposed that, in parallel with the customs union, the Community would restore freedom of movement of textiles in line with the position it had adopted *vis-à-vis* all its trading part-ners during the Uruguay Round (i.e. for a gradual phasing out of the Multi Fibre Arrangement). The return to the Association arrangements would, the Commission indicated, also involve greater liberalization of trade in agricultural products.

Special policy treatment

The Commission proposed co-operation in a wide range of fields, in-cluding industry, agriculture, financial services, transport, energy, en-vironment, science and technology.

Financial provisions

A·new agreement would also include the resumption and extension of the financial protocol which was suspended in 1981. This would pro-vide ECU 600 million of aid, though this would be mainly in the form of loans.

5.3 Assessment of the proposals

The main conclusions on the 1963 Association Agreement were that its economic provisions were inadequate for the declared objective of preparing Turkey for full EC membership, and that the economic policies pursued by Turkey were inappropriate. The failure of the Association Agreement was, therefore, predictable. Have the lessons from this been learned, or is there again a triumph of political wishful thinking (and mutual misperception) over economic reality?

Access to the EC market can provide a motor for Turkish economic development, indeed it has already done so. The problem for Turkey is that conditions are changing. The SEM will dismantle a range of non-tariff barriers. This will provide a stiffer competitive challenge for producers inside the SEM but will also allow the more efficient amongst them to take advantage of the bigger market. Producers outside the SEM may therefore be put at a disadvantage, though if the SEM suc-ceeds in raising EC incomes this may draw in more imports from out-side the Community. Turkey, whose exports – as already noted – are strongly oriented towards the EC, is closely affected by this process. The EFTA countries, aware of the dangers, have negotiated a special deal in the European Economic Area which effectively put them inside the SEM, though without real decision-making influence. Even so, a number of EFTA countries took the further step of applying for full EC membership. In addition to the SEM effect, the EC's relations with the Central and Eastern European countries have undergone a dramatic change in recent years, with the negotiation by the EC of association agreements with these countries. Although these agreements certainly do not give unrestricted access to the EC market, they do improve the position of Turkey's potentially rival suppliers.

In view of these changes, it is difficult to regard the proposed EC measures in relation to Turkey as at all adequate to the task of preparing Turkey for full EC membership in the foreseeable future. The financial provisions are ungenerous and the trade arrangements neglect the vitally important area of non-tariff barriers, including anti-dumping measures. Certainly, closer integration would involve adjustment problems for both parties. Some industries in Turkey which are regarded as symbolic of economic advancement may not be able to survive unrestricted competition from EC producers. At the same time, in EC labour-intensive industries such as clothing, some standardized manufactured goods such as synthetic fibres, as well as agricultural products, adjustments to Turkish competition might be painful. These latter adjustments are, however, inevitable if the EC genuinely intends to play its part in encouraging the transformation of the Eastern European economies, let alone the economies of Mediterranean countries and the Third World generally. In a dynamic world economy it is, moreover, in the EC's own interest to move away from the bulk production of simple manufactured products in which it has lost its one-time comparative advantage towards more sophisticated items.

The EC is now cautious about entering any agreement which might lead to a large-scale immigration, particularly of the traditional rural–urban type, fearing that at a time of high unemployment in many EC countries this would aggravate social tensions. Current EC intolerance towards large-scale immigration has been reflected in attacks on foreign workers, including Turkish workers in Germany. But the population pressures of neighbouring countries will not go away. This indicates that the EC needs to increase its efforts to promote job creation in the countries on its eastern and southern peripheries. Similar issues arise in relation to the EC Budget. To create a real impact on the economic development of neighbouring countries would involve massive financial transfers, particularly given the poor development of their basic infrastructures. But this would have an economic and political payoff: in

economic terms the neighbouring countries are promising markets for
EC production, whilst politically the economic development of the neighbouring countries might help to avert political instability towards which
the Community could not be indifferent.

6 CONCLUSIONS

The 1963 Association Agreement between the EC and Turkey was
supposed to pave the way for Turkey's eventual full membership of
the Community. However, the economic provisions of the agreement
were inadequate for this purpose, given the magnitude of the gap between living standards in Turkey and the original EC members. Moreover, the economic policies pursued by Turkey were inappropriate, with
their emphasis on import substitution. In short, political aspirations
were allowed to overshadow economic reality, and the reality was that
the Turkish economy lagged far behind those of the EC members.

In the wake of the problems with the European Monetary System
and the continued uncertainty over the plans for monetary union, the
future evolution of the EC is particularly unclear. The balance between deepening the Community through economic and monetary union,
and widening it by admitting more countries may change. The set-
backs towards the deepening process may focus more political effort
on widening, a change of course likely to be welcomed among some
governments, including the UK's. However, Turkey has not been at
the head of the queue for new members: Austria, Sweden and Finland
joined the EC in 1995.

Given that the EC has indicated the eligibility of Turkey for eventual EC membership but that this will not happen in the immediate
future, what is the best way forward? The EC's 1990 proposals represented very little improvement on the existing position. Turkey may,
of course, be able to combine these measures with changes in other
directions such as closer links with fellow Black Sea economies. But
it is difficult to see these markets as in any way comparing with that
of the EC. Turkey's best strategy may, therefore, be to try to negotiate
membership of the European Economic Area (EEA). Membership of
the EEA would offer Turkish goods better access to the EC market in
the very important area of non-tariff barriers. Also, the commitment to
a programme of policy co-ordination within the EEA would enhance
the credibility of Turkey's EC membership bid, as Portugal's membership of EFTA helped to ease its entry to the EC. Recent events

have called into question the monolithic view of the Community: in a variable geometry Europe, Turkey's most advantageous position may be as part of a second tier which embraces both Central and Southern European countries.

APPENDIX

TABLE 7.A   *Inflation rates in relation to per-capita incomes*

Economies	GDP per capita ($US, 1984)	Average annual inflation rate	
		1965–73	1973–84
China and India	290	1.0	4.0
Other low-income economies	190	4.6	14.9
Middle-income economies	1250	5.5	38.0
Upper middle income	1950	5.6	44.0
Industrial market economies	11 430	5.2	7.9
Turkey	1160	10.5	42.4
Portugal	1970	4.9	20.5
Yugoslavia	2120	10.9	24.6
Greece	3770	4.4	17.3
Spain	4440	7.0	16.4
Ireland	4970	8.5	14.4
Italy	6420	5.1	17.2
UK	8570	6.2	13.8
Belgium	8610	4.4	6.4
Austria	9140	4.5	5.3
Netherlands	9520	6.4	5.9
France	9760	5.3	10.7
Finland	10 770	7.2	10.7
Germany	11 130	4.7	4.1
Denmark	11 170	7.6	9.4
Sweden	11 860	5.3	10.2
Norway	13 940	6.3	9.4
Switzerland	16 330	5.5	3.9

SOURCE: *World Development Report* (1986, Table 1).

NOTES

1. I am grateful to John Redmond for his helpful comments on an earlier draft of this chapter. As usual, I take responsibility for any remaining errors and omissions.
2. Despite large-scale expenditure on national regional policies.
3. Verdoorn's law associates higher rates of productivity growth with higher rates of growth of output (Verdoorn, 1949).
4. However, the damage could be offset by remittances from emigrants.
5. Even EFTA, with its preference for the non-bureaucratic, pragmatic approach, found it necessary to have rules relating to state aids and other aspects of competition policy (see Curzon, 1974).
6. In the EC, this was recognized from the outset and indeed economic integration was seen by some as a means of generating political integration.
7. For an excellent discussion of the political and economic issues in EC–Turkey relations see Redmond (1993).
8. Redmond (1993, p. 25).
9. The generosity of this move can be questioned. Depending on the size of the quotas, there might be no impact on the volume of exports, since beyond the quota the full rate applied; however, exporters might be able to realize a higher price.
10. Quoted by Redmond (1993, p. 347).
11. Customs duties may have been reduced but other barriers have replaced them; for example, 44 per cent of products subject to the tariff are also covered by an import surcharge; in 1988 receipts from customs duties were 3.4 per cent of the cif value of imports but stamp duty, wharfage and contributions to special funds raised this to 12.2 per cent, compared to 6.7 per cent in 1980.
12. For example, half of the children receive no education beyond the age of 11, and the illiteracy rate is 34 per cent (compared with 21 per cent in Portugal, 10 per cent in Greece and 7 per cent in Spain (all figures for 1981).
13. Hourly wage costs in manufacturing are estimated to be 13 per cent of those in the EC (EC Commission, 1989).

REFERENCES

Birand, M. A. (1988), 'A Turkish View of Greek–Turkish Relations', *Journal of Political and Military Sociology*, vol. 16, no. 2.
Curzon, V. (1974), *The Essentials of Economic Integration* (London: Macmillan).
EC Commission (1989), *Commission Opinion on Turkey's Request for Accession to the Community*, SEC (89) 2290 Final (Brussels: EC Commission).
Greenaway, D. and Hine, R. C. (1991), 'Intra-Industry Specialisation, Trade Expansion and Adjustment in the European Economic Space', *Journal of Common Market Studies*, December, pp. 603–22.

Hirschman, A. O. (1958), *The Strategy of Economic Development* (New Haven, CN: Yale University Press).

IKV (1988), *The Relative Structural Advancement of Turkey in the Context of Becoming a Full Member of the EEC* (Ankara: IKV).

Kaldor, N. (1970), 'The Case for Regional Policies', *Scottish Journal of Political Economy*, vol. 17, pp. 337–48.

Kaldor, N. (1971), 'The Dynamic Effects of the Common Market', in D. Evans (ed.), *Destiny or Delusion: Britain and the Common Market* (London: Gollancz), pp. 59–91.

Krugman, P. R. and Venables, A. J. (1990), 'Integration and the Competitiveness of Peripheral Industry', Chapter 3 in C. Bliss and J. B. De Macedo (eds), *Unity with Diversity in the European Economy* (Cambridge: Cambridge, University Press).

MacDougall Report (1977), *Report of the Study Group on the Role of Public Finance in European Integration* (Brussels: EC Commission).

Molle, W. (1990), 'Will the Completion of the Internal Market Lead to Regional Divergence?', in H. Siebert (ed.), *The Completion of the Internal Market* (Kiel: Institut für Weltwirtschaft).

Myrdal, G. (1957), *Economic Theory and Underdeveloped Regions* (London: Duckworth).

Redmond, J. (1993), *The Next Mediterranean Enlargement of the European Community. Turkey, Cyprus and Malta* (Aldershot: Dartmouth).

State Planning Organisation (1988), *Reports of the Ad Hoc Committee on the Competitiveness of Turkish Industry with Respect to the EC* (SPO: Ankara).

Summers, R. and Heston, A. (1984), 'Improved International Comparisons of Real Product and its Composition, 1950–1980', *Review of Income and Wealth*, series 30, no. 2, pp. 207–62.

Summers, R. and Heston, A. (1988), 'A New Set of International Comparisons of Real Product and Prices: Estimates for 130 Countries, 1950–1985', *Review of Income and Wealth*, series 34, no. 1, pp. 1–26.

Verdoorn, P. J. (1949), 'Fattori che Regalono lo Sviluppo della Produttivita del Lavoro', *L'Industria*, vol. 1, pp. 45–54.

Wijkman, P. M. (1990), 'Patterns of Production and Trade', Chapter 5 in W. Wallace (ed.), *The Dynamics of European Integration* (London: Pinter).

Yannopoulos, G. N. (1988), *Customs Unions and Trade Conflicts* (London: Routledge).

8 Export Expansion, Capital Accumulation and Distribution in Turkish Manufacturing, 1980–9

Fatma Taskin and A. Erinc Yeldan

In the early 1980s, Turkey started to pursue an export-oriented growth strategy centred on manufactured exports. Stimulated mainly by a vigorous export promotion strategy which consisted of high export subsidies, competitive devaluations of the Turkish lira, and repression of domestic demand, Turkey increased the total value of its merchandise exports fourfold by the first half of the 1980s. While the economic and political effects of this episode are in general well-documented, (for example, Celasun and Rodrik, 1989; Senses and Yamada, 1990; Onis and Riedel, 1993), its income distribution consequences remain unexplored. Indeed, throughout the decade, the observed rapid surge in manufacturing exports appear to have been accompanied by faltering rates of capital accumulation and a deterioration in the purchasing power of the working classes. Although there are references to the problem in the Turkish literature (see, for example, Celasun, 1989; Yeldan, 1993; Boratav, 1992), a formal analysis of the linkages between export expansion and income redistribution is yet to be undertaken.

In this chapter we analyse the historical links between exports, growth, employment and (functional) distribution of income within the Turkish manufacturing sector which was the main target of export promotion policies exclusively targeted. The paper consists of three sections: the first section provides an overview of the manufacturing export performance, with special emphasis on the economic policies that shaped the formation of price and cost structure within the sector; Section 2 provides a more detailed sectional analysis of the export drive, while Section 3 analyses the trend in export expansion, accumulation and distribution.

1   EXPORT PERFORMANCE OF THE MANUFACTURING SECTOR

The introduction of the stabilization program in 1980s induced a sharp increase in exports. Between 1980 and 1990, the total merchandise exports quadrupled and the export value which was 2910.0 million US dollars in 1980 reached 12 959.3 million US dollars by 1990. During the period, the average annual growth rate for exports reached 17 per cent; the ratio of exports to GNP (in current prices) was only 5 per cent in 1980, reached 15.6 per cent in 1985 and was at 16 per cent by the second half of the decade (see Table 8.2). This export boom has been the most important factor in the recovery of Turkish economy since 1980. It has also had a major role in increasing the creditworthiness of Turkey.

In addition to the increase in absolute levels of exports, there were structural changes. The period witnessed a transformation both in the composition and geographical destination of Turkish exports. At the beginning of the period 57.4 per cent of the total exports was agricultural goods and only 35.9 per cent was industrial goods, but by the end of the decade the composition changed in favour of industrial goods. The share of industrial goods reached 79.3 per cent of the total exports, whereas only 18 per cent of total exports were agricultural goods. Furthermore, Turkey expanded its trade with the non-OECD countries, mainly the Middle East. Thus, the share of Middle Eastern and North African markets in total exports jumped from 17.8 per cent in 1980 to 41.9 per cent in 1982, eventually stabilizing around 33.0 per cent by 1985. This phenomenal improvement in export performance was the result of both decisive changes in economies policies and external effects, such as the emergence of the Middle Eastern market with the eruption of the Iran–Iraq war in the early decade.

Table 8.1 documents important aspects of the relevant policy tools. As can be observed, real currency depreciation seems to be the primary instrument in the promotion of export targets and the achievement of balance in the current account. The exchange rate is devalued by 30 per cent between 1979 and the end of 1980. Starting from May 1981, the exchange rate was adjusted daily and the parity was tied to a sliding crawling-peg. Consequently the Turkish lira depreciated by another 30 per cent in real terms between 1981 and 1985.

In addition to adjustments in the real exchange rate, efforts at trade liberalization included incentives such as tax rebates, credit subsidies, an exchange retention scheme, and duty-free imports for the production

TABLE 8.1 *Prices and costs in Turkish manufacturing*

	1980	1981	1982	1983	1984	1985	1986	1987	1988	1989	1990
1. Wage rate[a]	100.0	106.8	102.6	93.6	78.4	71.3	63.1	79.2	61.3	74.1	
2. Interest rate[b] (%)	-33.1	2.9	7.8	6.7	-4.5	7.6	12.5	5.9	-3.6	-2.1	-3.1
3. Profits[c] (%)	100.0	96.6	95.9	109.8	153.5	215.2	175.6	229.3	202.5	185.3	
4. Energy price	100.0	155.7	225.8	283.6	497.5	982.7	1333.0	1644.5	2306.4	3828.5	6167.4
Producer prices											
5. Private	100.0	131.1	166.2	219.9	323.3	453.1	613.8	860.3	1546.8	2530.8	3637.7
6. Public	100.0	131.2	165.2	213.7	311.5	451.8	576.8	702.4	1219.1	2033.3	3241.7
7. Exchange rate[d]	-23.0	-13.3	-10.5	-3.1	-0.4	-0.7	-12.8	-6.7	-1.6	9.7	12.2
8. Protection rates[e] (%)				81.8	85.4				61.8		36.2
9. Consumer goods				129.1	133.9				88.1		52.3
10. Intermediates				57.9	59.2				38.0		25.9
11. Investment goods				61.5	68.0				87.9		37.8
12. Subsidy Rates[f] (%)				47.1	32.1		24.5		25.6	24.4	21.1
13. Consumer goods				33.3	22.7		12.5		13.3	15.8	13.9
14. Intermediates				50.6	36.1		32.3		32.2	29.6	25.7
15. Investment goods				67.9	40.7		25.9		31.2	27.6	20.4

SOURCES: Rows 1–3, Yeldan (1994); rows 4–6, *SIS Statistical Yearbooks*; row 7, Aşikoğlu and Uçtum (1992); rows 8–15, Olgun and Togan (1991).

NOTES: [a] Real wages in manufacturing deflated by CPI.
[b] Real interest rate on annual deposits, deflated by CPI.
[c] Aggregate profits in 500 largest firms, deflated by CPI.
[d] Annual percentage change of the real effective exchange rate index of the Central Bank, a negative sign indicates depreciation.
[e] Nominal protection rates (%), row 8 refers to manufacturing average.
[f] Nominal subsidy rates (%), row 15 refers to manufacturing average.

of exportables. Non-traditional exporting sectors such as metal products, machinery and transport equipment have had further preferential
treatment. Import liberalization measures, such as reduction of quantitative restrictions, were introduced in 1980. Another critical reform in
the trade regime was further liberalization of imports, announced in
December 1983. The tariff rates were decreased, a substantial amount
of quantitative restrictions were eliminated, and instead of the previous practice, which listed only the commodities which were free
of all duties, a prohibitive list which was significantly less binding
was put into practice. These changes in trade policies increased the
role of market forces and decreased the anti-export bias in the trade
regime.

As a consequence of a series of bold reforms towards financial liberalization, domestic financial markets gained depth and flexibility. Market
rates of interest turned positive in real terms. This, however, resulted
in a reduction in the share of entrepreneurial profits in the non-wage
value added because of increased interest costs. Concurrently, a price
reform was implemented, which aimed at correcting the existing distortions in the domestic price system which were especially prevalent
in the state enterprise sector.

A closer look at the behaviour of these policy variables for the second half of the decade, however, shows a weakening of managerial
activity of the bureaucracy. We witness what seems to be a reversal of
macro-policies – a phenomenon for which Ersel (1991) coins the term
'reform fatigue'. In particular, if we examine the overall patterns of
protection, we see that trade protection, even though curtailed to a
large extent, continued, standing at an average rate of 36.2 per cent in
1990. A similar pattern is observed in the care of export promotion
policy, with a secular downward movement in the subsidy element
reaching an average of 21 per cent of manufacturing exports.

During this period, the inflation rate soared and the exchange rate
began to appreciate in real terms. Real rates of interest turned negative. An important consequence of the loss of momentum in the implementation of price reforms is apparent: until 1985, the price indexes
for the public and private manufacturing sector moved together. However, from 1986, the spread between the two widened in favour of the
private sector. This observation suggests that the pricing policy in the
state sector from 1986 onwards failed to exploit the market signals,
while the private sector succeeded in doing so.

In sum, the Turkish export-led growth strategy failed to generate an
indigenous momentum of its own, and receded into a phase of uncertainty

in which 'political rationalities' finally came to grips with 'economic realities'. The limits of classic liberalization, based on statistical efficiency gains, seem to have been reached with cyclical growth patterns in the product and factor markets. We analyse the sectoral consequences of this episode in more detail in the next section.

2   SECTORAL COMPOSITION OF TURKISH EXPORTS

The success of Turkey's new outward-oriented growth policy is attributed to the spectacular increase in its exports and significant changes in the composition of Turkish exports during the 1980–90 period. Export-led development strategy with sizeable export subsidies and real exchange rate policies led to a much faster expansion in the industrial product exports. While the overall exports increased fourfold, the industrial product export increased tenfold during the decade (Table 8.1). With rapid increase in the share of industrial goods exports, the composition of the total exports changed drastically in favour of industrial goods. At the beginning of the period, 57.5 per cent of the total exports were agricultural goods and only 35.9 per cent were industrial goods. By the end of the period, the share of industrial goods had reached 79.4 per cent of the total exports whereas only 18 per cent of total exports were agricultural goods.[2] Turkey moved from being mainly an agricultural goods exporter to an industrial goods exporter (see Table 8.2).

It is widely accepted that export expansion exerts a positive impact on economic growth and that the composition of exports is an important factor in the economic growth process. Ever since the effect of the enunciation of the Singer–Prebish thesis – that primary commodity exports suffer a long-term deterioration in terms of trade – the commodity composition of many of the developing countries exports has changed in favour of manufactured exports. Among all the developing countries which changed their development strategy and increased the share of manufactures in exports, there is no other country which has achieved as rapid a transformation of its export composition as Turkey during 1965–85.[3]

Prior to 1980, Turkey followed an import-substitution development strategy which advocates industrialization with high protection of the domestic industry. The required protection was obtained through high tariffs and quantity restrictions on imports and with overvalued exchange rates. After 1980, the change in the development strategy towards a market-oriented export-led growth emphasized the importance

TABLE 8.2 *Exports by commodities (million US$)*

	1980	1981	1982	1983	1984	1985	1986	1987	1988	1989	1990
Total	2910	4703	5746	5728	7134	7958	7457	10 190	11 662	11 625	12 959
	100.00	*161.62*	*197.46*	*196.84*	*245.15*	*273.47*	*256.25*	*350.17*	*400.76*	*399.48*	*445.33*
I. Agriculture	1672	2219	2140	1881	1749	1719	1886	1853	2341	2128	2347
	100.00	*132.72*	*127.99*	*112.50*	*104.61*	*102.81*	*112.80*	*110.83*	*140.01*	*127.27*	*140.37*
II. Mining and quarrying	191	193	175	189	240	244	247	272	377	413	327
	100.00	*101.05*	*91.62*	*98.95*	*125.65*	*127.75*	*129.32*	*142.41*	*197.38*	*216.23*	*171.20*
III. Industry	1047	2290	3430	3658	5145	5995	5324	8065	8943	9083	10 285
	100.00	*218.72*	*327.60*	*349.38*	*491.40*	*572.59*	*508.50*	*770.30*	*854.15*	*867.53*	*982.33*
A. Processed agricultural products	209	412	568	670	809	647	667	954	885	907	937
	100.00	*197.13*	*271.77*	*320.57*	*387.08*	*309.57*	*319.14*	*456.46*	*423.44*	*433.97*	*448.33*
B. Processed petroleum products	39	107	344	232	409	372	178	232	331	255	291
	100.00	*274.36*	*882.05*	*594.87*	*1 048.72*	*953.85*	*456.41*	*594.87*	*848.72*	*653.85*	*746.15*
C. Industrial products	799	1771	2518	2756	3928	4976	4479	6879	7728	7922	9057
	100.00	*221.65*	*315.14*	*344.93*	*491.61*	*622.78*	*560.58*	*860.95*	*967.21*	*991.49*	*1133.54*
Cement	40	198	207	81	56	44	27	7	7	33	77
	100.00	*495.00*	*517.50*	*202.50*	*140.00*	*110.00*	*67.50*	*17.50*	*17.50*	*82.50*	*192.50*
Chemical industry products	76	94	148	120	173	266	350	527	735	774	618
	100.00	*123.68*	*194.74*	*157.89*	*227.63*	*350.00*	*460.53*	*693.42*	*967.11*	*1018.42*	*813.16*
Rubber and plastic industry products	16	72	61	77	97	108	141	258	352	313	238
	100.00	*450.00*	*381.25*	*481.25*	*606.25*	*675.00*	*881.25*	*1612.50*	*2200.00*	*1956.25*	*1487.50*

Product											
Hides and skin products	50	82	111	192	401	484	345	722	514	605	750
	100.00	*164.00*	*222.00*	*384.00*	*802.00*	*968.00*	*690.00*	*1444.00*	*1028.00*	*1210.00*	*1500.00*
Forestry products	4	20	33	15	24	106	52	32	22	23	23
	100.00	*500.00*	*825.00*	*375.00*	*600.00*	*2650.00*	*1300.00*	*800.00*	*550.00*	*575.00*	*575.00*
Textile products	424	803	1057	1299	1875	1789	1851	2707	3201	3503	4060
	100.00	*189.39*	*249.29*	*306.37*	*442.22*	*421.93*	*436.56*	*638.44*	*754.95*	*826.18*	*957.55*
Glass, ceramics, brick–tile products	36	102	104	108	146	189	158	205	233	258	326
	100.00	*283.33*	*288.89*	*300.00*	*405.56*	*525.00*	*438.89*	*569.44*	*647.22*	*716.67*	*905.56*
Iron and steel products	34	100	362	407	576	969	804	852	1457	1348	1612
	100.00	*294.12*	*1064.71*	*1197.06*	*1694.12*	*2850.00*	*2364.71*	*2505.88*	*4285.29*	*3964.71*	*4741.18*
Non-ferrous metal products	18	30	45	79	86	115	111	134	226	256	250
	100.00	*166.67*	*250.00*	*438.89*	*477.78*	*638.89*	*616.67*	*744.44*	*1255.56*	*1422.22*	*1388.89*
Metallic goods industry products	8	20	27	19	16	73	60	107	52	34	38
	100.00	*250.00*	*337.50*	*237.50*	*200.00*	*912.50*	*750.00*	*1337.50*	*650.00*	*425.00*	*475.00*
Machinery	22	65	116	103	118	378	203	681	333	195	204
	100.00	*295.45*	*527.27*	*468.18*	*536.36*	*1718.18*	*922.73*	*3095.45*	*1513.64*	*886.36*	*927.27*
Electric machinery and equipment	11	26	75	69	100	119	130	293	294	235	440
	100.00	*236.36*	*681.82*	*627.27*	*909.09*	*1081.82*	*1181.82*	*2663.64*	*2672.73*	*2136.36*	*4000.00*
Motor vehicles, parts and accessories thereof	50	117	110	126	135	147	82	110	118	1554	212
	100.00	*234.00*	*220.00*	*252.00*	*270.00*	*294.00*	*164.00*	*220.00*	*236.00*	*3108.00*	*424.00*
Other industrial products	10	42	62	61	125	189	166	246	184	192	210
	100.00	*420.00*	*620.00*	*610.00*	*1250.00*	*1890.00*	*1660.00*	*2460.00*	*1840.00*	*1920.00*	*2100.00*

SOURCE: *Foreign Trade Bulletin*, Ankara Undersecretariat of Treasury and Foreign Trade.

NOTE: Numbers in italics show the index value of export growth (1980–90).

TABLE 8.3   *Commodity composition of exports (% of total exports)*

	1980	1981	1982	1983	1984	1985	1986	1987	1988	1989	1990
I. Agriculture	57.5	47.2	37.2	32.8	24.5	21.6	25.3	18.2	20.1	18.3	18.1
II. Mining and quarrying	6.6	4.1	3.0	3.3	3.4	3.1	3.3	2.7	3.2	3.6	2.5
III. Industry	36.0	48.7	59.7	63.9	72.1	75.3	71.4	79.1	76.7	78.1	79.4
A. Processed agricultural products	7.2	8.8	9.9	11.7	11.3	8.1	8.9	9.4	7.6	7.8	7.2
B. Processed petroleum products	1.3	2.3	6.0	4.1	5.7	4.7	2.4	2.3	2.8	2.2	22
C. Industrial products	27.5	37.7	43.8	48.1	55.1	62.5	60.1	67.5	66.3	68.1	69.9
Cement	1.4	4.2	3.6	1.4	0.8	0.6	0.4	0.1	0.1	0.3	0.6
Chemical industry products	2.6	2.0	2.6	2.1	2.4	3.3	4.7	5.2	6.3	6.7	4.8
Rubber and plastic industry products	0.5	1.5	1.1	1.3	1.4	1.4	1.9	2.5	3.0	2.7	1.8
Hides and skin products	1.7	1.7	1.9	3.4	5.6	6.1	4.6	7.1	4.4	5.2	5.8
Forestry products	0.1	0.4	0.6	0.3	0.3	1.3	0.7	0.3	0.2	0.2	0.2
Textile products	14.6	17.1	18.4	22.7	26.3	22.5	24.8	26.6	27.4	30.1	31.3
Glass, ceramics, brick–tile products	1.2	2.2	1.8	1.9	2.0	2.4	2.1	2.0	2.0	2.2	2.5

Iron and steel products	1.2	2.1	6.3	7.1	8.1	12.2	10.8	8.4	12.5	11.6	12.4
Non-ferrous metal products	0.6	0.6	0.8	1.4	1.2	1.4	1.5	1.3	1.9	2.2	1.9
Metallic goods industry products	0.3	0.4	0.5	0.3	0.2	0.9	0.8	1.1	0.4	0.3	0.3
Machinery	0.8	1.4	2.0	1.8	1.7	4.7	2.7	6.7	2.9	1.7	1.6
Electric machinery and equipment	0.4	0.6	1.3	1.2	1.4	1.5	1.7	2.9	2.5	2.0	3.4
Motor vehicles, parts and accessories thereof	1.7	2.5	1.9	2.2	1.9	1.8	1.1	1.1	1.0	13.4	1.6
Other industrial products	0.3	0.9	1.1	1.1	1.8	2.4	2.2	2.4	1.6	1.7	1.6

SOURCE: Undersecretariat of Treasury and Foreign Trade, *Economic Indicators* (Ankara).

of exports, specifically manufactured exports. Accordingly, a series of export-promotion schemes was put into effect during the period. These schemes were sector specific and had differing impacts on the various sectors. The nominal rates of subsidy show that the manufacturing sector received preferential treatment with the highest nominal subsidy rates compared with the agriculture and mining and energy sectors. Within industry, intermediate and investment goods had the highest subsidy rates. The subsidies for consumer goods were low but, among these, durables and non-durables received relatively high subsidies (Togan, 1992).

There are wide differences in the growth rates of sectoral exports within manufacturing industry. Textiles, the traditional manufactured exports of Turkey, maintained their importance. In 1980, 14.5 per cent of the total exports were textile products, whereas in 1990 31.3 per cent of the total exports were from this industry. Textile products became the major export item of Turkey, with their value exceeding the value of total agricultural product exports by a factor of two. The fastest export growth was observed in two non-traditional export sectors: iron and steel products and electrical machinery and equipment (Table 8.3). By 1990, iron and steel products became the second most important manufactured exports with 12.4 per cent of total exports. In 1980, only 1.2 per cent of exports were from this industry. Electrical machinery increased its share of total exports to 3.4 from 0.4 per cent during the same period.

Among the rest of the industrial products, traditional exports such as hides and skin products, and non-traditional export items like rubber and plastic industry products and non-ferrous metal products are the sectors whose exports grew faster than average industrial export growth. By 1990, after the change in the composition of exports, the hides and skin products industry (which comprise 5.8 per cent of total exports), chemical industry (4.8 per cent) electrical machinery and equipment (3.4 per cent), and glass, ceramic and brick–tile products (2.5. per cent) became the important industrial goods exports of Turkey (Table 8.3).

The main objective of the new development strategy was industrialization through export growth. Resources were reallocated from the agricultural sector to industry and the importance of industrial goods exports increased. However, the desired diversification of manufactured exports was not achieved during this period. Textile products, with 39.5 per cent of total manufactured exports, continued to be the major export item. Only a limited amount of diversification was obtained through growth in the share of iron and steel, hides and skins

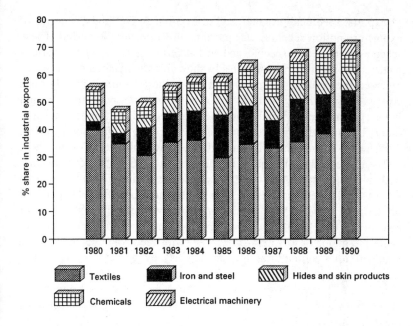

FIGURE *8.1*   *Composition of Turkey's manufacturing exports*

and chemical industry product exports. The iron and steel products share was 15.7 per cent of total industrial exports in 1990. With these changes, the important manufactured exports became hides and skin products (7.3 per cent), chemical industry exports (6 per cent) and electrical machinery and equipment (4.3 per cent). These five manufacturing exports constitute 72.4 per cent of the total industrial product exports by 1990, compared with a share of 56.5 per cent in 1980 (Figure 8.1).

The expansion in manufactured exports was concentrated in relatively labour intensive sectors such as textiles, clothing and leather. There are some new export sectors, such as iron and steel and chemicals which increased in importance both in value of absolute exports and their share in total manufactured exports that are more capital intensive in their production technology. But their relative importance in total exports is not high (see Table 8.4).

Next, we turn to the sectoral properties of manufacturing industry and changes in production conditions, in order to illustrate the interaction between necessary output growth and export supply growth. The commodity classification of industrial products in the foreign trade and manufacturing industry data do not tally, but by using the information

TABLE 8.4 *Commodity composition of manufacturing industry exports (% of industrial exports)*

	1980	1981	1982	1983	1984	1985	1986	1987	1988	1989	1990
A. Processed agricultural products	20.0	18.0	16.6	18.3	15.7	10.8	12.5	11.8	9.9	10.0	9.1
B. Processed petroleum products	3.7	4.7	10.0	6.3	7.9	6.2	3.3	2.9	3.7	2.8	2.8
C. Industrial products	76.3	77.3	73.4	75.3	76.3	83.0	84.1	85.3	86.4	87.2	88.1
Cement	3.8	8.6	6.0	2.2	1.1	0.7	0.5	0.1	0.1	0.4	0.7
Chemical industry products	7.3	4.1	4.3	3.3	3.4	4.4	6.6	6.5	8.2	8.5	6.0
Rubber and plastic industry products	1.5	3.1	1.8	2.1	1.9	1.8	2.6	3.2	3.9	3.4	2.3
Hides and skin products	4.8	3.6	3.2	5.2	7.8	8.1	6.5	9.0	5.7	6.7	7.3
Forestry products	0.4	0.9	1.0	0.4	0.5	1.8	1.0	0.4	0.2	0.3	0.2
Textile products	40.5	35.1	30.8	35.5	36.4	29.8	34.8	33.6	35.8	38.6	39.5
Glass, ceramics, brick–tile products	3.4	4.5	3.0	3.0	2.8	3.2	3.0	2.5	2.6	2.8	3.2

Iron and steel products	3.2	4.4	10.6	11.1	11.2	16.2	15.1	10.6	16.3	14.8	15.7
Non-ferrous metal products	1.7	1.3	1.3	2.2	1.7	1.9	2.1	1.7	2.5	2.8	2.4
Metallic goods industry products	0.8	0.9	0.8	0.5	0.3	1.2	1.1	1.3	0.6	0.4	0.4
Machinery	2.1	2.8	3.4	2.8	2.3	6.3	3.8	8.4	3.7	2.1	2.0
Electric machinery and equipment	1.1	1.1	2.2	1.9	1.9	2.0	2.4	3.6	3.3	2.6	4.3
Motor vehicles, parts and accessories thereof	4.8	5.1	3.2	3.4	2.6	2.5	1.5	1.4	1.3	17.1	2.1
Other industrial products	1.0	1.8	1.8	1.7	2.4	3.2	3.1	3.1	2.1	2.1	2.0

SOURCE: Undersecretariat of Treasury and Foreign Trade, *Economic Indicators* (Ankara).

on the manufacturing industry it is possible to capture some of the crucial elements of the sectors whose products are major export items.

In an open economy, supply of exports can be increased either through increased production or reduced domestic absorption. Between 1980 and 1989, value added increased in all sectors (see Table 8.3 for the manufacturing sector data). Even though the rate of growth was slightly higher in the sectors whose outputs were also the main export items, such as basic metals and textiles, and slightly lower in sectors whose export growth was below average, such as forestry products, there is no definite relationship between the rate of export growth and output growth. It is clear that the growth of value added in all sectors lagged behind the growth of total exports from the sector. This provides some support for the contention that depressed domestic demand contributed to rapid export expansion.

Although at a slower pace than the expansion in exports, the increase in manufacturing output led to changes in the capital and labour use of sectors. The incremental capital output ratio in all sectors increased in the first half of the period and showed a decline towards the end of the decade. The largest increase in the incremental capital–output ratio was observed in textiles and basic metals, the two most important export items.

Although the incremental capital output ratio grew in all sectors, there were wide differences in the rate of capital accumulation between sectors. There are no clear relationships between the differential investment rate, export performance and the export subsidies given to the various sectors. All manufacturing industry, except for food processing and mining, was receiving above-average export subsidies during the period. Exports of iron and steel, non-ferrous metals, electrical machinery, chemicals, and rubber and plastic products received relatively high subsidies and showed rapid increase in exports. But among these sectors, the additions to capital stock was highest in iron and steel and electrical machinery. In the chemicals, rubber and plastic industries, with highly capital intensive production technology, the net additions to capital stock per unit of value added was the lowest among all sectors. On the other hand, forestry products, with high subsidy rates, showed a meagre expansion in exports, and output growth and investment per value added was the lowest among all the manufacturing sectors. Declining incremental capital–output ratios for the period proves that the export drive did not create enough impetus for expansion in capacity of the sectors and the initial expansion in output was achieved through the use of excess production capacity.

In order to examine the employment effect of export expansion in the manufacturing industry, one can evaluate the data for labour per unit of value added in all the sectors. If there are no changes in the production technology, this ratio will indicate the impact of output growth on employment in an industry. The most noticeable fact is that in all sectors, both labour-intensive sectors such as textiles, food processing and machinery and capital-intensive sectors such as chemicals and basic metals, labour per unit of value added declined throughout the period. Part of this decline can be attributed to labour productivity increase. Another explanation is that at the outset of export promotion policies, the sectors had both excess capacity and the labour employed was not fully utilized. The necessary expansion in output was achieved with increased utilization of the existing capital equipment and increased labour demand at a proportionately slower rate than the increase in output. Both the sectoral diversification created in the exports sectors towards capital intensive production, and the decline in labour per value added present a pessimistic picture in terms of the employment creation effects of export expansion.

Similar conclusions about the capacity expansion and employment effects follow from the performance of the capital–labor ratio in manufacturing. In most of the manufacturing sectors K/L ratios declined during the period. This was observed in the case of both labour-intensive products, such as textiles and clothing, leather and food processing, and capital-intensive sectors, such as basic metals. In chemicals, rubber and plastics the K/L ratios increased slightly during the first half of the decade and declined during the latter half. This also indicates that increased output was achieved with increased utilization of available excess capacity. The expansion of exports did not lead to a permanent increase in investment and capacity of production. These issues are elaborated upon in the next section.

3   INTERFACE OF EXPORT EXPANSION, ACCUMULATION AND DISTRIBUTION

We now turn to an analysis of the sectoral implications of export expansion to deduce the informal economic linkages between exports, employment, capital accumulation and distribution at the functional level. In so doing, we follow the consumer versus producer manufacturing dichotomy. We believe such a distinction is relevant, as it underscores the relative effectiveness of the non-traditional export expansion as opposed to that of the traditional sectors.

More formally, we study two distinct routes of interface throughout the export-led growth episode; first is the exports–employment–
exchange rate linkage. Second, we investigate the linkage between sectoral
capital accumulation and the profit–wage frontier. We do not, however, analyse cause–effect relationships, since it is our contention that
the movements of each indicator are intermixed with each other to
such a degree that isolation of any one as the 'causal' link may be misleading.

Figure 8.2 depicts the first mechanism we are interested in. Here we
plot export per worker (*X/L* on the left-hand scale), and depreciation
versus wage costs (on the right-hand scale) in the consumer (Figure
8.2a) and the producer (Figure 8.2b) manufacturing industries from
1980 to 1989. The exports per worker indicator takes account of both
sectoral export expansion and employment expansion. Thus, a steep
rise in the *X/L* ratio is a mixed blessing in that, while it shows successful export performance, it also signals meager employment creation in the sector. On the right-hand scale, we treat labour as our numerate
entity, and we normalize the nominal exchange rate by the nominal
wage rate. Here again, the observed indicator is the result of two effects: while exports are promoted by depreciation of the exchange rate,
rising wage costs inhibit export performance. The latter effect occurs
both because of increased production costs and increased domestic
consumption demand which diverts producers away from export markets towards domestic markets.

Figures 8.2a and b show a direct relationship between exports per
worker (*X/L*) and the exchange rate over wage ratio (*ER/W*). This is
true for both the consumer and the producer manufacturing, yielding
almost the same *X/L* ratios over time. *Per contra*, the *ER/W* ratio is
observed to rise until 1985 and to taper off with a sudden fall in 1989.
Here, the ratio follows a higher numerical value in the consumer manufacturing. This reveals that the wage renumerations were higher in
the non-traditional (producer manufacturing) industries; or, to put it differ-
ently, traditional sectors, which are labour intensive in character, exploited
wage reductions quite successfully. As Table 8.1 attests, average wage
rates in manufacturing fell by as much as 40 per cent in real terms between 1980 and 1988. Yeldan (1993) confirms that this trend was more
pronounced in the private sector since, in most cases, public enterprises
continued to employ labour at politically regulated wage rates. While
it is a widely recognized fact that the quality of such data on factor
incomes is limited and suffers from severe shortcomings. Many independent researchers confirm a severe decline in the share of wage income,

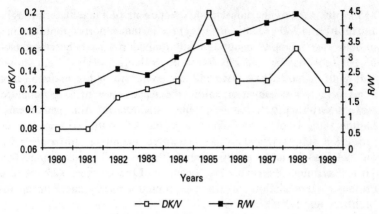

DK/V : ratio of gross additions to capital stock to aggregate value added
R/W : ratio of aggregate profits to aggregate wages

FIGURE 8.2a   *Capital accumulation and the profit–wage frontier in consumer manufacturing*

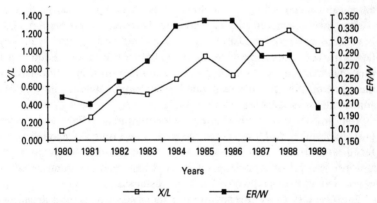

X/L : real exports (in 1980 million TL) per worker employed
ER/W : exchange rate (TL/$) – wage rate (in current thousands TL) ratio

FIGURE 8.2b   *Exports per worker and depreciation versus wage costs in producer manufacturing*

and of the size of the non-labour component of manufacturing value added in the 1980s. Ozmucur (1991) for instance, argues that the share of non-wage income in non-agricultural value added increased from 65 per cent in 1980 to 72 per cent in 1991.

It is to be noted that price inflation was one of the major components of this mechanism enabling the wage squeeze to be captured both as surplus profits for the producers and as inflation tax revenues for the state. Implemented under a regime of continued currency depreciation supplemented by direct export incentives, inflation policy did not lead to any loss of competitiveness of Turkish exportables. This mechanism, however, lost steam by 1988 as the possibilities of prolonged depreciation and wage suppression finally came up against 'political reality' (Onis, 1991).

The interaction of the exchange-rate administration with the wage cost realization documents a three period categorization of the export-led path in the 1980s: the first sub-period covers 1980 through mid-1983, when the sector 'recovered' and responded to the market signals which were transmitted through depreciation of the currency and the price reforms. Here, X/L starts to gradually pick up, while the downward movement in ER/W occurs at a modest scale. However, in the second sub-period, from 1983 to the end of 1986, both series disclose an abrupt acceleration. We believe it is in this sub-period that the classic mechanism of surplus extraction for export promotion could have been exploited in Turkish manufacturing: wage costs were held down in real terms; liberalization provided new sources of funding in financial markets; and exchange rate administration had 'matured' in the sense that the process responded to incentives without the need for sudden devaluation on a massive scale.

The strategy began to disintegrate beginning in 1987, and the export performance of the sector faltered. The domestic economy was faced with the uncertainties which we have earlier referred to as the 'reform fatigue' phenomenon. In other words, policies contributing to export-led growth paths could not be sustained.

We now turn to an investigation of the pattern of capital accumulation in the face of developments in the profit–wage frontier over the decade. For this purpose we utilize information exhibited in Figures 8.3a and 8.3b. On the left-hand scale of Figures 8.3*a* and 8.3*b*, we plot the ratio of 'gross additions to capital stock' to sectoral value added (dK/V). This data covers expenditures made on new or used fixed assets purchased from the domestic market, fixed assets imported, and fixed assets produced by the establishment's own staff. Major repairs

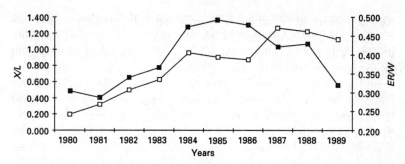

X/L   : real exports in (in 1980 million TL) per worker employed
ER/W   : exchange rate (TL/$) – wage rate (in current thousands TL) ratio

FIGURE 8.3a   *Exports per worker and depreciation versus wage costs in consumer manufacturing*

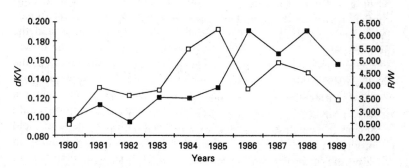

DK/V   : ratio of gross additions to capital stock to aggregate value added
R/W   : ratio of aggregate profits to aggregate wages

FIGURE 8.3b   *Capital accumulation and the profit–wage frontier in producer manufacturing*

and expenditures made on plant studies and plans as well as on land improvements are included in this category.

We compare this ratio with the historical path of profits–wages ratio (R/W) which appears on the right-hand scale. Thus we adopt an accelerationist approach to capital accumulation, in response to signals of profitability and labour costs. Data reveal a secular upward movement in the dK/V ratio in both sectors, reaching a peak of approximately 0.2 in 1985. It is interesting to note that from 1985 the consumer goods and producer goods industries exhibit divergent factor-industries.

Re-interpreting dK/V values as incremental capital–output ratios, we observe that in the first half of the decade, consumer manufacturing displays a lower score, as is to be expected given its labour-intensive character. After 1985, however, dK/V of consumer manufacturing exceeds that of producer manufacturing, with the single exception for the year 1987. This suggests a sluggish growth of capital investments in the producer manufacturing industries, with consequences for productivity growth in the longer run. Clearly, much remains to be understood with regard to the meagre performance of capital accumulation over the decade. As Rittenberg (1991) reports, private fixed investments grew at about half the rate of growth of the pre-crisis period, returning to its 1979 level only after 1986. Thus, aggregate manufacturing investments increased by only 15 per cent in real terms at the end of the decade as compared to their 1980 values.

However, the industrial enterprises appear to have capitalized on the on-going export expansion through sharp shifts in the profit–wage frontier, which can be regarded as a necessary condition for the adoption of the new strategy by the capital owners. The growth of the R/W ratio was especially pronounced in producer manufacturing.

In sum, the export-led growth strategy accomplished an important transformation in the composition of Turkey's exports and promoted resource reallocation from the agricultural sector to industrial sectors. However, the necessary level of diversification of strategy did not lead to the hoped-for industrial product exports. The traditional manufactured exports items continued to account for the bulk of exports. The distinguishing characteristic of the Turkish export performance during the period was that it rested on the extraction of resources for exports by suppressing domestic demand through wage reduction and currency devaluation. This surplus was exported to foreign markets with the provision of generous subsidies and led to increasing profits. This process, however, had limited resource-pull effect on the rest of the economy, and could not lead to rapid labour employment. Coupled with an overall decline in the share of physical investments in traded goods, such export expansion based on wage reductions and price incentives hit its political limits in the late 1980s and began to falter. It is unlikely that in the near future this rapid increase in exports will continue and the newly emerging export sectors will increase their overall significance in the economy.

The new 'strategy' of export-led expansion, however, biased incentives towards export-oriented manufacturing capital, but this lasted for only a relatively short time span, which was not long enough to lift the economy on to a sustainable growth path.

NOTES

1. Note that the quoted figure is an amalgam of various 'officially' set rates of tariffs, tax-like surcharges and various levies. Thus, the 'actual' rate of protection which includes concessions and/or evasions, yields a smaller figure. For elaboration of this point, see Celâsun (1992).
2. Industrial good exports include 7.2 per cent of processed agricultural products, 1.3 per cent of processed petroleum products and 27.5 per cent of industrial product exports. The increase in the industry exports share was due to the increase in the industrial products. The share of the processed agricultural goods exports and petroleum products remained the same through the period, but the share of the industrial products increased to 69.9 per cent of the total exports.
3. The only country which came close to changing its export composition towards manufactured good exports as rapidly is Taiwan, which increased the share of the manufactured export from 41.3 to 80.2 per cent between 1965 and 1976 (Sarkar and Singer, 1991).

REFERENCES

Asikoğlu, Y. and Uctum, M. (1992), 'Exchange Rates in Turkey', *World Development*, vol. 20, pp. 1501–14.
Boratav, K. (1992), *1980'li Yillarda Turkiye'de Sosyal Siniflar ve Bolusum* (Istanbul: Gercek Yay).
Celâsun, M. (1989), 'Income Distribution and Employment Aspect of Turkey's Post-1980 Adjustment', *METU Studies in Development*. vol. 16, nos 3–4, pp. 1–32.
Celâsun, M. (1992), 'Trade and Industrialization in Turkey: Initial Conditions, Policy and Performance in the 1980s', paper presented at the Bilkent–Lancaster Joint Conference on the 'Turkish Economy since Liberalization', Ankara, October 1992 (mimeo).
Celâsun, M. and Rodrik D. (1989), 'Debt, Adjustment and Growth: Turkey', Book IV in J. Sachs and M. Collins (eds), *Developing Country Debt and Economic Performance: Country Studies* (Chicago, IL: The University of Chicago Press).
Ersel, H. (1991), 'Structural Adjustment: Turkey, 1980–1990', paper presented at the IMF–Pakistan Administrative Staff College Joint Seminar, Lahore, 26–28 October 1991 (mimeo).
Olgun, H. and Togan, S. (1991) 'Trade Liberalization and Structure of Protection in Turkey in the 1980s: A Quantitative Approach', *Weltwirtschaftlishes Aerchiv*, **vol.** 127(1), pp. 152–70.
Onis, Z. (1991), 'Political Economy of Turkey in the 1980s: Anatomy of Unorthodox Liberalism', in M. Heper (ed.), *Strong State and Economic Interest Groups: The Post-1980 Turkish Experience* (Berlin: de Gragter) Ch. 2.
Onis, Z. and Riedel, J. (1993), *Economic Crises and Long-Term Growth in Turkey* (Washington, DC: World Bank).

Ozmucur, S. (1991), 'Price and Income Distribution', Bogazici Universitesi Research Papers, No. 155/EC 91-17.

Rittenberg, L. (1991), 'Investment Spending and Interest Rate Policy: The Case of Financial Liberalization in Turkey', *Journal of Development Studies*, vol. 27, pp. 151–67.

Sarkar, P. and Singer, J. W. (1991), 'Manufactured Exports of Developing Countries and Their Terms of Trade Since 1965', *World Development*, vol. 19, no. 4, pp. 333–40.

Senses, F. and Yamada, T. (1990), *Stabilization and Structural Adjustment Program in Turkey* (Tokyo: Institute of Developing Economics Research Programme Series, no. 85).

State Institute of Statistics (SIS), *Statistical Yearbook of Turkey* (various years), Ankara.

Togan, S. (1992), *Foreign Trade Regime and Liberalization of Foreign Trade in Turkey during 1980s* (Ankara: Turkish Eximbank).

Yeldan, E. (1994), 'The Economic Structure of Power under Turkish Structural Adjustment: Prices, Growth and Accumulation', in F. Senses (ed.), *Recent Industrialization Experience of Turkey in a Global Context* (London: Greenwood Press) Ch. 6, pp. 75–80.

9 Liberalization, Export Incentives and Exchange Rate Policy: Turkey's Experience in the 1980s

Oktan H. Aktan

1 INTRODUCTION

The year 1980 marked the beginning of a new era in Turkey in terms of economic policies. On 24 January 1980, the Turkish Government announced a major economic reform programme. In addition to the inauguration of a stabilization programme backed by the International Monetary Fund, a multitude of accompanying policies, with a wide and varying impact on many sectors of the economy, were introduced. All these policies had components of earlier policy packages of 1958 and 1970. The main novelty of the policies of 24 January was, however, that in addition to the usual stabilization measures, the Government intended to liberalize the economy generally, and place greater reliance on market forces rather than state intervention.

The consequences of the stabilization policies are beyond the scope of this paper (see Krueger and Aktan, 1992). It suffices to remark here that the achievements of the programme of trade liberalization and the pursuit of an outer-oriented trade regime are remarkable by any standard. Exports have become a major engine of growth. Turkey's exports, measured in US dollars, grew at an average annual rate of 22.2 per cent from 1980 to 1985 at a time when world trade was almost stagnant. They continued to grow rapidly in the latter half of the 1980s, reaching just under US$13 billion in 1990 from $2.9 billion in 1980. Imports showed a similar trend: the rate of growth of imports reached 11 per cent per annum in the 1980–90 period, compared to the average rate of 1.7 per cent in the preceding five-year period, reaching $22 billion in 1990 from $7.9 billion in 1980. Consequently, exports' share in GNP increased from 5 per cent in 1980 to 12 per cent in 1990, and that of imports from 13.9 per cent to 20.6 per cent.

The major factors contributing to the success story of exports were undoubtedly the liberalization of the trade and exchange regimes on the one hand, and heavy reliance on export subsidies, on the other. The crucial role of exchange-rate policy in eliminating the overvaluation of the currency, especially during inflationary periods, for the success of the exports performance was also recognized by the policy-makers. A more flexible exchange rate policy was introduced right from the beginning as an integral part of the liberalization policy of the 1980s. Following the major devaluation of the Turkish lira in January 1980 (whereby the dollar rate of the lira was increased from TL 47 to TL 70), eleven mini-devaluations were affected in the following 16 months. Starting from 1 May 1981, the exchange rate has been adjusted on a daily basis, with a view to compensate for fluctuations in purchasing power parity of the lira.

The flexible exchange-rate policy has been successful in eliminating the differences between the official and black market (later free market) rates. However, the much more interesting question is whether this policy has also been successful in eliminating the bias against exports. In other words, whether the goal of the policy changes in the trade and payments regime in the 1980s, with the express purpose of making exports more attractive to domestic producers and import-substituting production somewhat less profitable than it has been in the preceding decades, has been realized. This chapter addresses the issue.

In the first part of the chapters the liberalization efforts will be reviewed very briefly with a view to quantifying the changes in protection for import-competing industries. In the second part, export subsidies and incentives will be analysed to estimate the real exchange rates for manufactured exports. The behaviour of the real exchange rate during the 1980s will be examined in the third part of the paper. On the basis of these calculations, the change in relative profitability and, therefore, the bias of trade and payment regime resulting from the reforms of the 1980s may be analyzed.

2   LIBERALIZATION OF THE IMPORT REGIME

2.1   Changes in tariffs and surcharges on imports

Imported goods are subject to customs duty and various other charges in Turkey. Some of these charges are made for revenue purposes, and others for protecting domestic industries. In addition to customs duty, the charges include municipality tax, stamp duty, wharf tax, value added

TABLE *9.1   Total charges on imports*

Customs duty collected (*cd*) = *c.i.f.* × t
Municipality tax (*mt*) = *cd* × *m*
Stamp duty (*sd*) = *c.i.f.* × *s*
Funds (*f*) = specific rates
Wharf tax (*wt*) = (*c.i.f.* + *cd* + *mt* + *f* + *sd*) × *w*
Value-added tax (*vat*) = (*c.i.f.* + *cd* + *mt* + *f* + *sd*) *v*
Deposit requirements for importation (*g*)

where
  t = the rate of nominal tariff
  m = 15 per cent through the entire period
  s = 1 per cent, 1980 – May 1985
       4 per cent, June 1985 – December 1986
       6 per cent, January 1987 – October 1988
       10 per cent, November 1988 to date
  w = 15 per cent throughout
  v = 0 until January 1985[a]
       10 per cent, January 1985 – October 1985
       12 per cent, November 1986 – October 1988
       10 per cent, November 1988 – 1990
  g = 3.8 per cent, 1980
       10 per cent, 1981 and 1982
       7 per cent, 1983
       7.8 per cent, 1984
       5.2 per cent, 1985
       0.6 per cent, 1986
       2.7 per cent, 1987
       4.3 per cent, 1988
       12.0 per cent, April 1989
       7.0 per cent, May 1989
       5.0 per cent, June 1989
       0 per cent, 1990

Total charges against imports = *cd* + *mt* + *sd* + *f* + *wt* + *vat* + *g*

NOTE: [a]Before 1985 production tax with variable rates.

tax (prior to 1985, production tax), and charges for funds. Table 9.1 presents a schematic representation of these levies.

There is no time-series data of nominal protection rates which would permit an analysis of their growth over time, and such a calculation is outside the scope of this chapter. Furthermore, the duty rates were so specific and changed so frequently and, especially prior to 1985, there were so many exemptions that the only way to provide an estimate of their effect was to take a sample of commodities and trace the evolution

TABLE 9.2 Total protection: import duties and other charges, 1980–91

	1980	1981	1982	1983	1984	1985	1986	1987	1988	1989	1990	1991	Change 1980–91
Food and beverages													
Soy oil	60.1	66.3	66.3	9.0	12.5	7.4	25.1	41.4	16.4	64.8	32.0	32.0	−28.1
Whiskey	226.7	232.9	232.9	205.8	731.6	242.6	227.4	233.8	240.6	247.8	247.8	247.8	21.1
Tomato paste	72.2	78.4	78.4	75.4	76.2	30.7	35.7	40.7	48.2	78.3	162.0	162.0	89.8
Minerals													
Calcium phosphate	10.8	27.0	12.0	24.0	24.8	17.2	12.6	19.0	23.1	37.0	27.0	27.0	16.2
Cement	57.0	63.2	63.2	60.2	15.8	24.7	21.6	19.0	23.1	27.0	43.7	44.7	−12.3
Asbestos	44.9	51.1	51.1	48.1	48.9	42.8	33.7	40.1	46.8	54.1	54.1	54.1	9.2
Copper ore	17.8	24.0	24.0	21.0	9.8	24.7	21.6	28.0	34.8	42.0	27.0	27.0	9.2
Aluminium ore	17.8	24.0	24.0	21.0	9.8	24.7	21.6	28.0	34.8	42.0	27.0	27.0	9.2
Mineral fuels													
Coal	84.3	90.5	90.5	87.5	88.3	25.9	29.5	37.9	35.4	39.3	39.3	39.3	−45.0
Lignite	84.3	90.5	90.5	87.5	88.3	25.9	12.6	19.0	42.0	45.9	45.9	45.9	−38.4
Coke	84.3	90.5	90.5	87.5	15.8	25.9	22.8	29.2	36.0	27.0	27.0	27.0	−57.3
Chemicals													
Phosphoric acid	47.9	54.1	54.1	51.1	39.9	36.8	33.7	40.1	46.8	48.0	27.0	27.0	−20.9
Sodium hydroxide	66.0	72.2	72.2	81.3	52.0	48.9	96.4	90.0	37.7	28.6	42.0	42.0	−24.0
Sodium sulphure	66.0	72.2	72.2	81.3	141.3	99.0	88.0	90.9	107.3	113.6	42.2	42.2	−23.8
Teraflatic acid	66.0	72.2	72.2	69.2	39.9	36.8	42.9	37.7	44.4	39.9	37.0	37.0	−29.0
Phetsalic anhydrite	66.0	72.2	72.2	69.2	52.0	63.2	65.7	65.3	69.7	77.0	58.5	58.5	−7.5
Ammonium sulphate	36.0	42.2	42.2	39.2	40.0	48.9	56.1	53.5	45.8	42.1	37.0	37.0	1.1
Organic dyes	51.0	57.2	57.2	54.2	37.9	36.8	33.7	40.1	46.8	54.1	43.2	43.2	−7.7

Rubber and plastic													
Polyester chips	97.2	103.4	103.4	100.4	57.6	51.9	47.0	53.5	61.7	54.1	43.2	43.2	-54.0
Silicons	97.2	103.4	103.4	52.1	45.9	36.8	33.7	40.1	46.8	54.1	43.2	43.2	-54.0
Latex	54.9	61.1	61.1	58.1	39.8	30.7	27.6	34.0	36.0	42.0	27.0	27.0	-27.9
Tires (truck)	68.1	74.3	74.3	71.3	103.2	76.9	57.0	63.4	70.2	54.1	48.0	48.0	-20.1
Leather, hides and fur													
Hides	23.9	30.1	30.1	21.0	15.8	24.7	12.6	19.0	23.1	37.0	27.0	27.0	3.1
Sole leather	132.6	138.8	138.8	135.8	136.6	42.8	32.1	19.0	41.7	47.0	40.6	40.6	-92.0
Leatherwear	192.9	199.1	199.1	196.1	196.9	205.8	122.4	76.3	102.6	121.8	60.1	60.1	-132.8
Paper and products													
Wood pulp	29.9	36.1	36.1	48.1	9.8	24.7	12.6	19.0	23.1	37.0	27.0	27.0	-2.9
Newsprints	25.8	27.0	27.0	60.2	27.0	63.7	50.7	44.9	34.8	43.2	44.1	44.1	18.3
Craft paper	74.1	80.3	80.3	77.3	67.0	68.9	66.4	69.5	64.2	57.5	48.1	48.1	-25.9
Cotton and cotton textiles													
Cotton	23.9	30.1	30.1	135.8	28.2	17.5	12.7	19.0	23.1	27.0	27.0	27.0	3.1
Long-fibre cotton	23.9	30.1	30.1	27.1	27.9	36.8	33.7	40.1	46.8	54.1	27.0	27.0	3.1
Cotton textiles	114.3	120.5	120.5	117.5	52.0	48.9	45.8	52.2	58.9	46.2	42.0	59.7	-54.6
Cotton T-shirts	150.6	156.8	156.8	183.9	76.1	73.0	69.9	76.3	83.1	72.7	60.6	60.6	-89.9
Glass ceramic													
Tiles	152.6	158.8	158.8	155.8	156.6	60.9	33.7	40.1	46.8	60.2	58.5	58.5	-94.0
Porcelain tableware	152.6	158.8	158.8	155.8	156.6	60.9	69.9	76.3	83.1	127.9	109.8	109.8	-42.8
Glass, col., uncol.	162.6	168.8	168.8	165.6	166.6	73.0	57.8	64.2	71.0	66.2	54.1	54.1	-108.5
Ordinary glass	72.2	78.4	78.4	75.4	76.2	85.1	57.8	64.2	58.9	66.2	54.1	54.1	-18.1
Iron and steel													
Blooms, billets	44.9	51.1	51.1	37.1	25.0	26.4	33.3	39.7	46.5	37.0	58.3	58.3	13.4
Coils for rerolling	32.8	39.0	39.0	37.1	25.0	26.3	31.2	37.6	36.4	44.7	44.7	44.7	11.8
Non-ferrous metals													
Blister copper	53.9	60.1	60.1	81.2	37.0	25.9	22.8	29.2	36.0	27.0	27.0	27.0	-26.9
Aluminium	53.9	60.1	60.1	39.0	9.8	17.2	12.6	19.0	23.1	27.2	27.0	27.0	-26.9

cont. on page 182

182

TABLE 9.2 *continued*

	1980	1981	1982	1983	1984	1985	1986	1987	1988	1989	1990	1991	Change 1980–91
Metal products													
Saw blades	82.2	88.4	88.4	85.4	74.1	73.0	69.9	76.3	83.1	99.2	54.1	54.1	−28.1
Drill bits	82.2	88.4	88.4	85.4	86.2	60.9	57.8	64.2	71.0	99.2	48.0	48.0	−34.1
Non-electric machinery													
Grinders, mills	109.3	115.5	115.5	112.5	113.3	60.9	57.8	64.2	71.0	78.2	60.1	60.1	−49.1
Electric machinery													
Refrigerators	88.3	94.5	94.5	91.5	116.0	88.8	69.9	76.3	68.0	57.1	61.5	61.5	−26.7
Dishwashers	56.0	62.2	62.2	53.2	114.1	96.9	81.2	87.6	97.4	57.1	99.1	99.1	43.1
Transformers	97.2	103.4	103.4	100.4	50.0	48.9	45.8	52.2	58.9	72.7	55.0	55.0	−42.2
Hairdryers	94.3	100.5	100.5	97.5	98.3	73.0	69.9	76.3	83.1	120.2	69.8	69.8	−24.4
Radios	77.2	83.4	83.4	85.4	219.5	178.0	174.9	181.3	191.1	95.4	63.4	63.4	−13.8
TVs (colour)	92.2	98.4	88.4	100.4	121.9	93.0	89.9	96.3	106.0	78.5	60.2	60.2	−32.0
Transport equipment													
Motor cars	112.4	118.6	115.6	115.6	119.3	121.8	127.0	88.4	98.1	69.2	95.4	95.4	−17.0
Buses	112.4	118.6	118.6	115.6	119.3	121.8	127.0	88.4	83.1	66.2	65.4	65.4	−47.0
Others													
VCR	104.3	110.5	110.5	107.5	121.4	127.1	106.7	113.1	122.8	84.9	67.6	67.6	−36.7
Magnetic tapes	80.1	86.3	86.3	107.5	62.0	60.9	57.8	64.2	71.0	78.2	75.1	75.1	−5.0

of their treatment through time. The results for customs duties and other charges are given in Table 9.2.

2.2 Quantitative restrictions

The most significant steps in the liberalization process were the abolition, in 1981, of quotas representing 12 per cent of 1980 imports, and the change in the protection mechanism. Prior to 1984, imports were regulated by several lists, which were announced every year and which listed goods, the importation of which were either allowed (liberalized lists) or restricted quantitatively (quota list). The importation of an item no listed in either of these lists was, therefore, prohibited. The 1984 import regime adopted a negative list actually specifying the prohibited items. The gradual liberalization of imports may be traced by examining Table 9.3. The number of goods whose importation was subject to prior approval was reduced from 1137 in 1984 to 33 in 1988, and was abolished altogether in 1990. Those items which were listed under the fund list could be imported freely, but were subject to specific charges earmarked for the Housing Fund.

The abolition of import prohibitions (with the exception of narcotics, weapons and ammunition) was realized in 1985. In 1990, the fund list was abolished, making importation (with the exception of three groups of commodities) virtually free. (A further liberalization occurred in 1990, when the number of items subject to fund charges was reduced from 1180 in 1989 to 598).

These measures virtually abolished import licensing in Turkey as an effective means of maintaining domestic prices of import-competing goods above international prices. Without careful analysis of detailed data on domestic and foreign prices and duty rates on imported commodities, however, it is impossible to estimate with any degree of confidence the extent to which liberalization reduced the protection afforded to import competing goods. It would be highly misleading, however, to estimate effective exchange rates without recognizing the impact of quantitative restrictions on imports. Somewhat arbitrarily, therefore, it has been assumed that quantitative restrictions imposed an additional 50-percentage-point wedge between the landed cost of import-competing items and their domestic prices in 1980, 40 per cent in 1981, 30 per cent in 1982 and 1983, 20 per cent in 1984, 10 per cent in 1985, and zero per cent thereafter. The effects of both customs duties and other charges, and of quantitative restrictions are presented in Table 9.4.

TABLE 9.3 *Liberalization of trade regime: numbers of commodities on various import lists, 1979–90*

	1979	1980	1981	1982	1983	1984	1985	1986	1987	1988	1989	1990
A. 'Positive' List System[a]												
1. Liberalized List I	1600	653	942	956	956							
2. Liberalized List II		958	835	821	821							
3. Quota List	345	312	–	–	–							
4. Fund List[b]		–	–	23	35							
B. 'Negative' List System[c]												
1. Prior Approval List						1137	638	245	111	33	37	–
2. Fund List						67	153	347	570	784	1180	598
3. Prohibited List[d]						459	3	3	3	3	3	3

SOURCE: *Official Gazette*, various years.

NOTES: [a] Abolished at the end of 1983.
[b] Introduced with 1982 import programme.
[c] Introduced January 1984.
[d] Virtually abolished in May 1985.

TABLE 9.4 Total protection: impact of import duties and quantitative restrictions, by commodity group 1980–91 (estimated percentage c.i.f. price)

	1980	1981	1982	1983	1984	1985	1986	1987	1988	1989	1990	1991	Change (1980–91)
Food and beverages[a]	116.1	112.3	102.3	72.2	64.3	29.1	30.4	41.0	32.3	71.6	97.0	97.0	−19.2
Minerals	79.7	77.9	64.9	64.9	41.8	36.8	22.2	26.8	32.5	40.4	35.8	36.0	−43.7
Mineral fuels	134.3	130.5	120.5	117.5	84.1	35.9	21.6	28.7	37.8	37.4	37.4	37.4	−96.9
Chemicals	107.0	103.2	93.2	93.6	77.5	62.9	59.5	59.6	56.9	57.6	41.0	41.0	−66.0
Rubber and plastic	129.3	125.5	115.5	100.5	81.6	59.1	41.3	47.8	53.7	51.1	40.4	40.4	−89.0
Leather, hides and fur	166.5	162.7	152.7	147.6	136.4	101.1	55.7	38.1	55.8	68.6	42.6	42.6	−123.9
Paper and products	93.3	87.8	77.8	91.9	54.6	62.4	43.3	44.5	40.7	45.9	39.7	39.7	−53.5
Textiles, clothing	129.4	125.6	115.6	140.3	67.6	53.7	39.5	45.5	51.8	49.0	40.3	43.9	−85.5
Glass, ceramic	185.0	181.2	171.2	168.2	159.0	80.0	54.8	61.2	65.0	80.1	69.1	69.1	−133.3
Iron and Steel	88.9	85.1	75.1	67.1	45.0	36.4	32.3	38.7	41.4	40.8	51.5	51.5	−6.8
Non-ferrous metals	110.3	106.5	96.5	87.2	52.9	44.7	35.1	41.5	47.4	39.6	34.0	34.0	−56.4
Metal products	132.2	128.4	118.4	115.4	100.1	77.0	63.9	70.3	77.0	99.2	51.1	51.1	−72.2
Non-electric machinery	159.3	155.5	145.5	142.5	133.3	70.9	57.8	64.2	71.0	78.2	60.1	60.1	−103.8
Electric machinery	134.2	130.4	118.7	118.0	139.9	106.4	88.6	95.0	100.7	80.2	68.2	68.2	−58.1
Transport equipment	162.4	158.6	147.1	145.6	139.3	131.8	127.0	88.4	90.6	67.7	80.4	80.4	−88.2
Others	142.2	138.4	128.4	137.5	111.7	104.0	82.2	88.6	96.9	81.6	71.3	71.3	−66.9
Mean protection	129.4	125.6	115.2	113.1	93.1	68.3	53.5	55.0	59.5	61.8	53.7	54.0	−72.7

NOTE: [a]Whiskey was omitted from the food and beverages group because of its dominance with regard to the total.

3   INCENTIVES FOR INDUSTRIAL EXPORTS

Although export-oriented policies in Turkey date from 1980, there were several measures intended to promote exports throughout most of the two decades preceding 1980s. Even under the import-substitution regimes, there were some measures of export promotion. These included rebates on customs duty paid by exporters, (which were, in reality, reductions in the disincentives that exporters would otherwise have faced). In like manner, exporters were exempted from paying the production tax on final goods in the 1970s and early 1980s. When the tax was replaced with a value added tax in 1985, exports continued to be exempted from the value added tax.

When the new economic policies were being considered in 1980, the export-promotion measure of the past were seized upon as instruments which could quickly be enchanced to strengthen incentives for exports. Export subsidy rates were increased, provisions for foreign exchange retention were liberalized, and export credit provisions were enchanced.

In what follows, the main tools of export promotion measures which are employed in Turkey will be outlined (Krueger and Aktan, 1992) In general, the export incentives of the 1980s applied primarily to industrial exports. In those few instances where the incentive measures are applicable to other activities, it is so noted.

3.1   Export incentive measures

3.1.1   Export tax rebates

Tax rebates started in the 1960s in Turkey, and were designed, at least in principle, to provide a refund to exporters for taxes paid at earlier stages of production. There had been significant elements of 'export encouragement' in the rebate rates, especially for non-traditional export commodities.

Prior to 1975, export rebate rates were awarded separately for each commodity. Starting from that date, a major simplification occurred; all eligible commodities were divided into eleven 'lists', with rebate rates established for each list. Rebate rates were altered in line with changes in economic policies, and the number of lists were changed. Starting from 1984, the tax rebate rates were reduced systematically. The number of lists was reduced from ten to five in 1987. Finally by 1989, export rebates was phased out. Turkey's signing of GATTs Subsidy Code on 1 February 1985, was instrumental in the Government's decision to abolish tax rebates.

3.1.2 Export credits

Credits have been available to exporters at rates below that for ordinary loans since mid-1960s. Credit rationing prevailed in Turkey until mid-1980s, so that credit availability for local firms was valuable. For exporters, however, access to credit was important because Turkish interest rates were well above world interest rates, and the exchange rate was fixed throughout the 1960s and 1970s. When the trade and payments regime was re-oriented to provide increased incentives to exports in the 1980s, several of the earlier export credit schemes were extended and new ones added. Several separate funds were used for this purpose. One was entitled the *Export Promotion Fund,* which was established in the 1960s as the *Special Export Fund.* It provided credit for exporters of fresh fruit and vegetables, marine products, export trading companies, and construction contractors working overseas. A second fund was the *Interest Differential Rebate Fund.* As the name implies, it was intended to compensate for differences in costs attributable to higher interest rates payable in Turkey, and the rate was differentiated by product category. In 1980, the requirements for eligibility for export credits were relaxed. One consequence in the early 1980s was that export credits were received by individuals who used them to finance activities other than exporting. This resulted in a reduction in the differential in favour of export credits by 3 per cent in 1983, but that did not stop the practice. The authorities therefore abolished the entire export credit mechanism in 1985. However, in 1986, the export credit system was reinstated, and new institutions were created.[1] In mid-1987, the *Turkish Export Credit Bank* was charged with the responsibility of supplying credits to, and providing insurance for exporters, and contractors abroad. In 1988, a *Special Exports Credit Facility* was established, which, in turn, was replaced by the *Foreign Trade Corporate companies Rediscount Credit Facility* in 1989. It extended credits through the Exim Bank to Foreign Trade companies whose exports exceeded $100 million per year. Export credits were readily available at lower rates. Until the liberalization of exchange control to permit foreign borrowing, the availability of export credits, at preferential rates was regarded as a valuable incentive by exporters. However, it lost some of value with the liberalization of foreign exchange, and some exporters stopped accessing the Exim Bank credits altogether.

3.1.3   Exemption from taxes and duties

In Turkey, there is a tax on all financial transactions, in addition to a banking commission and a stamp duty. Exporters are exempted from these charges, as well as from the contribution to the *Resource Utilization Support Fund* which replaced, in 1984, *Interest Differential Rebate Fund.*

3.1.4   Foreign exchange retention

During the entire import-substitution period, all exporters were required to surrender their export proceeds to the Central Bank within 3 months of exportation, or 10 days after the date at which they received foreign exchange, whichever came first. However, a foreign exchange retention scheme for exporters was introduced in 1980. Under that scheme, exporters were permitted to retain up to 5 per cent of their proceeds, or $40 000, whichever was greater. In addition, under the incentive schemes, exporters were permitted to retain foreign exchange equal in amount to the value of the importers imputs used in exporting, plus the amount of their export credits, including interest payments. Beyond that, exporters of industrial and mining products were granted the right to transfer a certain percentage of their export proceeds for financing the importation of goods used in export production. In 1980, the scheme was extended to Turkish construction contractors abroad, and exporters of fresh fruit, vegetables and marine products, though the retention ratio for that group was lower.

After 1980, the premium on foreign exchange diminished and exchange regulations were relaxed. Many of these measures, therefore, became less valuable; they were abolished in 1983, although the foreign exchange retention right was set at 20 per cent for all exporters, provided that they surrendered the remaining 80 per cent within 3 months of exporting. Subsequently, the holding time for foreign exchange was raised to 6 months in 1988, and in 1989, the retention ratio was raised to 30 per cent if surrender was within 3 months.

The foreign exchange retention rights were clearly valuable to exporters in the 1970s and early 1980s, when foreign exchange was scarce and delays in receiving import licenses could disrupt production and delivery schedules. The value of the scheme clearly diminished as the trade regime was liberalized. Finally, in June 1989, it became irrelevant as further liberalization of the payments regime permitted Turkish citizens to purchase and hold foreign exchange, and the surrender provisions because inoperative.

3.1.5 *Foreign exchange allocation and duty-free importation of inputs*

Although the foreign exchange retention scheme provided exports with some leeway for obtaining needed imports, it clearly was not adequate to finance all imports. Two related policies were affected to cover these needs. On one hand, a *foreign exchange allocation* programme was introduced to provide financing for imports used to produce exports. On the other hand, provisions were made so that exporters could import these commodities without paying duty one their inputs.

Turning first to the foreign exchange allocation scheme, any exporters with an Exporter's Certificate could apply for a foreign exchange allocation to cover imports needed in production of exports. The maximum allowable percentage of the value of exports that could be used for this purpose was altered from time to time. As it stands, the value of imported inputs cannot exceed 60 percent of the value of exports committed. In addition, materials and spare parts required for the production can also be imported duty-free, in which case, the cost of imports cannot be more that 2 per cent of the value of exports committed.

Retroactively, imported goods, including packaging materials, that are physically incorporated in the exported product, plus machine and equipment that are directly used in the production of export goods, can be exempted from customs duties and other charges on imports. The value of imports in that case cannot exceed 10 per cent of the exports realized. Only manufacturer–exporters can benefit from this provision. Domestic sales which are regarded as exports or other foreign exchange earning activities may also benefit from duty-free imports of inputs. However, the rate of exemption in these cases varies between 25 and 50 per cent of the CIF value of imports.

3.1.6 *Exemption from fund charges*

Transit trade of certain petroleum products are subject to charges ($3 per ton) at the entry and exit of customs ports. Provided that the above goods are transported by road, and the exporter has an export certificate, these charges for the Housing Fund can be waived.

3.1.7 *Corporate tax reductions for exports*

Starting in 1981, exporters were permitted to claim an exemption from their corporate profits taxes equal to 20 per cent of the value of their exports, and to pay a much lower rate of tax on the exempted portion. Export volume has to be at least $250 000 in order to qualify for the exemption.

3.1.8   The Support and Price Stabilization Fund (SPSF)

The SPSF was founded in 1980 and was thereafter reorganized several times, but has basically retained the same function. Until 1987, payments from the SPSF were relatively minor, providing small subsidy payments to exporters to help finance sales promotion, export-oriented investments, and export insurance schemes. Starting in 1987, an increasing number of export products became eligible for payments from the fund on a specific basis. At the outset, 45 products were eligible for SPSF subsidies (of which 24 were manufactured goods). At the beginning of 1988, the number of eligible products rose to 83 (62 manufactured) and in mid-1989, to 122. At the beginning of 1991, however, the number was reduced to 89. During 1986 and 1987, abuses of the SPSF became evident with over-invoicing of exports and reporting of non-existent exports. Consequently, at the end of 1988, maximum payment rates in terms of percentages of export value were established. The payments from the fund (financed, *inter alia*, from levies on imports) were important for individual commodities, but never constituted more than two per cent of the value of manufactured exports as of 1989.

3.1.9   Foreign Trade Corporations

Foreign Trade Companies (FTC), meeting specified values of exports were granted several privileges. One of them was the 'additional' tax rebate, equal to a percentage of export sales. This rate could reach as high as 10 per cent of the value of exports. Other privileges were as follows.

(a) There were preferential credits at the Export Promotion Fund, with more favourable rates and terms than those available to exporters generally.

(b) The requirements for obtaining foreign exchange were simplified. In addition, in the early 1980s, priority foreign exchange was even allocated for production for the domestic market – a privilege of considerable value at the time.

(c) Foreign exchange could be allocated for imports of investment goods, materials and spare parts without regard to their connection to export production.

(d) Trading companies could sell any goods they imported under the temporary import regime to any domestic industrial producer.

(e) In principle, trading companies were not supposed to engage in production activities. In fact, however, they were permitted to invest in the development of ancillary export facilities such as packaging, storing and transportation. Those investments were granted customs duty exemptions and other investment incentives not available to other investors.

In 1984, when incentive measures were gradually being scaled down, the first four specific incentives for the foreign trading companies were also eliminated. However, an additional incentive was provided which proved to be important. That is, they were the only entities legally entitled to trade with the socialist countries and others where state trading occurred.

As the tax rebate scheme was phased out, FTCs lost one of their incentives, i.e. additional rebates. As compensation, the Money and Credit Council decreed in 1989 that a basic 2 per cent premium should be extended to FTCs which realized a minimum of $100 million exports in 1988 and which pledged to export the same amount in 1989. This premium was to be paid out of SPSF resources through the Exim Bank.

3.2 Impact of export incentives

Table 9.5 shows that subsidy element of various export incentive measure enumerated above. The subsidy element conferred by the tax rebate scheme depends on: (a) the share of the eligible goods in total exports; (b) the average tax rebate rate; and (c) the actual indirect taxes paid which the scheme is supposed to compensate for. As data on actual proportion of taxes in value of exports for different industries are not available, it is assumed that in 1980 tax rebates represented the true compensation of the actual indirect taxes incurred. In fact, from when this scheme was introduced in 1960s, until 1975, export rebate rates had been calculated separately for each commodity at factory sites by the government officials. Starting from 1975, all eligible

TABLE 9.5 Total subsidies and offsets: 1980–89, weighted average subsidy rates[a]

	1980	1981	1982	1983	1984	1985	1986	1987	1988	1989
Subsidies										
Tax rebates	5.9	3.6	9.5	11.8	11.3	3.1	1.9	0.2	-0.9	-3.8
SPSF	0.0	0.0	0.0	0.3	0.3	0.2	0.2	1.6	2.1	12.7
Export credits	5.5	6.4	7.2	7.9	6.0	3.2	3.6	5.9	9.1	9.1
Cor. tax deduction	0.0	0.4	0.6	1.2	1.7	1.6	2.1	2.5	3.0	3.0
Freight subsidy	0.0	0.0	0.0	0.0	0.0	0.0	0.08	0.15	0.15	0.15
Advance payment	0.0	0.0	0.0	0.0	0.0	0.0	0.0	1.1	1.0	0.0
RUSF	0.0	0.0	0.0	0.0	0.0	4.0	2.2	0.0	0.0	0.00
Total subsidies	11.4	10.4	17.3	21.2	19.3	12.1	10.1	11.5	14.5	21.2
Offsets										
V.A.T. Exemption	0.0	0.0	0.0	0.0	0.0	7.5	8.1	9.5	8.4	7.8
F.E. Retention	1.9	1.6	2.5	5.1	0.9	0.5	0.9	1.1	0.8	0.5
F.E. Allocation	3.9	3.3	4.2	7.9	3.1	3.4	5.6	6.2	5.5	4.3
Total subsidies and offsets	17.2	15.3	24.0	34.2	23.3	23.5	24.7	28.3	29.2	33.8

NOTE: [a] Weights are the export shares of manufactured goods in total exports.

commodities were divided into eleven lists with rebate rates established for each list. Therefore it is not too misleading to assume that the rebate rates in 1980 approximate to true rates. Therefore, any rebate in excess of the 1980 rates is assumed to be the subsidy elements of the scheme.

The subsidy elements of the export credit is the difference between the credit rates applicable for exports and those of normal short-term credit, minus the exemption from taxes and duties applicable to normal credits.

The subsidy element of foreign exchange allocation and retention schemes is the difference between the free market and official exchange rates minus the deductions for various taxes and charges applicable to normal foreign exchange transactions.

In the absence of the actual data, the subsidy element of the duty free importation of inputs is calculated from the input–output tables to determine the input requirements of the industries, then the import duties and other charges are calculated for those inputs.

Specific rates for the direct payments from the SPSF are converted into *ad valorem* rates, making use of the average export values for each item eligible for the payment.

The results of these calculations are summed up in Table 9.5. A close examination of the table indicates that the subsidy conferred by the tax rebate scheme increased in the 1980–4 period, but as the rates were scaled down starting from 1985 and were eliminated altogether in 1989, the subsidy element of this scheme became negative in 1988. On the other hand, payments from the SPSF have gradually increased in importance and largely compensated for the elimination of the tax rebate scheme. The export credits system has been another scheme which provided significant incentives for exporters.

Among the offsets, exemptions from the VAT and foreign exchange allocation schemes conferred considerable subsidy for the manufactured exporters.

4   NOMINAL AND EFFECTIVE OFFICIAL EXCHANGE RATES

As was noted above, with the implementation of the liberalization policies, the exchange rate of Turkish lira was adjusted frequently and, starting from May 1981, its rate has been adjusted daily to maintain the real value of foreign exchange to exporters. In fact, there was a deliberate policy to devalue the currency by somewhat more than the inflation differential between Turkey and her trade partners.

Table 9.6 presents the official exchange rate, the Turkish consumer price index, the US dollar price index, and a weighted average (by share of Turkish exports) of price indexes of Turkey's major trading partners (loosely called G-7 in Table 9.6 for the sake of brevity) for the period 1975–90. The purchasing power parity (PPP) exchange rate can be calculated *vis-à-vis* the US and Turkey's partners. The table indicates that there was significant real appreciation of the Turkish lira in the late 1970s, especially against the currencies of Turkey's seven trading partners. In terms of the dollar, the official rate of lira appreciated by 18.5 per cent between 1975 and 1979, compared with a weighted average of Turkey's G-7 trading partners, the appreciation was 20.6 per cent.

After 1980, the real value of foreign currency rose continuously and significantly both in dollars and in the weighted currency basket of seven countries. In dollar terms a real depreciation of 42.7 per cent was effected between 1980 and 1984. In terms of G-7 currencies, the real depreciation was 45 per cent. After 1985, the lira seems to have been held fairly constant – with adjustments in the nominal exchange rate just about sufficient to offset changes in relative price levels – until 1989. After that year the nominal depreciation of the lira was at a far slower rate than the inflation differential; so a real appreciation of over 26 per cent – in terms of dollars – took place. Overall appreciation of the lira for the 1985–90 period was 50 per cent in terms of dollars and 57 per cent in terms of the currencies of the G-7 countries.

5   EFFECTIVE EXCHANGE RATES FOR EXPORTABLES AND IMPORT-COMPETING GOODS

Table 9.7 provides estimates of the effective exchange rates (EERs) to producers of manufactured exportable goods and for producers of import-competing commodities. Export subsidies appear to have been at best a partial offset to the protection accorded to imports. In general, the average import EER was well above that for exporters of manufactures.

Exporters of agricultural and mineral commodities not eligible for the export incentives were subject to a bias introduced by the trade regime even greater than that indicated in Table 9.7. Even for manufactured exports, the bias of the regime in 1980 and 1981, immediately after the devaluation (and, therefore, the presumed large drop in the extent of the bias) is estimated to have been of the order of 96 per cent that is, on average import-competing producers received 1.96 times

TABLE 9.6 Nominal and PPP exchange rate for Turkey, 1975–90

	Ner (TL/$)	Turkish CPI	USA CPI	PPP NER Turkey–USA	G-7 CPI	PPP NER Turkey–G-7	Overvaluation of TL/$	
							G-7	USA
1975	14.44	2.74	50.03	263.66	50.03	263.66	-2.1	-0.1
1976	16.05	3.22	52.93	263.83	54.03	269.31	3.2	6.4
1977	18.00	4.09	56.32	247.86	58.03	255.39	7.4	6.5
1978	24.28	5.94	60.60	247.71	61.33	250.69	16.9	11.4
1979	31.08	9.42	67.45	222.54	66.24	218.55		
1980	76.04	19.81	76.55	293.83	73.13	280.71	-22.1	-24.3
1981	111.22	27.06	84.44	347.06	80.22	329.71	-14.9	-15.3
1982	162.55	35.39	89.68	411.91	86.72	398.31	-17.2	-15.7
1983	225.46	46.50	92.55	448.74	91.84	445.30	-10.6	-8.2
1984	366.68	69.01	96.53	512.91	96.06	510.41	-12.8	-12.5
1985	521.98	100.00	100.00	521.98	100.00	521.98	-2.2	-1.7
1986	674.51	134.60	101.90	510.64	101.08	506.53	3.0	2.2
1987	857.21	186.96	105.67	484.50	103.94	476.57	6.3	5.4
1988	1422.35	327.93	110.00	477.11	106.85	463.45	2.8	1.5
1989	2121.70	556.17	115.28	439.77	111.34	424.74	9.1	8.5
1990	2608.60	909.89	121.51	348.36	116.23	333.22	27.5	26.2

SOURCES: Official Turkish exchange rates: *Quarterly Bulletin*, TCMB. Consumer price index: SIS, *Urban Consumer Price Index*. G-7 consumer price index is calculated from UN, ECE, *Economic Survey for Europe in 1990–1991*, Appendix Table A.9.

NOTE: Exchange rates are the yearly averages of selling rates. PPP exchange rates are calculated by taking the ratio of the partner country consumer price index to the Turkish price index and multiplying the resulting number by the Turkish official nominal exchange rates. The G-7 countries are Germany, the Netherlands, France, Italy, the United Kingdom, Switzerland and the United State Weights are calculated as exports from Turkey to each country as a share of Turkey's total exports to the G-7.

TABLE 9.7   *Effective exchange rates for producers of import-competing goods and manufactured exports, 1980–9*

	NER (TL/$) (1)	Export subsidy (2)	EER for exports (3)	Import charges (4)	EER for imports (5)	Bias (5)/(3) (6)
1980	76.04	13.1	89.1	98.4	174.4	1.96
1981	111.22	17.0	128.2	139.7	250.9	1.96
1982	162.55	39.0	201.6	187.3	349.8	1.74
1983	225.46	77.1	302.6	255.0	480.5	1.59
1984	366.68	85.4	452.1	341.4	708.1	1.57
1985	521.98	122.7	644.6	356.5	878.5	1.36
1986	674.51	166.6	841.1	360.9	1035.4	1.23
1987	857.21	242.6	1099.8	471.5	1328.7	1.21
1988	1422.35	415.3	1837.7	846.3	2268.6	1.23
1989	2121.70	717.1	2838.8	1311.2	3432.9	1.21

SOURCE: Column 1 from Table 10.6. Column 2 from Table 10.5 (total subsidies and offsets multiplied by column 1). Column 4 from Table 10.3 (unweighted average multiplied by column 1).

more liras per dollar of foreign exchange produced than did producers of exportable manufactures.

There is little doubt that there was a significant reduction in the bias of the trade and payments regime against exports during the first half of the 1980s. It appears, however, that the momentum of liberalization was lost by 1986. In the last 4 years of the 1980s, the bias against the exports remained above 20 per cent.

6   CONCLUSION

The 1980s witnessed strong tendencies of liberalization of the trade and payments regime as import licensing virtually ceased and controls over financial transactions abroad diminished significantly. Furthermore, there was some tendency for the protection accorded to producers of import-competing goods to decline. In addition, exporters of manufactured goods enjoyed a variety of incentive and support schemes.

However, the policies of the 1980s were not sufficient to eliminate the bias against exporters. The momentum for maintaining the real EERs for exporters equal to that of EERs for imports, was lost in the second part of the decade. The reduction of the export subsidies, especially direct payments to exporters of manufacturers in the form of tax rebates, is in line with the competition rules of the international community and Turkey signed the subsidy code of the GATT in 1985. However, there has been an upward trend in the payments from the SPSF, another direct payment which clearly violates GATT rules. It would be appropriate to replace those schemes which are not compatible with the international competition rules with those measures that would accord incentives to exporters without violating the said rules. Exchange-rate policy during the early 1980s accorded significant incentives for exporters of manufactured products. The loss of momentum in this policy in the second half of the 1980s may, at least in part, be responsible for the slowing down of the growth of Turkish exports.

NOTE

1. This was apparently in response to the failure of Iraqi importers to pay for their sales. With Communiqué Number 1 of 1 November 1986, the Central Bank opened its rediscount credit facility for short-term export credits. Later, the Turkish Export Credit Bank (Turkish Exim Bank) was established under Decree no. 87/11914, *Resmi Gazete,* 21 August 1987.

REFERENCE

Krueger, A. O. and Aktan, O. H. (1992), *Swimming against the Tide: Turkish Trade Reform in the 1980s* (San Francisco, CA: ICS Press).

Index